MURDER AND MYSTERY IN THE LAST FRONTIER

True Crime and Mystery in Alaska

ROBIN BAREFIELD
ALASKA WILDERNESS MYSTERY AUTHOR

PC PUBLICATION
CONSULTANTS
WE BELIEVE IN THE POWER OF AUTHORS

PO Box 221974 Anchorage, Alaska 99522-1974
books@publicationconsultants.com, www.publicationconsultants.com

ISBN Number: 978-1-63747-130-2
eBook ISBN Number: 978-1-63747-131-9

Library of Congress Number: 2022923079

Manufactured in the United States of America

CONTENTS

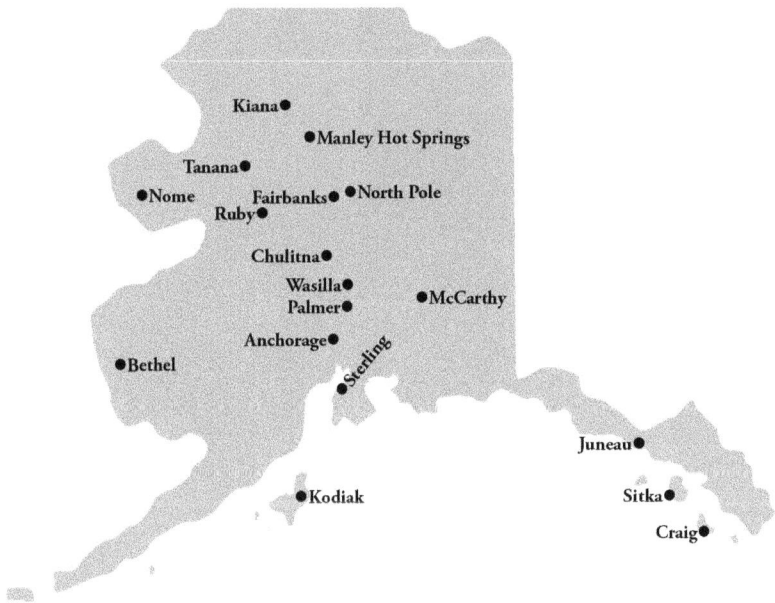

Kiana●

●Manley Hot Springs

Tanana●

●Nome   Fairbanks● ●North Pole

Ruby●

Chulitna●

Wasilla●
Palmer●

Anchorage●   ●McCarthy

Sterling

●Bethel

Juneau●

●Kodiak

Sitka●

Craig●

ALASKA: AN INTRODUCTION

Alaska is big, and it's impossible to lump the many regions of the state together for any purpose. From the rainforests of Southeast Alaska to the tundra of Kotzebue to the windswept Aleutian Islands, geography, habitats, and cultures vary widely. The state measures 2,400 miles from east to west and stretches 1,420 miles from north to south. With an area of 663,268 square miles, Alaska is larger than the next three biggest states (Texas, California, and Montana) combined. Despite its vast area, as of 2020, Alaska had a population of only 736,000 people, or 1.26 people per square mile. This last statistic is misleading because most of the population lives in the three largest cities of Anchorage, Fairbanks, and Juneau.

Alaska is wild, beautiful, and unlike any other place on the planet. Unfortunately, it also suffers from unique patterns of crime. People move to the state for many reasons, including adventure, money, the desire for a wilderness lifestyle, and as an escape from their problems. Alaska is not the best place to run from your problems, though. Harsh winters and long winter nights can be depressing. If people have psychological issues to begin with, they are likely to get worse in Alaska.

Alaska is a state rich in natural resources, including minerals, oil, fish, and crab. Mining these resources has produced several economic booms throughout the state's history. Young men, and a few young women, flocked to Alaska during the gold rush days of the early 1900s. Money again flooded the state during the 1970s with the construction of the Trans-Alaska Pipeline. Commercial fishing has seen several boom-and-bust periods, and the allure of making big money for only a few months of hard work appeals to many young people.

As workers rushed to Alaska to mine for gold, build the oil pipeline, or crew on a fishing boat, a wave of criminals followed in their wake. These criminals found ways to relieve the workers of their hard-earned paychecks, and crime spiked.

Crime is more prevalent in the densely populated cities, but much of the rest of the state has limited law enforcement. A few cities and large towns in Alaska support police departments, but the Alaska State Troopers are responsible for patrolling most of the state. Three hundred commissioned troopers must patrol a state one-fifth the size of the continental United States. In other words, Alaska has one state trooper for every million acres of land. Also, approximately 180,000 Alaskans lack access to a modern 911 system, and even if residents of the many small, remote villages could call an emergency response number, the troopers would still take hours, if not a day or longer, to respond to a violent situation.

Alaskans suffer deplorable statistics for violence against women. The Violence Policy Center ranks Alaska as the most dangerous place in the United States for women. According to a University of Alaska Justice Center victimization survey, fifty-nine out of every one hundred women residing in Alaska have experienced intimate partner violence, sexual violence, or both. A 2016 report by the Violence Policy Center ranked Alaska as the state with the highest homicide rate among female victims killed by male offenders. Alaska Native women are the most at-risk group to become victims of violent crimes. Alaska Natives comprise only 20 percent of the state's population, but Alaska Native women represent 54 percent of Alaska's sexual assault victims. Compared to all other women in the US, Alaska Native women are ten times more likely to experience domestic violence.

Alcohol and substance abuse contribute to these staggering statistics. According to the Alaska State Troopers, approximately 37 percent of all crimes they investigate annually involve alcohol or sub-stance abuse, and drugs and alcohol contribute to 62 percent of all violent crimes.

Alaska abolished the death penalty in 1957, before the terri-tory became the forty-ninth state. Alaska's first-degree murder stat-ute states that a person convicted of first-degree murder can be sen-tenced to prison for a term between twenty and ninety-nine years. Throughout this book, you will note judges handing down ninety-nine-year prison sentences to convicted murderers. A judge can sen-tence a convicted murderer who kills more than one person or com-mits other crimes to a prison term longer than ninety-nine years. A judge can also impose a sentence and then "suspend" part or all of the sentence. A suspended sentence allows the defendant to leave custody sooner than the original remand.

It is essential to keep these facts in mind as we travel through the state and look at specific cases involving murder and mystery in the "Last Frontier."

Southeast Alaska

O ften called the Alaska Panhandle, Southeast Alaska is bordered to the east by the northern half of British Columbia. Southeast Alaska has a mild, rainy maritime climate. The largest cities in the area are Juneau, Sitka, and Ketchikan. Most of this region of the state is part of the Tongass National Forest, the largest national forest in the United States. The region is home to the Tlingit and Haida and, more recently, to a settlement of Tsimshian.

Although no roads connect Juneau to the rest of the state, Juneau is the capital of Alaska. Rugged terrain surrounds the city, and all goods must come in or out by boat or plane. Many of the other towns in Southeast Alaska are found on the islands of the Alexander Archipelago, a three-hundred-mile-long island chain consisting of approximately eleven hundred islands. These islands form the northern part of the Inside Passage, and the largest are Prince of Wales, Admiralty, Baranof, Chichagof, Revillagigedo, and Kupreanof.

British naval officer George Vancouver named Prince of Wales Island in honor of George, Prince of Wales, who would later become King George IV of England. He named Admiralty Island in honor of his Royal Navy employers. Baranof, Chichagof, and Kupreanof Islands were all named after Russian naval officers and explorers, although oddly, Admiral Vasili Chichagov never visited Alaska. Since a Spanish explorer was the first European to "discover" Revillagigedo

Island, George Vancouver named the island in honor of Juan Vincente de Güemes, Second Count of Revillagigedo in Spain. The town of Ketchikan is on Revillagigedo Island, and Sitka is located on both Baranof and Chichagof Islands. Haines is the largest town on Prince of Wales.

The first story in this section occurred in and around the Juneau area. The next two tragic tales happened in tiny Haines (2020 population: 1,863) on Prince of Wales Island, and the last two stories are centered in Sitka.

ED KRAUSE: ALASKA'S FIRST SERIAL KILLER

Many serial killers have called Alaska home, and if you apply the broadest definition to the term, then serial killers terrorized settlers here long before profilers coined the expression "serial killer." A near-total lack of law enforcement in Alaska in the early 1900s allowed human predators to prowl the territory and prey on settlers and gold miners. Imagine the nervous miners who had managed to amass a quantity of gold. How did they sleep? Fear must have gripped them during the long trek from their claim to the nearest town with a bank where they could deposit their gold.

Ed Krause was a vile predator who killed with no remorse and took what he wanted. We will never know how many people Krause murdered or how much money, gold, fox furs, land, and other valuables he stole, but what we do know paints Krause as one of the darkest figures in Alaska's history.

The area in Southeast Alaska around Juneau where Krause operated provided the perfect location for his crimes to go undetected. Deep, fjord-like bays and passes indent the coastline and surround the numerous islands in the area. If a murderer had access to a boat, he (and they were almost always men) could quickly dispose of a body and cover up a crime. Prosecutors in the early 1900s shied away from charging a suspect with murder when they had no body even to prove the victim was dead. Circumstantial murder cases were too difficult to prove. During that era, miners and businesspeople came and went frequently in Southeast Alaska, so just because someone was there one day and gone the next did not mean the person had been murdered.

Between 1912 and 1915, several single, prominent businessmen vanished in Southeast Alaska, and the increasingly alarmed citizens pressed law enforcement officials to investigate. When the federal authorities failed to spring into action, the fraternal societies of Juneau stepped in and raised $1,500 to hire a private detective. More than anything else, this move spurred the federal authorities into action. They worried that if mob violence erupted in the Alaska wilderness, their superiors might decide to replace them with law enforcement agents less reticent to respond to the reports of missing men.

Kato Yamamoto, a Japanese foreman at a mine near Petersburg, was one of Krause's first suspected victims. Yamamoto owned property in British Columbia and was educated and prosperous. When he vanished, the mine where he worked owed him $700 in wages. If he meant to leave the area, why wouldn't he first collect his paycheck from the mine? It made no sense for the responsible Yamamoto to quit his job without telling anyone or collecting his wages.

A while after Yamamoto disappeared, a man who called himself George Hartman wrote to the bankers in Vancouver, British Columbia, where Yamamoto owned real estate. Hartman told the bankers that he had offered Yamamoto a mortgage on his property. Hartman now demanded a foreclosure on the property, which he wanted to be placed in his name. He said Yamamoto had drowned and would not be able to pay the mortgage. The man calling himself George Hartman produced forged documents to back up his claim, and the banker signed over the property to him.

In addition to Yamamoto, several other men disappeared, and soon after they were gone, Krause ended up with their possessions and money. Many Juneau residents suspected Krause and his gang of thugs of murdering the men, but they had no proof because they had no bodies. The missing men were all single and had no close family to raise the alarm and convince the authorities that their loved ones had met with foul play. People believed their friends would not leave without saying goodbye, but they could not prove the men hadn't simply packed their bags one day and headed south.

* * *

In the early 1900s, fox farming was a popular industry in Alaska. Fox farms were usually located on islands, where the animals could run free but remain captive on the isolated piece of land. Fox farming could be a lucrative business, and blue fox pelts were especially precious. Europeans paid $175 for one hide, and a fox farmer might bring in $20,000 a year, an impressive income at that time.

Fox farmer Calvin Barkdull carefully guarded his foxes, but on a cold, stormy night in 1915, he knew trouble had arrived on his island, and he had no doubt who the intruders were. Barkdull knew he had to hold off Krause and his gang of poachers, or they would take his foxes and kill him.

A few weeks earlier, a fellow fox farmer named Callahan visited Barkdull. Callahan said Ed Krause told him he was building fox pens on an island and intended to fill the pens with the foxes he planned to take from farmers on neighboring islands. Callahan told Barkdull to keep an eye out for the devil. Callahan disappeared a short while later, and Krause and his gang took over Callahan's fox farm. With no law enforcement present, it proved simple to kill a man and take over his life.

Now, late at night, Barkdull's foxes awoke him with their barking, and Barkdull looked out the window and watched Krause's boat approach his small island. Krause dropped the anchor and began rowing ashore through the choppy ocean. Krause did not choose a good night to raid Barkdull's farm. Two feet of snow covered the ground, and the thermometer read 0°F. A strong southeasterly wind tossed the seas and battered the island. Barkdull loaded his automatic rifle and waited in the warmth of his house. He believed he had the advantage as he sat in his home and watched Krause approach.

When Krause reached the island, Barkdull saw him hide behind a woodpile. Several shots rang out a few minutes later from the other side of the island, and Barkdull watched Krause peer around the woodpile, his rifle ready. Barkdull knew that Krause had ordered one of his gang members to fire the shots, hoping Barkdull would hurry out of his cabin, his attention focused on the other side of the island. While he was looking the other way, Krause would have no problem picking him off with his rifle. Barkdull did not rise to the bait. Instead, he remained in his warm, dark cabin, his gaze fixed on the woodpile and Ed Krause.

Barkdull stoked his fire, giving Krause and his cohorts a subtle hint that he was watching them and would shoot them if they came near his home. After a while, Krause and his gang gave up and returned to their boat. Barkdull was relieved to see them go, but he knew they would soon return and try to steal his valuable pelts. Barkdull quickly packaged 125 blue fox furs worth nearly $22,000 and caught a ride the following day on a halibut boat heading to Petersburg. He shipped his package through the Wells Fargo Express Office and breathed a sigh of relief.

A short while later, Barkdull saw Ed Krause standing on the sidewalk speaking to a group of men. Barkdull pushed through the crowd until he faced Krause. Barkdull reportedly said,

> Krause, you're a cold-blooded, low-down sneak-thief and a murdering skunk. There's a yellow streak up and down your back a foot wide. You won't come out in the open and fight in daylight alone. You have a gang to help you in your dirty work and the murdering of innocent, hardworking people at night. I could have killed you a half-dozen times last night, but I didn't want to. I want to see the time when the law will catch up with you, and you are hanged by the neck until you're dead.

When Barkdull finished speaking, Krause stared at him and then turned and walked away. Krause did not bother Barkdull or his foxes again.

Captain James O. Plunket, fifty-five, owned the *Lue*, a cabin cruiser available for charter in Juneau. On October 24, 1915, patrons at McCall's cigar store on Front Street in Juneau overheard a man ask Plunket if he could charter the *Lue* to take him to the nearby town of Snettisham. Plunket told the man he could not take him because he had already promised to take a passenger to a mysterious location. This passenger did not want to reveal his intended destination until the last minute. A few days later, the *Lue* left Juneau, and it did not return. No one saw the boat or its captain again. Four days later, the US customs office in Juneau received a letter reporting that the *Lue* had burned. The letter included the *Lue*'s license and was signed: *James O. Plunket.*

On October 29, five days after the last reported sighting of Plunket and his boat, a man appeared at the Treadwell Mine on Douglas Island near Juneau and introduced himself as a deputy marshal. He said he had orders to take William Christie, a mine worker, to see the marshal. The man assured the mine foreman that he would bring Christie back to the mine in the afternoon. The foreman released Christie into the man's custody, and Christie vanished.

Krause accomplished his abductions and murders in a cold, calculating manner. Although many in Juneau suspected him of violent crimes, they could not prove he had done anything wrong. Krause made few mistakes and operated under the cloak of darkness and secrecy. His attack on William Christie was unlike any of his other crimes. He abducted Christie in broad daylight, and workers at the mine saw his face. He impersonated a police officer, an indisputable crime that would give investigators a reason to hold him while they sorted out his more serious offenses. Worst of all, Krause's acquaintances knew he hated William Christie, and they knew he wanted to make Christie disappear.

Christie had recently married a young German woman named Cecile. Cecile and Krause had previously dated, and Krause grew jealous when Cecile broke off her relationship with him to begin dating Christie. Although he mostly kept his feelings to himself, his hatred of Christie grew when Christie married Cecile. Krause seethed and plotted revenge against his rival.

When Christie failed to come home for dinner, Cecile wondered where he was. Soon she received a note, supposedly from Christie, explaining his absence. Neighbors spotted Krause near the Christie home around the time the message arrived. Krause soon became the prime suspect in the disappearance of William Christie, so he jumped on a boat bound for Ketchikan. From there, he booked passage to Seattle on the passenger ship the *Jefferson*. Instead of using his real name, he traveled under the assumed name of O. E. Moe. Moe was another one of the missing men from Juneau whom many believed Krause had killed.

The police waited for the *Jefferson* to dock in Seattle and watched the disembarking passengers, planning all the while to arrest Krause when he walked past them. Krause disguised himself, though, and the officer standing by the gangplank did not recognize him. Krause walked off the *Jefferson* and onto the streets of Seattle. Luckily, a former Alaskan, now a salesman in Seattle, saw Krause on a city street and pointed him out to the police. Krause was arrested and incarcerated in Seattle.

Krause fought extradition back to Alaska, but he lost the battle and was sent back to Juneau, where he faced trials for a long list of crimes, including kidnapping and murder. Juries quickly found Krause guilty of kidnapping Christie and several frauds involving the property of the missing men. But the prosecutor knew that without a body, he faced a difficult task in securing a murder conviction against Krause.

The Plunkett case seemed to have the best circumstantial evidence. The prosecutor admitted to the jury that the body of James Plunkett was missing. He pointed out how easy it was to dispose of a body in the water-rimmed region of Southeast Alaska. He even speculated that Plunkett's final resting spot could be under many fathoms of water near Taku Glacier. The prosecutor made sure the jury understood how long Plunkett had resided in Juneau, and witnesses emphasized that Plunkett had no plans to leave the area. They also said Plunkett was a sober man of good character who had no relatives outside to visit. He seemed content in Juneau and had not told anyone he planned to leave.

The prosecutor pointed out that Krause had had some of Plunkett's property in his possession when the police arrested him. He speculated that Krause had planned to use Plunkett's documents to acquire and control his assets. According to expert testimony, the note to the US customs office had been typed on Krause's typewriter, and the signature at the bottom of the message matched Krause's handwriting. The prosecutor called Krause a "sneaking wolf and a monster" in his closing argument. Although he provided compelling circumstantial evidence, the attorney was afraid the jury would not find Krause guilty of murder in the absence of a body.

The prosecutor and the citizens of Juneau rejoiced when the jury returned a verdict of murder one. They recommended no mercy, and in February 1917, a judge sentenced Ed Krause to hang. The judge set the execution date for May 11, 1917.

Accused murderers in Alaska in the early 1900s often saw their death sentences commuted to life in prison. Ed Krause did not stick around to see if someone would commute his sentence. The federal jail in Juneau held five prison cells. When the jailers opened the cell doors, the prisoners could exit their solitary cells and mingle with the other prisoners in a large, locked room called the "big tank." A narrow hallway led from the big tank to a door that opened into the jailer's office. A door in the jailer's office led outside the jail. Guards typically allowed prisoners to move back and forth from their cells to the big tank during the day, but at 9:00 p.m., they ordered the prisoners to return to their cells and then locked the cell doors.

Krause somehow obtained a knife and fashioned it into a saw. He then placed a wooden plug at the bottom of the door to his sleeping cell. The plug kept his door from closing securely when the jailers ordered the prisoners back to their cells. At night, Krause freely left his cell and used his saw to cut through the bars of the big tank.

At 9:00 p.m. on the night of April 12, 1917, the two guards on duty entered the big tank and began the nightly ritual of securing the prisoners in their cells. Once the guards had their backs turned, Ed Krause calmly slid through the hole he'd cut in the bars and walked down the narrow hall. The guards had carelessly left open the door leading from the hallway into the jailer's office, so Krause entered the office and exited the jail. Moments later, they discovered his absence.

Governor J. F. A. Strong met with the guards and law officers, and they immediately dispatched armed parties in every direction. Men in automobiles searched the streets of Juneau, and the Treadwell Mine provided launches that searched from Petersburg to Sitka to the end of Douglas Island. Juneau is an isolated community nestled between the ocean and the mountains. Krause would know his chances of escape were better by sea than on land, and he had experience with boats. The police concentrated on the islands near Juneau. They suspected Krause would hide somewhere among the islands of the Alexander Archipelago until he found an opportunity to sneak away from the area.

The authorities soon learned that Krause had stolen a rowboat at Norway Point, just two miles from the city's center, and many believed Krause would go to Admiralty Island, fifteen miles from Juneau. Arvid Franzen was a Juneau shopkeeper who worked and stayed in Juneau during the week but returned to his family in Doty's Cove on Admiralty Island on the weekends. Franzen had a wife and six small children in Doty's Cove. When he heard about Krause's escape and the speculation that Krause might head to Admiralty Island, Franzen quickly returned to Doty's Cove and his family. Not long after he arrived home, on the afternoon of Sunday, April 15, Franzen and his wife noticed a man in a small boat rowing to shore. They watched as he pulled the boat up on the beach and walked toward their house.

Franzen told his wife to go out and sweep the front porch. He assured her that he would be behind her, hidden in the brush, with his rifle trained on the man. Mrs. Franzen trusted her husband and even remained calm enough to greet the stranger as he approached their house. When the man drew close, Franzen stepped out of the brush and leveled his rifle.

Franzen asked the man if he was Krause, and the exhausted man replied, "Yes." Krause continued to approach the Franzens, and Arvid Franzen did not hesitate. He shot Krause twice. One bullet pierced Krause's heart, and the other entered his head. Ed Krause died immediately.

Franzen sent a message to Juneau telling the authorities he had killed Ed Krause. An inquest the following day exonerated Franzen, and he received the $1,000 reward from the Territory of Alaska for the capture, dead or alive, of Ed Krause.

Ed Krause alone knew the full extent of his crimes, and he took that knowledge to the grave. Since he mostly preyed on single men with no families, few people missed his victims when they disappeared. Law enforcement personnel determined that Krause had murdered at least nine men and then stole their property. Some historians believe Ed Krause killed many more men; some even think he was one of the most prolific serial killers in American history.

THE INVESTOR MURDERS

What happened on a foggy September day in 1982 in the small fishing village of Craig, Alaska? Many believe they know who killed the crew and passengers of the *Investor*, but only the killer knows why the massacre occurred.

Craig, the largest town on Prince of Wales Island, had 550 residents in 1982, and it depended on the Alaska State Troopers for major crime investigations. The troopers are spread thin across the vast state of Alaska, and they can't be everywhere at once. The police response, in this case, was slow, and the investigation far from perfect.

Commercial fishing is one of the most economically important industries in Alaska, and the three-month salmon season in the summer is among the most lucrative fisheries. In the 1970s and 1980s, when salmon prices were at their highest, three months of hard work could earn the captain and crew of a fishing boat a half-million dollars or more. Crew members of a salmon seiner can make good money, but they must work hard and put in long hours. Crewing on a fishing boat is a job for young people, willing to work and ready to play on those rare nights when the season is closed and their boat pulls into port.

In Alaska, gill netting and purse seining are the two most common methods of commercial salmon fishing. A gill net operation is land-based, and the fishermen (and the majority are men) use small boats to pull salmon from a long net attached to the shore. Fishermen use a larger boat to "purse seine," and the crew sleeps, eats, and lives on the vessel. Purse seiners actively search for schools of salmon, encircle the fish with their net, and then pull the fish on board. The events of this story happened on a purse seiner.

On Sunday, September 5, 1982, the *Investor*, a fifty-eight-foot purse seiner owned by Mark Coulthurst, from Blaine, Washington, pulled into Craig and unloaded the crew's recent catch of 77,000 pounds of pink salmon onto a Holbeck Seafoods tender. The payload from just a few days of fishing was worth $33,000, but the cannery wouldn't pay Coulthurst for this or his other catches of the summer until the end of the season.

The Alaska Department of Fish and Game had temporarily closed the commercial salmon season but planned to reopen it the following day for the final salmon opening of 1982. This closure ensured that some salmon would escape the fishing nets and swim upstream to spawn.

When the *Investor* pulled into Craig, the crew planned to spend a leisurely evening in the small town. Besides Mark Coulthurst, the crew and passengers on the boat included Mark's wife, Irene, twenty-eight; their two children, Kimberly, five, and John, four; Dean Moon, Jerome Keown, and Mark's cousin Mike Stewart, all nineteen; and Chris Heyman, eighteen. Irene was three months pregnant.

After unloading its catch, the *Investor* pulled up to the North Cove Dock in Craig, and the crew tied the boat outside a seiner named *Decade*, which in turn was tied outside the seiner *Defiant*. The *Defiant* was tied to the dock. To get back and forth to the dock, the crew from the *Investor* had to climb across the decks of the other two boats.

Dean Moon and Jerome Keown went ashore soon after the boat docked. According to troopers, the two men later bought a small quantity of drugs from a friend named John Kenneth Peel. Peel had been a crewman for Mark Coulthurst the previous summer on another boat, but Coulthurst had fired him, and Peel was now crewing on the seiner the *Libby 8*. The *Libby 8* was also tied to the dock near the *Investor*.

While ashore, Jerome Keown called his brother, who later stated that Jerome sounded normal and didn't indicate anything was wrong. Mike Stewart and Chris Heyman left the *Investor* together, but the troopers were unable to find anyone in Craig who remembered seeing the two men that night. Stewart called his home in Bellingham, Washington, and didn't mention any trouble.

Mark Coulthurst apparently had no money on the boat because he wrote a $100 check to a friend for cash so he could take his family out to dinner at Ruth Ann's Restaurant in Craig to celebrate his twenty-eighth birthday. Later, people at the restaurant reported nothing unusual had happened while the family dined, although one witness did say that John Kenneth Peel had briefly stopped at the family's table to talk to them. Peel later denied he was ever at the restaurant.

The Coulthursts left the restaurant at 9:30 p.m., and a crewman on the *Decade* remembered four-year-old John sticking his head inside the pilothouse to say hi on his way back to the *Investor*.

During the night, a storm with high winds and heavy seas pounded the dock, and the crew of the *Decade* celebrated the end of the salmon season with a loud party. With all the noise, no one on the *Decade* or the *Defiance* heard anything unusual, and no one on either boat remembered anyone coming or going to the *Investor*.

At 6:00 a.m. on Monday, a *Decade* crewman went out on the deck and saw the *Investor* slowly idling away from the dock. He noticed that the *Investor*'s expensive tie-down lines remained on the *Decade*'s deck. Typically, the crew would retrieve these lines and stow them onboard. The *Decade*'s crewman waved at a man in the *Investor*'s pilothouse, who then returned the wave. A few minutes later, the *Decade*'s skipper also came out on deck and saw a man on the *Investor*'s deck.

At 7:30 a.m., a crewman on another seiner saw the *Investor* anchored across the harbor from Craig, near Fish Egg Island. Around that same time, another witness saw the seine skiff from the *Investor* tied to the cold storage dock in Craig.

By 10:30 a.m., heavy fog had rolled into Craig, obscuring the *Investor* from everyone in town. As the fishing fleet prepared for the opening of the salmon season later in the day, they forgot about the *Investor* for the moment. The *Investor*'s seine boat, however, was in the way at the cold storage dock and had to be moved several times during the day.

The captain of the *Decade* thought the *Investor* had left the dock because of the loud party on his boat, and he radioed the *Investor* to apologize. There was no reply. As boats headed out to wait for the salmon season to reopen, the dense fog remained, and most captains used radar to navigate.

The fog finally lifted the following morning, and observers in Craig were surprised to see the *Investor* still anchored near Fish Egg Island. Why hadn't Mark Coulthurst gone fishing with the rest of the fleet?

Witnesses saw a young man buy two and a half gallons of gasoline—a suspiciously small amount. He then climbed into the *Investor*'s skiff with the gas and motored out to the boat.

At 4:00 p.m., the crew of the fishing boat *Casino* noticed smoke rising from the *Investor*. After alerting the authorities, the *Casino* headed toward the *Investor* to offer help. On the way, the *Casino* captain saw the *Investor*'s seine skiff leave the boat and motor toward Craig. The captain nearly had to ram the boat to make it stop, and when he asked if anyone was on the burning boat, the seine skiff operator said, "Yeah, there's people on the boat," and then he sped toward Craig.

Once the mysterious man in the *Investor*'s skiff reached the dock at Craig, he spoke to at least three people before walking into town and disappearing with the fog. Later, a state trooper investigator said the man had "slipped into a time warp at the end of the dock."

By the time the *Casino* reached it, the *Investor* was fully engulfed in flames and was too hot for the *Casino* crew to approach. Alaska State Trooper Bob Anderson was the first law enforcement official to arrive. No one in Craig had the proper equipment to fight a fire on the water, so the responders issued a Mayday call, and nearly two hours later, a tug with one small pump arrived and started spraying water on the blaze. Anderson called the Coast Guard to airlift additional pumps to the scene.

Trooper Anderson returned to Craig and called his sergeant in Ketchikan, telling him the fire was spreading quickly, and he was sure the blaze was arson. His sergeant said he would send an arson investigator to the scene.

At 7:30 p.m., the tug captain radioed the Coast Guard to tell them the fire was under control. Anderson returned to the *Investor* and found it had burned to the gunnels and was listing twenty degrees. He and a few volunteers boarded the wreckage and found the charred human remains of four people in what had been the boat's galley. Experts later identified Mark and Irene Coulthurst, their daughter Kimberly, and Mark's cousin, Mike Stewart. All four had sustained multiple gunshot wounds.

As soon as the searchers removed the bodies, the fire flared again and destroyed the rest of the cabin. Anderson returned to Craig, where a police officer told him that he had interviewed a witness who'd seen the suspicious man in the *Investor*'s seine skiff. The witness said the man was twenty or twenty-one years old with light-brown or blond hair. He weighed 150 to 160 pounds and was wearing glasses and a baseball cap with a logo. Since the man was seated in the boat, the witness couldn't guess his height.

The following morning, two more law enforcement officials arrived. The fire was still burning, so the troopers finally summoned a helicopter used for fighting forest fires, and it dumped water on the burning boat. The boat was listing badly, so the officers towed it ashore and left it there until the arson investigator could examine it. Oddly, the authorities left the *Investor* unguarded, allowing anyone to poke around in the wreckage. Also, the rising tide likely destroyed most of the remaining evidence.

When the arson investigator finally examined the wreckage, he found more bone fragments, and the medical examiner positively identified Jerome Keown's remains. Investigators believed some of the remaining teeth and bones belonged to Chris Heyman and Dean Moon, but they could not make any definitive matches. No trace of four-year-old John Coulthurst was ever found, and the authorities believed the blaze had entirely consumed his small body.

The detectives did not think the killer was among the missing crew members because eyewitnesses stated that the man they saw operating the skiff was not a member of the *Investor*'s crew. Since neither Chris Heyman nor Dean Moon was ever seen again after the fire, they were presumed dead, and the police concluded that someone had murdered eight people on the *Investor* on the night of September 5 or in the early-morning hours of September 6, 1982.

As mentioned earlier, the authorities did a poor job investigating this crime, especially during the critical first few days. Even the prosecuting attorney admitted at trial that the authorities had badly mishandled the investigation. The police couldn't extinguish the fire on the *Investor* until the day after it had started. By then, little forensic evidence remained, and the troopers didn't even know how many victims had died on the boat. After the responding officer learned that the skiff tied to the cold storage dock was the one seen leaving the burning vessel, he examined it briefly but decided the rain would have washed away any fingerprints. He didn't bother to impound the boat and look at it more closely, and he didn't even realize the skiff in question belonged to the *Investor*.

The authorities had the eyewitness descriptions of the man who'd bought the gasoline and sped away from the burning boat. Considering the number of people who saw and even spoke to the man, you would think their descriptions would have led the authorities to a suspect. Remember, in 1982, Craig had a population of only 550 people. Unfortunately, the eyewitness descriptions of the young suspect were vague. Although Craig is small, a stranger in town at the end of the fishing season is the norm, not an exception. Twenty-something crew members of both sexes flood the town during the fishing season, and the locals don't know everyone.

Investigators believed the killer shot the crew members of the *Investor* one or two at a time as they returned to the boat Sunday night. They determined that the killer shot Mark, Irene, and Kimberly Coulthurst and Mike Stewart with a .22-caliber weapon.

Did the killer remain on the *Investor* the entire night, or did he leave and return the following morning when he ran the *Investor* to Fish Egg Island? When he arrived at Fish Egg Island, he anchored the *Investor* in deep water and opened the sea cocks (the valves in the boat's hull), expecting the boat to sink. He almost certainly was surprised to see the *Investor* still floating when the fog cleared, and he quickly purchased gasoline and took the seine skiff back to the *Investor* to set it on fire.

For over a year, investigators chased leads with little luck, but when the authorities finally released an artist's rendering based on eyewitness accounts of the suspicious man from the *Investor's* seine skiff, several fishermen came forward to say they recognized the man in the sketch. They identified him as John Kenneth Peel, a Bellingham man who had once crewed for Mark Coulthurst.

The authorities questioned the crew of the *Libby 8*, the boat where Peel was living and working as a crewman. Initially, his fellow crew members were reluctant to say anything that might land Peel in prison for the murders. Eventually, though, Larry Demmert, the captain of the *Libby 8*, told troopers that he was sleeping aboard his boat the night (or early morning) of the murders when he awoke suddenly at 2:00 a.m. He heard a "pop, pop, pop, pop" sound and said it resembled the backfiring of a small engine. Then, he said he heard the bloodcurdling scream of a woman. He said he looked out the cabin door of his boat and saw a man walking across the decks of the *Decade* and *Defiant*, carrying a rifle. He recognized the man as John Peel. Demmert said he was scared and returned to his stateroom, where he locked the door. He then heard someone jump onto the deck of the *Libby 8*. Demmert feared for his life but said the person left the boat a few minutes later. He added that he'd known Peel for many years and considered him a good friend. He felt very hesitant about testifying against him.

Dawn Holmstrom, a crew member on the *Libby 8* and John Peel's former girlfriend, was even more reticent than Demmert to tell investigators what Peel had said to her after the murders. When the troopers pressed her, she finally admitted to her conversation with Peel soon after the massacre. She said Peel started crying and told her, "It all happened so fast; I can't believe I did it."

The authorities arrested John Kenneth Peel nearly two years to the day after the murders, and two years after that, in January 1986, the trial proceedings began in Ketchikan. Jury selection took more than a month, with the prosecution and defense fighting over every juror. The animosity between the prosecution and defense carried over into the trial. While both sides argued over evidence, the case dragged on for six months, becoming the longest-running trial in Alaska history. The Superior Court trial judge admonished both the prosecution and defense for their backhanded tactics.

The state admitted to having only circumstantial evidence against Peel. Much of the evidence was either based on witnesses who said they'd seen Peel in the *Investor*'s skiff or purchasing gasoline before the blaze started on the *Investor*. The state said Peel's motive was revenge because Coulthurst had fired him the previous year.

Larry Demmert and Dawn Holmstrom were the core witnesses for the prosecution. Demmert claimed he saw John Peel walking away from the *Investor* carrying a rifle, and according to Holmstrom, Peel confessed to her that he'd murdered the crew of the *Investor*. Unfortunately, neither witness was reliable, and neither wanted to be responsible for putting Peel in prison for the rest of his life. Both Demmert and Holmstrom changed their testimony several times.

Peel's defense attorney picked apart the eyewitness testimony, pointing out the inconsistencies and making it clear that some of the witnesses had changed their stories or had trouble remembering the events from four years earlier. The defense also suggested the killings had resulted from a drug deal gone wrong, but the defense never introduced any drug evidence into the trial record. The defense also hinted that either Heyman or Moon could have been the murderer since their remains were never positively identified.

After six months of testimony, the jurors deliberated for six days before declaring themselves deadlocked. The jurors agreed not to talk to the press, but according to journalists, they voted seven to five for acquittal.

Two years later, the state brought Peel back to trial. This time, the trial was held in Juneau. The second trial lasted only three months, mainly because the defense decided not to call witnesses after the prosecution had presented its case. The jury deliberated for four days before acquitting Peel on all charges of murder and arson. The investigation and two trials cost the state of Alaska nearly $3 million. Even after a jury had acquitted Peel, state officials insisted he had murdered Mark Coulthurst, his family, and crew. No one else has ever been charged with the massacre aboard the *Investor*.

In 1990, Peel sued the state of Alaska for $175 million for wrongful prosecution. He based his suit on a 1984 memo from one of the lead investigators indicating that no direct evidence tied Peel to the crime. In 1997, Peel agreed to a $900,000 settlement.

The authorities and the district attorney stated early in the investigation that drugs were not involved in the *Investor* murders. Still, rumors flowed, suggesting there *were* drugs on the boat, and some people believed drugs were the reason for the killings. No foundation for this rumor was ever proven, though. People in Craig did not know the Coulthursts and their crew well since they usually didn't deliver their fish to the cannery in Craig, and they probably only did so this time because they were on their way back to Washington State, where they lived. The *Investor* was a beautiful boat owned by a young man, and rumors floated that Mark Coulthurst had used drug money to buy it. No one has ever supplied evidence to support this claim.

Two crewmen who worked with John Peel the year after the murders claimed he'd admitted to them that he had murdered the crew of the *Investor*, but their statements were suspect. The Coulthurst family believes John Peel killed Mark Coulthurst and the others on the *Investor*. Mark's mother, Sally, told a reporter she thought Peel had "freaked out" and did it because he was jealous of Mark and the boat and was mad because Mark had fired him from his previous vessel.

THE TROUBLED TEEN

Most teenagers fight with their parents, and during a heated argument, some kids might even scream, "I hate you!" Still, few teens order a hit on a parent simply because the child feels the parent is too strict.

Matricide, the killing of one's mother, is uncommon, and matricide by a girl under eighteen is extremely rare. Of the few cases in recent history where a girl under the age of eighteen killed her mother, the mother either had abused the offender or the killer exhibited extremely antisocial behavior. Rachelle Waterman was neither abused nor antisocial, despite what she told her friends. She appeared to be a typical high-achieving junior in high school. Rachelle sang in the school choir and played on the volleyball team. Residents of Craig, the same small town featured in the last story, adored Rachelle's mother, Lauri, who was active in her church, worked as a teacher's aide, and was always the first to volunteer to help with any community function. Rachelle's father, Carl "Doc" Waterman, was a well-liked and successful real estate agent in Craig.

Not only was Lauri Waterman an unlikely murder victim, but Craig seems like the last place such a crime would occur. As mentioned in the previous story, Craig is not immune to violent crime, having experienced the worst mass murder in Alaska's recent history just a few years before, in 1982. The massacre still haunts the residents of Craig because no one was ever convicted of the crime, and now again in 2004, another horrible murder affected this small town.

On Sunday, November 14, 2004, Alaska State Trooper Bob Claus received a call from a deer hunter hunting in a remote area of Prince of Wales Island. The hunter said he noticed smoke on the side of a cliff, and since he knew there were no homes or cabins in the area, he investigated the cause of the smoke and found a van that had tumbled off the road and was pinned against a log. The van was partially burned, and when the hunter peered through a broken window, he saw a skull resting beside a blackened human torso on the van's back seat. The body was so severely burned that he could not tell if it was a man, woman, or child.

When Trooper Claus reached the van, he knew this was a murder scene. How else could he explain a charred corpse in the back seat of a vehicle? He immediately called his supervising lieutenant in Ketchikan and requested help investigating a likely homicide. He needed a crime scene technician, a fire investigator, and a homicide investigator. These specialists would arrive the following morning, so in the meantime, Claus and a wildlife trooper guarded the crime scene, and Claus called the police in Craig and asked them to notify him if anyone called to report a missing person on the island.

At 9:45 p.m., the Craig Police Department dispatcher called Claus to inform him that real estate broker Doc Waterman had just reported his forty-year-old wife, Lauri, and her purple minivan missing. Lauri wasn't home when Doc had returned at 3:30 p.m. from a weekend business trip to Juneau, and his concern deepened with every passing hour Lauri did not return. When she still was not home by nightfall, he decided to call the police. The news stunned Claus. Was Lauri Waterman the burned corpse in the van? The Waterman and Claus families were friends, and Waterman's daughter, Rachelle, and her older brother, Geoffrey, had attended elementary school with Claus's two daughters. Claus's wife was a schoolteacher in Craig, Lauri Waterman worked as a teacher's aide, and Doc Waterman was the school board president.

Claus called Doc Waterman, and Doc explained that he was in Juneau for the weekend at a Girl Scout council meeting, and Rachelle had spent the weekend in Anchorage at a volleyball tournament. Since Geoffrey was away at college, Lauri spent the weekend alone at their house. Doc said he'd tried to call his wife several times on Sunday, but she never answered the phone. He and Rachelle both returned to Craig at nearly the same time, and when they arrived home, they found that Lauri and her van were missing from their home.

Since Doc did not see Lauri's purse where she usually kept it, he assumed she must have been running errands and would be home soon. The previous night, Lauri had volunteered to help with the chamber of commerce dinner, and Doc thought she now might be assisting with the cleanup from the event.

In their kitchen, Doc discovered an empty wine bottle on the counter, and since Lauri rarely drank alcohol, he found the presence of the wine bottle curious. In the master bedroom, Doc noticed the bed was unmade, and Lauri always made the bed first thing in the morning. He found his wife's wedding ring set in the bathroom, and he said that while she often took off her rings before going to bed, she always wore them when she left the house. Still, Doc was not too worried about his wife, and he believed that when she returned home, she would be able to explain her unusual behavior. As the hours passed and she still failed to return, his concern turned to fear and even dread. Doc called friends and neighbors to ask about Lauri, and they told him they'd seen her on Saturday night at the chamber of commerce dinner, but no one remembered seeing her after she'd left the event.

Trooper Claus knew the corpse in the burned-out van must be Lauri Waterman. Minivans were rare on Prince of Wales Island, and no one else had been reported missing. But because neither the remains nor the van had been officially identified, Claus refrained from telling Doc Waterman about the wreckage. As Claus guarded the van while he waited for the other investigators to arrive, he wondered who would want to kill sweet Lauri Waterman. In most investigations, the husband is the first suspect, but Doc Waterman had been 220 miles away in Juneau for the weekend. Lauri's children had also both been gone that weekend. Who on their sparsely populated island would want to kill Lauri Waterman?

On Monday morning, homicide investigator Sergeant Randy McPherron, a deputy fire marshal, and a crime scene tech arrived at the scene of the presumed homicide. The fire marshal determined the blaze had started in the van's back seat, and most of the flames had stayed inside the vehicle. The thorax, the pelvic girdle, the leg bones above the knees, and the large arm bones were all that remained of the body. The skull was also intact but was very brittle due to the heat of the fire, followed by rapid cooling from the near-freezing ambient temperature. Investigators found several teeth among the ashes of the van. The fire marshal noted the scent of gasoline in the rock and soil samples he collected for analysis.

Sergeant McPherron found the VIN (vehicle identification number) tag in the wreckage. Claus called the DMV and confirmed the van was registered to Carl and Lauri Waterman. Chief See with the Craig Police Department volunteered to deliver the bad news to Doc Waterman.

On Monday, November 15, Rachelle Waterman went to school rather than stay home and worry about her missing mother. Rachelle was a good student and a talented singer and athlete. She was popular with her peers, but over the past year, she had changed. She began wearing all-black clothes and polished her nails black. She still spent time with her girlfriends at school, but the previous summer, she'd worked at a computer store and had started hanging out with a new circle of friends, including two men in their twenties. These friends shared an interest in video games and the fantasy role-playing game Dungeons & Dragons. Even after the computer store went out of business, Rachelle had continued to spend time with the D&D crowd.

Rachelle's behavior at school on Monday morning seemed odd for a teenage girl whose mother was missing. Students reported that she remained quiet and sullen for most of the day, but she casually asked one of her friends if she had seen her mother. All the kids had heard about the burned-out van and knew the corpse found in the back was probably Rachelle's mother. Rachelle told at least one friend that she feared her mother had died in a drunk driving accident, citing as evidence the empty wine bottle Rachelle and her father had found when they returned home on Sunday. When several friends gave her a sympathy card for the loss of her mother, Rachelle lost control. The high school secretary called Don Pierce, a friend and neighbor of the Watermans' and a special-education teacher. Don came to the office and told Rachelle he would take her home. Rachelle declined his offer and said she was waiting for her friend, Jason Arrant, who was coming to the school to be with her.

Pierce knew Jason was one of Rachelle's friends from the computer store. Jason was a heavyset man in his midtwenties who worked as a janitor at the school in Klawock, another town on the island. Jason had a reputation as a "washout" who still lived with his parents and spent his time playing video games, and Pierce knew Lauri Waterman had not been happy when Rachelle started spending time with Jason.

When Jason arrived at the school, he told Pierce he would take care of Rachelle, but Pierce said Police Chief See wanted to talk to Rachelle and her father at her home, and he would drive her there. As Pierce and Rachelle walked out of the school, Jason ran after them, yelling at Pierce, but Pierce ignored him. Jason followed them to the Waterman home and tried to follow Rachelle into the house, but when Chief See arrived, he told Jason to leave, and he finally complied.

Chief See wasted no time breaking the news to Doc and Rachelle. He told them the burned-out vehicle was Lauri's van. He explained that they had not identified the remains yet, but he thought the body was probably Lauri's. Experts would compare Lauri's dental records to the teeth found in the van to confirm the identification.

Doc Waterman listened calmly to what Chief See said and then asked him to follow him upstairs. Doc pointed out blood on the bedsheets in the master bedroom and showed See the items he'd found tangled in the blankets, including what looked like the tip of a finger of a rubber glove and a five-inch-long fiber from a rope. Chief See suddenly realized that the house was a crime scene, and he told Doc and Rachelle they would have to temporarily move out of the house until crime scene techs could comb the premises. Doc and Rachelle packed a few clothes and went to stay next door at the home of Don and Lorraine Pierce.

Investigators believed Lauri Waterman had been abducted from her home sometime after 10:00 p.m. Saturday, when she'd left the chamber of commerce dinner, and before early Sunday morning, when Doc had tried to phone her at home. The blood on the sheets, the rubber glove tip, and the piece of rope all suggested an intruder had entered the house in the middle of the night when Lauri was asleep. The intruder had either murdered Lauri in the home or had abducted her and killed her later. Rachelle said she'd last spoken to her mother on the phone around 4:00 p.m. on Saturday. She said she and her mother had a good conversation, and her mother seemed happy. Rachelle admitted she sometimes argued with her mother, who didn't like her hanging out with the much older Jason Arrant.

A forensic odontologist in Anchorage compared the jaw and teeth found in the van to dental X-rays of Lauri Waterman's teeth and conclusively identified the corpse as Lauri Waterman.

Trooper Bob Claus knew the Waterman family well, and he knew Lauri had been unhappy when Rachelle began dating Jason Arrant. Jason was best friends with her boss at the computer store, Brian Radel, and Jason had spent much of his time at the store playing video games. From the beginning of the investigation, Claus suspected Arrant was somehow involved in the murder of Lauri Waterman. Rachelle began dating Jason during the summer, but once school started, they were rarely seen together, and many around town assumed Rachelle had come to her senses and broken up with the older man. Both Jason and Brian were big men. At the time of Lauri Waterman's murder, Brian stood six foot five and weighed 280 pounds, and Jason also weighed well over 200 pounds. When Trooper Claus began to suspect Jason might have been involved in Lauri's murder, he wondered if Brian also had participated in the crime. The two big men easily could have subdued and abducted the much smaller Lauri Waterman.

Troopers questioned both Jason Arrant and Brian Radel. Jason told them that he and Rachelle had dated for a while, but they'd broken up because Rachelle's parents were not happy about their relationship. Jason and Brian claimed they had been together at Brian's house drinking all night on Saturday, November 13, during the abduction and murder.

At 7:30 p.m. on November 17, Sergeant Randy McPherron and Troopers Bob Claus and Dane Gilmore arrived at the Waterman house to interview Doc and Rachelle again. McPherron told Doc he would like for Gilmore to stay at the home to interview him while he and Claus took Rachelle to the police station for an interview. Doc readily gave McPherron permission to talk to Rachelle without him present, and Rachelle went willingly with the troopers to the police station. Since Rachelle was sixteen years old, the troopers did not technically need her father's permission to interview her. Still, McPherron hoped that by asking her father for consent, he would ease Doc's mind and keep him from calling a lawyer to accompany Rachelle to the station.

Once the officers reached police headquarters, they took Rachelle to an interrogation room and videotaped her interview. McPherron began by asking the teen about her mom, and the easy questions seemed to relax her. McPherron then asked Rachelle about her relationship with Jason Arrant, but she said they were only friends. She said her mother had not liked her hanging out with Jason, and she agreed with her mother and began spending less time with him. McPherron suspected Rachelle was less than truthful about her relationships with her mother and Jason, but he moved on to another topic.

A while later, McPherron reminded Rachelle of her rights and said she could end the interview at any point. He then told Rachelle that he thought Jason Arrant might be responsible for her mother's death, and he again asked her about her relationship with Jason and told her he needed to know the details of their relationship. McPherron and Claus asked her if she'd ever had sex with Jason Arrant or Brian Radel. She said she had done nothing more than kiss Jason on the cheek. McPherron lied to Rachelle and told her that both Jason and Brian had claimed they'd had sex with her. Rachelle initially denied the claims, but as the questioning grew more intense, she finally admitted to having sex with Jason several times during the summer and once with Brian Radel the previous spring.

McPherron then asked Rachelle if she'd ever said anything to Jason or Brian about fights she'd had with her mother. She said she might have mentioned being mad at her mother a few times, and she'd told Jason her mother sometimes hit her, but she claimed she'd never told Jason or Brian anything to make them want to kill her mother; she did not believe either man would want to harm her mom. As McPherron and Claus pressed her, Rachelle finally admitted she and her mother had frequently argued about her clothes, her choice of boyfriends, and her recent interest in Wicca, a religion some believe to be related to witchcraft. Rachelle said her mother had hit her legs with a baseball bat and had once tried to push her down the stairs. Rachelle also claimed her mother had threatened her with a knife. She confessed to reporting these incidents to Jason and Brian.

McPherron and Claus believed Rachelle was trying to portray herself as the innocent victim of an abusive mother. Rachelle seemed to suggest that if Jason and Brian had killed her mother to protect Rachelle from more beatings, then the murder was their idea, and she'd had nothing to do with it. The troopers did not believe in Rachelle's innocence. They thought she'd used sex to manipulate the older men into killing her mother for her.

The troopers interviewed Rachelle's other friends, including past boyfriends. Some said Rachelle also had told them her mother abused her, but none believed Rachelle's claims and said she was prone to exaggeration. Doc Waterman flatly denied that Lauri had abused Rachelle. He said they sometimes argued, but Lauri had never gotten physical.

The murder of Lauri Waterman made national news when reporters discovered Rachelle had been blogging about her life for the past two years. In 2004, blogging was in its infancy, and although teenagers around the world would embrace the idea of writing an online journal to share their thoughts, habits, and lives with total strangers, most parents remained unaware of what their children did on their computers. The Waterman case and Rachelle's blog alerted the media, and this small-town murder case spawned waves that spread far beyond the shores of Prince of Wales Island.

Rachelle Waterman loved to blog and did not censor her feelings about her family or her town. She titled her blog *My Crappy Life* and referred to Craig as "Hell, Alaska." She candidly discussed sex, used profanity, and described arguments with her parents and her disdain for her community. Her last entry in the blog, on Wednesday, November 18, 2004, shocked the Craig community and the entire country and caused many residents there to suspect Rachelle had ordered her mother's murder:

> Just to let everyone know, my mother was murdered. I won't have computer access until the weekend or so because the police took my computer to go through the hard drive. I thank everyone for their thoughts and e-mails, I hope to talk to you when I get my computer back.

Five thousand people commented on Rachelle's post, and people in Craig were stunned when the blog came to their attention. Rachelle casually mentioned her mother's murder as the reason she would not have access to her computer for the next few days.

Sergeant McPherron soon cracked Jason Arrant. In his third interview, Jason said Brian Radel had killed Lauri Waterman, but Jason insisted he had known nothing about the murder until it was over. Jason said Rachelle was not involved in the murder of her mother. When McPherron and Claus interviewed Jason again, he admitted that he had helped plot the murder. Rachelle had told Jason that her mother was abusing her, and Rachelle also mentioned that she and her dad would be out of town for the weekend. Jason said he was in love with Rachelle and couldn't bear to think of her enduring more abuse. He said the opportunity had presented itself, and he'd asked Brian to murder Lauri Waterman. His friend had agreed to do the murder because he didn't think Jason had what it would take to kill another human being.

When investigators arrested Brian Radel, he told McPherron and Claus that he planned to plead guilty and was willing to make a video statement, explaining in detail how he'd kidnapped and killed Lauri Waterman. Brian said he broke into the Watermans' garage at 12:30 a.m. on Sunday, November 14. He entered the house and climbed the stairs to the top level, where he saw Lauri asleep in the master bedroom. He hovered outside her bedroom until 3:00 a.m. and then decided to act. He approached the bed, put a cloth over Lauri's mouth, and pinned her to the bed. He duct-taped the cloth to her mouth and made Lauri change from her nightgown into street clothes.

Brian said he had initially planned to make Lauri's death look like a drunk driving accident, so he took her downstairs, opened a bottle of wine, and told her to drink the entire bottle. Lauri meekly complied. He then took the keys to her minivan from her purse and told her to lie in the back seat of the van. He bound her hands and feet so she could not move and then drove for an hour to a secluded area of the island. He took Lauri out of the van and set her down on the gravel on her knees. He hoped to break her neck, put her back in the van, and send the van over the edge of the cliff, making it look as if she'd broken her neck in the crash. He said he tried to break her neck with his bare hands, but although he heard a crack, she was still breathing. Next, he pummeled her neck with a flashlight, but still, she did not die, so he covered her mouth with a cloth and pinched her nose until she stopped breathing.

Brian said that during the assault, Lauri never resisted or screamed. She just kept repeating the words, "Can I ask you a question?" Brian asked her what the question was, but she repeated, "Can I ask you a question?" Once she was dead, Brian put Lauri back in the vehicle, drove the minivan to the cliff's edge, doused Lauri and the vehicle with gasoline, and set it on fire. The minivan slid partway down the embankment. Brian said Jason was not with him until the very end, when he set the van on fire. He claimed Jason had taken no part in the murder and that Rachelle had been unaware of the murder plan.

McPherron and Claus did not believe Brian Radel when he said Jason and Rachelle had not been involved in the murder. They thought Brian was trying to protect his friends. They interviewed Jason again and convinced him that Rachelle had lied to him about being abused. McPherron told Jason he believed Rachelle had asked him to kill her mother, and he'd enlisted Brian Radel's help. Jason finally caved and admitted that Rachelle had told him she wanted her mother dead. He said she'd called him before she left for Anchorage to go to the volleyball tournament and asked Jason if he and Brian were all set. She called Jason again when she arrived home and found her mother missing, and he said he told her it was done.

Jason told McPherron and Claus that he and Brian had tried to kill Lauri one other time. Their plan was to gun down Lauri after she'd dropped off Rachelle for volleyball practice, but when Brian experienced problems with his gun, they were forced to abort the plan. After the plan failed, Jason said he emailed Rachelle and told her they had to cancel the hunting trip but promised they would try again.

Jason confessed he'd lied when he claimed he'd met up with Brian after Lauri was dead. He now said he'd joined Brian when Lauri was still bound and in the back of the van. Jason repeated Brian's sickening story of Lauri's murder, and Jason said that at one point, he told Lauri that she would never hurt Rachelle again.

Investigators knew the case against Rachelle Waterman was weak, so they interviewed her one more time. Rachelle willingly accompanied McPherron and a Sergeant Habib to the police station.

McPherron read Rachelle her Miranda rights and asked Rachelle if she understood her rights and knew she could have her father present for the questioning. Rachelle said she wanted to talk to the investigators without her father or lawyer present.

McPherron told Rachelle that both Jason and Brian had admitted to killing her mother, and he said both men had implicated her in the plot. This last statement was not true. Jason said Rachelle had asked him to kill her mother, but Brian Radel steadfastly maintained that Rachelle had nothing to do with the plan. McPherron and Habib went at Rachelle hard for two and a half hours, and finally, she admitted to asking the two men to kill her mother, but she said they'd told her nothing about the plot. She suspected the murder would happen when she was at the state volleyball tournament and her father was in Juneau, but neither Jason nor Brian had shared any details of their plan with her.

Investigators arrested Rachelle Waterman, and her bail was set at $150,000. Since her father could not raise the money, Rachelle stayed in prison until her trial. Jason Arrant and Brian Radel also remained incarcerated.

On Wednesday, June 8, 2005, Brian Radel pleaded guilty to first-degree murder. He was sentenced to a maximum of ninety-nine years in prison, but with time off for good behavior, he could be released in thirty-three years. Jason also pleaded guilty to first-degree murder, but since he had not committed the actual murder of Lauri Waterman, his sentence was capped at fifty years, making him eligible for parole in sixteen years.

Due to the notoriety of the Lauri Waterman murder case, the judge decided that a fair trial for Rachelle could not be held in either Craig or nearby Ketchikan, so the trial was moved to Juneau. Jury selection began on Monday, January 23, 2006. Both Brian Radel and Jason Arrant testified at Rachelle's trial. Brian stated that Jason had asked him to kill Lauri, and while Brian acknowledged that Rachelle had often complained about her mother abusing her, he stated she had never asked him to kill her mother.

Jason testified that Rachelle had told him she wanted her mother dead and that the two of them had talked about various murder plots. He said that, once she knew she would be in Anchorage and her father would be in Juneau for the weekend, she called Jason and told him it would be a good weekend to carry out the plan. When Rachelle called Jason after she returned home from Anchorage and found her mother and the minivan missing, Jason said Rachelle was disappointed to hear they'd destroyed the minivan because now she would not be able to inherit it. Jason said he'd asked Rachelle to wipe down the railing on the stairs and the doorknobs in her house in case Brian missed anything, and Rachelle agreed to do it.

Rachelle's defense attorney hammered McPherron for his harsh interrogation of a sixteen-year-old girl. Then a psychologist hired by the defense testified that Rachelle was immature for her age and did not fully understand her Miranda rights. The psychologist said McPherron had intimidated Rachelle, who was afraid to ask for her father. This characterization of Rachelle as a naive child did not match the smart-mouthed, intelligent, self-assured young woman McPherron remembered questioning. Rachelle's attorney portrayed her as a typical teenager who had complained to her friends about her mom. In his closing statement, her attorney stated that Rachelle had loved her mother and did not want her dead. He maintained that the real villain was Jason Arrant. He said Jason was angry because Lauri Waterman had not wanted her daughter to date him, so Jason convinced Brian to murder Lauri. Rachelle Waterman chose not to testify.

On Tuesday, February 14, 2006, the jury in the Rachelle Waterman case sent a note to the judge saying they could not reach a unanimous verdict, so the judge was forced to declare a mistrial. Ten jurors believed Rachelle was not guilty, while two thought she was guilty. Rachelle was released on reduced bail.

On January 24, 2011, Rachelle Waterman was retried for the murder of her mother. In the intervening years, she had attended college in Florida, as far away from Craig—the town she'd once dubbed "Hell, Alaska"—as she could get. The second trial took place in Anchorage. This time, the jury returned a unanimous verdict. Rachelle was acquitted of murder but found guilty of criminally negligent homicide. The jury determined that Rachelle was so negligent and deviated so far from what a reasonable person would have done that she caused her mother's murder. Rachelle was sentenced to three years in prison and is now a free woman.

THE UNHAPPY WIFE

S ome married couples thrive on discord. These are the people we avoid joining for dinner and the ones in whose presence we squirm as they argue, yell, and threaten. We wonder why they got married, and if they divorce, we're certain no one else would want either one of them. Still, some couples not only manage to survive their contentious relationships but enjoy sparring with their partners. Marriage is hard, but most of us try, at least for a while, to make a relationship work, and if it doesn't work, we leave and go our separate ways.

Jane and Scott Coville constantly fought, even before moving to Alaska and getting married, but Jane did not divorce Scott; she had no need to sever ties with him because Scott conveniently disappeared. Did he grow disillusioned with Jane, marriage, and life in Alaska? Did Scott take off on his own for an adventure somewhere else, a place far away from his current responsibilities, or did something much more sinister happen to Scott Coville?

Scott Coville and Jane Limm met while they were both students at La Sierra College in Riverside, California, near San Bernardino. Scott majored in biology, and Jane pursued a degree in physical therapy. The two started as friends, but they developed a romantic relationship over time. After his junior year, Scott dropped out of college and moved to Sitka, Alaska, where he found a job as a commercial fisherman and then worked in a cannery and at a pulp mill. Jane remained in Riverside and completed her physical therapy degree, but she stayed in contact with Scott. When Jane graduated from college, Scott traveled to Riverside for the ceremony. After her graduation, Scott asked her to marry him, and she agreed.

Sitka is unlike any other town in the US. For a young woman from sunny, populated California, the change in locale must have been jarring to Jane. Sitka comprises part of the Alaska Panhandle and sits on the western side of Baranof Island and the southern half of Chichagof Island in Southeast Alaska's Alexander Archipelago. The town spans a land area of 2,870 square miles and has a total area (including water) of 4,811 square miles, making it the largest city by landmass in the US. To give you a better idea of its size, the town of Sitka stretches across an area over four times the size of the state of Rhode Island. Despite its vast land size, fewer than 9,000 people lived in Sitka as of 2020.

The remote town of Sitka can only be accessed by water or air. Mountains carved by glaciers surround the village, which sits in the Tongass National Forest. Sitka has a wet maritime climate, but warm ocean currents moderate its temperatures. The average yearly rainfall in Sitka measures eighty-six inches, and the average snowfall reaches thirty-nine inches. The temperature averages around 62°F (17°C) in the summer and rarely drops below 30°F (−1°C) in the winter.

The frequent rainfall and dark days in a town shaded by the forest and the surrounding mountains probably weighed on Scott and Jane and possibly fueled their arguments and gloomy moods.

Jane joined Scott in beautiful but remote Sitka, where she found a job as a physical therapist. They married in a civil ceremony in Alaska in October 1987 and then had a formal church wedding in California in February 1988.

Scott and Jane lived in a mobile home on the edge of Sitka's main town area, and Scott continued to work at odd jobs. Scott's boss at the pulp mill fired him when he caught him smoking marijuana on the job, and Scott seemed to flounder, unsure what he wanted to do with his life.

The couple fought frequently, and Scott once told his mother that their relationship was like "fire and ice." In March 1988, Scott and Jane phoned Scott's parents and said they'd had a big fight and needed relationship advice. Jane admitted she thought marriage would be fun, but it seemed marriage was hard. Jane said she thought she would be "happy, happy, happy." Scott's mother, Rita, later said she did not know what had triggered the argument between Scott and Jane, but Rita and her husband counseled the young couple. They told them marriage is a compromise, and constant effort is required to make it work. They said marriage is both good and bad. Once they ended the call, the elder Covilles worried about the young couple. Scott would soon be twenty-six, and Jane was only twenty-three. Would their marriage last?

Rita didn't speak with Scott or Jane for a few weeks, but on April 12, she called her son to wish him a happy birthday. The phone at Scott and Jane's trailer repeatedly rang, with no answer. Rita wasn't concerned with her inability to reach Scott, but she still felt anxious about Scott and Jane's marriage.

On April 14, Scott was scheduled to appear before a judge in Sitka for a speeding ticket, but he failed to show. Rita continued to try to reach her son over the next few weeks, but no one answered the phone, and a check Rita sent Scott for his birthday remained uncashed. Finally, in early May, Rita called Scott and Jane's number and heard a recording announcing the number had been disconnected and was no longer in service. Now, Rita began to worry. Where were Scott and Jane?

Rita called one of her son's friends in Alaska, who told her he had not seen Scott since early April. The friend said Scott hadn't mentioned any plans to leave Alaska. While concerned, Rita and her husband knew Scott sometimes took off on his own, and if he and Jane were having marital problems, then perhaps he'd gone somewhere to think about his marriage and his life.

On Mother's Day, Rita received a card from Scott and Jane. The card was signed from both of them, but both signatures were in Jane's handwriting, and the envelope bore the postmark of San Bernardino, California. Rita knew Jane had family in San Bernardino, so perhaps she and Scott were visiting her relatives. Would Scott travel to California, though, without letting his parents know he was just hours from their home?

By May 30, when Scott's parents still couldn't reach him, they finally called the police in Sitka. The Covilles admitted to the authorities that their son might have left on his own, but they said they could not locate him and were worried about him. The Sitka police began to search halfheartedly for Scott, who was an adult and had a habit of wandering off without telling anyone. The authorities believed he would show up at any moment with a plausible explanation for where he'd been.

On June 8, 1988, law enforcement officials placed an article in the *Sitka Daily Sentinel* with Scott's photo. According to the piece, no one had seen Scott Coville since April 12, 1988, and anyone with information about Scott's location was asked to come forward. No one responded to the plea for information about his whereabouts.

The police then went to the trailer where Scott and Jane had lived. Jane's possessions were gone, but Scott's things were still there. The inside of the mobile home looked tidy, and the authorities found no clues there to Scott's whereabouts. Detectives tried to contact Jane in San Bernardino, but they couldn't find her.

The police then located Scott's truck at the Sitka airport, but they found no evidence that Scott had bought a plane ticket and left Sitka. Scott disappeared in 1988, though, when a passenger could more easily fly under an assumed name. Perhaps Scott used a false name, jumped on a plane, and flew someplace where no one could find him. As an adult, Scott had the right to disappear, and law enforcement officials felt little obligation to try to find him.

In the summer of 1988, Scott's parents received a rambling, three-page letter from Jane. She said she'd come home to their trailer in Sitka one day to find Scott and his truck gone, and she believed he'd given up on their marriage and left. She said she had no idea what had happened to him. She blamed him for the problems in their marriage. She said he'd begun acting strangely and smoking too much pot, and she told them the pulp mill manager had fired him for smoking marijuana on the job. She claimed he'd told her that he didn't want to be married to her any longer.

Jane gave Scott's parents her new phone number and told them to call her if they had any questions, but Rita said she didn't want to call Jane because she was suspicious of her and felt she may have had something to do with Scott's disappearance. Rita said, "I was afraid if I talked to her, I might say something a Christian shouldn't say."

A few months later, Jane called Scott's parents at their home in San Diego and said she planned to attend a party and thought she'd left a cocktail dress at their home. She asked if it would be okay for a friend to stop by and pick up the dress. Scott's father told Jane that she was welcome to come to their house to get the dress, but they would not allow a stranger to come into their home to search for it. Neither Jane nor anyone else came to look for the dress, and the Covilles never heard from her again.

In a notice in the June 21, 1989, *Daily Sitka Sentinel*, Jane announced she was suing Scott for divorce. Since Scott could not be found for the court to serve him divorce papers, Jane was required to file the notice in the newspaper. Scott never responded.

The case of Scott Coville's disappearance went cold, and ten years later, Scott's parents decided they needed to move on with their lives. They believed Scott was dead, because he would have contacted them by now if he were still alive. In 1994, the Covilles had Scott officially declared dead. Scott's father died in 2004, never knowing what had happened to his son.

Meanwhile, Jane moved to Southern California, where she worked as a physical therapist, and she became heavily involved in her Seventh Day Adventist church. She gave as much money as she could to the church and devoted time to missionary work in Nepal and China.

In 2000, Jane met Chris Reth, a corporate jet pilot, and the two married and moved to Maple Park, Illinois, a suburb of Chicago. Jane took a job working for the Geneva school district and was well liked by neighbors and fellow workers. Her marriage to Chris did not last, though, and the pair divorced in 2005. After their divorce, Chris moved back to California, while Jane stayed in Illinois.

In 2007, Chris Reth applied to have his marriage to Jane annulled by the Roman Catholic Church. The church takes marriage annulment very seriously, so they hired an investigator to run a background check on Chris and Jane. The man who investigated Chris and Jane's marriage happened to be a former LAPD homicide detective. Chris told the detective that Jane had once confessed to him that she'd murdered her first husband, Scott. The investigator was not bound by confidentiality, so he immediately called the Sitka Police Department and asked if they had any record of a missing person named Scott Coville.

Alaska's Cold Case Unit took charge of the case and convinced Chris Reth to phone his wife while authorities recorded the call. They wanted him to ask her about Scott's murder. Chris agreed and called Jane, who again admitted to him that she'd murdered Scott. The cold case detectives were thrilled when they heard Jane incriminate herself, but they knew Jane's recorded confession would not be enough to convict her. They had no physical evidence tying Jane to the murder of Scott Coville, and they didn't even have Scott's body to prove he had been murdered.

Alaska State Troopers flew to Illinois to talk to Jane. At first, she denied knowing anything about Scott's disappearance, but when the troopers played the recording of her conversation with Chris Reth, she finally admitted to killing Scott. She said she'd murdered him because he was abusive and said he wanted a divorce.

Jane told the detectives that on Scott's twenty-sixth birthday on April 12, 1988, she and Scott were talking in bed, and he said he was tired of being married to her and wanted a divorce. Jane waited for Scott to fall asleep and then took the .357 Magnum they kept in the trailer and shot him in the neck. Since Jane was much smaller than Scott, she then wielded a long-handled ax and hacked Scott into pieces as he lay on the mattress. She then stuffed his bloody remains into garbage bags. Next, she cut up the mattress, stuffed it into garbage bags, and then hauled the bags to several dumpsters. At the time, the city of Sitka incinerated its trash, so Scott's remains were burned to ash.

After disposing of her husband, Jane thoroughly cleaned the trailer, wiping away the blood and carefully erasing any sign of her crime in the bedroom. She then packed her clothes, drove Scott's truck to the Sitka airport, and flew to California.

Even after Jane's confession, the troopers did not feel they had enough evidence to arrest her. She could easily change her story and again claim she had no idea what had happened to Scott. They needed physical evidence to add weight to their case. They searched Sitka and were surprised when they located the trailer where Scott and Jane Coville had once lived. Investigators ripped up the carpet in the master bedroom and accessed the subflooring of the mobile home. They found a large bloodstain on the subflooring and took samples of it.

Luckily, Scott's mother had kept Scott's wisdom teeth after the dentist removed them when he was a child, and the crime lab compared the DNA extracted from the blood sample found in the mobile home to the DNA from Scott's wisdom teeth. The two samples matched, and the cold case detectives now had the physical evidence they needed to back up Jane's statement.

Twenty-two years after Scott Coville's disappearance, the State of Alaska indicted Jane for first-degree murder and tampering with evidence. Jane was arrested in Illinois and extradited to Alaska, where she pleaded not guilty to all charges. Jane's friends in Illinois were stunned by her arrest. She had been living a quiet life. She was devoted to her church and was working on her master's degree in social work. For her job, she helped people with developmental disabilities.

On October 8, 2010, Jane changed her plea to being guilty of second-degree murder, and the prosecution agreed to drop the tampering-with-evidence charge. Still, Jane knew she could receive a maximum sentence of ninety-nine years in prison. She described to the court how she'd murdered Scott on his twenty-sixth birthday, cut his body into pieces, and threw him away with the trash.

The court sentenced Jane on March 4, 2011, and Scott's mother, Rita, flew to Sitka for the hearing. Jane claimed she'd murdered Scott because he was abusive to her, and she said she'd even stayed at a women's shelter for a while. Her attorney could offer no proof of Jane ever seeking refuge at a shelter, though, and he provided no evidence that Jane had ever called the authorities to report spousal abuse. Jane's lawyer asked the judge to sentence her to no more than fifteen years.

The judge did not believe Jane's actions represented the behavior of an abused woman killing on the spur of the moment to escape further mistreatment. Instead, he said she had behaved in a cold, calculating manner. She shot Scott while he slept and then methodically cut him and the bloody mattress into pieces, stuffed everything into garbage bags, and disposed of the bags. Next, she carefully cleaned the trailer, packed her things, and flew to California to continue her life. The judge sentenced Jane to fifty-five years in prison, with nineteen suspended due to her lack of a previous criminal record and for the good deeds she'd done in recent years. Jane is now serving thirty-six years at the Highland Mountain Correctional Center in Seward, Alaska. With good behavior, she will be eligible for parole on January 28, 2034, when she is seventy years old.

FINDING THE MURDERER OF JESSICA BAGGEN

When a small Alaska town loses one of its children, the entire community grieves, and when a monster brutally rapes, murders, and discards the body of that child, the residents cry out for answers and justice. In the case of Jessica Baggen, the folks in the Sitka community would not have those answers for twenty-four years.

The people who loved and knew Jessica best described her as a "true Sitka kid." Most children who grow up in small, coastal Alaska towns and villages are unfazed by the wet climate and don't notice the short daylight hours in winter. Most love the outdoors and won't hesitate to swim in the frigid water of the North Pacific. They will happily unhook the fish they just caught and perhaps even kiss the slimy animal as they pose for a photo. Alaska kids are tough, and most have a strong support system of family and friends. They are raised not only by their parents but by their entire community.

After searchers discovered Jessica Baggen's body in May 1996, fifteen hundred Sitka residents gathered for a candlelight vigil at the spot where she was found. The townsfolk were grief-stricken, angry, and scared. Who would do such a horrible thing in their small community, and could the monster be one of them?

On May 4, 1996, Jessica's sister hosted a birthday party for her little sister, who was turning seventeen. Jessica's older sister lived in a trailer court on Sawmill Creek Road in Sitka, and when Jessica left the party to walk home a little after midnight, no one worried. Jessica lived with her parents less than a mile from her sister's place, and this was Sitka, where everyone knew everyone else and neighbors looked out for each other.

When Jessica failed to arrive home, her parents grew concerned and then frantic. Soon, searchers began combing the area near the path Jessica would have followed. Two days later, they found the T-shirt Jessica was last seen wearing; less than two hours after that, they located her body, seventy feet off a bike path parallel to Sawmill Creek Road. According to Major Dave Hanson with the Alaska State Troopers, "Jessica had been discarded and hastily buried under a log beneath the trunk of a hollowed-out tree."

Jessica was murdered just a few blocks from her home and near a main thoroughfare in the middle of Sitka. The Alaska Department of Public Safety Training sits just across the street from where searchers found her body. The perpetrator had sexually assaulted Jessica and shoved dirt in her mouth. Analysis indicated that the blood found on Jessica's shirt did not match her blood type, and the reddish-blond pubic hairs removed from her body were not hers.

The Sitka police suddenly had a murder to investigate, and they were in over their heads. At the time, not much more than petty crime occurred in Sitka. In 1993, the Associated Press released a humorous story about a few of the silly entries on the Sitka police blotter, including complaints of residents playing croquet too loudly. Murderers did not roam the streets of Sitka—at least, not until someone killed Jessica Baggen.

Not only did the Sitka Police Department not have experience in investigating murders, but Jessica's murder occurred before small-town police departments had sophisticated computer systems. The Sitka police detectives came up with a plan to use what they had. Because they'd recovered reddish-blond pubic hairs at the crime scene, the police combed through DMV records and made a list of men with red or reddish-blond hair, and they focused their attention on this list.

The public demanded answers. They expected the police to apprehend the murderer and quickly get him off the streets. People were angry and scared. They pressured the police to arrest Jessica's killer.

Into the middle of this chaos walked Richard Bingham, a longtime Sitka resident with a drinking problem and mental deficiencies. Bingham was highly suggestible. After a night of excessive drinking, he would often black out, and the following day, his friends liked to tease him by making up wild stories about what he'd done when he was drunk. Whatever the latest petty crime in Sitka happened to be, his friends told Bingham he did it. Bingham often believed his buddies and felt terrible, thinking he'd done the deed. While cruel to tease him, his friends mainly only accused him of harmless acts. Then, one of Bingham's so-called friends stepped way over the line and tried to convince Bingham he had raped and murdered Jessica Baggen.

Richard Bingham wandered into the Sitka police station and told the authorities he was drunk the night Jessica Baggen disappeared. He said, "I can't remember what happened. I want you guys to help me out." The Sitka police breathed a sigh of relief. They thought they had their man and could neatly wrap up this investigation. Unfortunately, while they concentrated on Bingham, the authorities overlooked another much more likely suspect, and this man was right under their noses.

The police used the controversial Reid technique to interrogate Bingham, named for psychologist and former Chicago police officer John E. Reid. Courts now question the Reid technique because it has spawned numerous false confessions in cases around the country. Interrogators who use this aggressive method often lie to suspects, claiming they possess nonexistent, incriminating evidence that suggests the person committed the crime. A suspect like Richard Bingham, who already doubted his actions, proved an easy mark when questioned in this manner. After several hours of relentless interrogation, Richard Bingham confessed to the rape and murder of Jessica Baggen.

Two months before someone murdered Jessica Baggen, an employee at a local Sitka grocery store found a teenage coworker crying in the breakroom. The girl claimed a local man named Steve Branch had raped her. With encouragement from her coworker, the girl reported the rape to the Sitka Police Department. The police convinced the girl to call Branch while they recorded the conversation. They wanted her to get Branch to confess to the rape, but he said nothing incriminating during the call. The police did not arrest Branch for the alleged rape until June, more than a month after Jessica's murder. They had already incarcerated Richard Bingham for raping and killing Jessica by then.

Despite the girl's accusation of rape against Branch, no evidence exists to suggest the Sitka police ever considered Branch a possible suspect in the rape and murder of Jessica Baggen. In a small town with little violent crime, the authorities must have assumed they had two rapists in their community, and one was also a killer. The prosecution even had a sample of Branch's blood, and with a search warrant, the police could have tested his DNA against the DNA found on Baggen's body. By 1996, DNA profiling had been around for ten years, but perhaps the budget of a small-town police force could not afford DNA analysis. They had found the money to test Richard Bingham's DNA, and they knew it did not match the DNA recovered from Jessica's body. The stated reason for drawing blood from Branch was to determine if he was HIV positive. Steven Branch also had reddish-blond hair, just like the pubic hairs found at the crime scene. Did the police have Branch on their list of suspects? They haven't said, but once Bingham confessed, they likely thought they had the killer in custody, and they stopped investigating the case.

In 1997, Branch went to trial for the rape of the teenage girl. When he took the stand, he cried and admitted he'd made a mistake, but he also insisted that the sex was consensual. After convening for a short time, the jury acquitted Steve Branch. Branch remained in Sitka for the next fifteen years and managed to stay out of trouble. In 2010, he moved to Austin, Arkansas.

The judge ordered Bingham's trial moved from Sitka to Juneau because he felt it would be impossible to find an impartial jury in Sitka. Richard Bingham suffered a miserable time in a Juneau jail while awaiting his trial. He spent the first several months in isolation, but then the warden moved him into the general population, where he feared for his life. Other inmates considered Bingham a child rapist and murderer, and they tried to lure him into secluded corners not monitored by video cameras. Bingham now remembers his time in prison as the worst period of his life.

Bingham's attorney, Galen Paine, knew she must somehow convince the jury to dismiss Bingham's confession. She hoped to guide them away from the confession and toward the physical evidence, so she called a "false confession" expert to testify about the Reid technique's propensity to produce such confessions. Paine also played a video of Bingham's interrogation, and a psychologist who had examined Bingham testified that Bingham suffered intellectual deficiencies and was vulnerable to suggestion. Paine then called a state crime lab technician to explain that the DNA recovered from the crime scene and Jessica's body did not match the DNA collected from Richard Bingham.

The jury convened for only two hours before acquitting Richard Bingham on all charges. With only a questionable confession and no physical evidence pointing to Bingham, the jurors believed Bingham was innocent and that the Sitka police had failed to apprehend the real killer.

Many in Sitka still believed Richard Bingham had killed Jessica Baggen, and fearing for his safety, Bingham quickly moved out of state, eventually settling in Washington. After Bingham's release, the Sitka police did not know what to do next, and the murder of Jessica Baggen soon landed on the stack of cold case files.

Over the years, the Sitka Police Department, the Alaska State Troopers, and a private detective hired by Jessica's family have investigated Jessica's murder. The authorities were able to clear more than a hundred potential suspects by comparing their DNA profiles to the profile obtained from evidence left on Jessica by her killer. Nothing brought investigators any closer to finding Jessica's murderer.

As the years passed, hope faded for the family and friends of Jessica Baggen. Her murderer seemed unlikely to ever be caught and convicted. Then, Cold Case Trooper Investigator Randy McPherron (featured in "The Troubled Teen") took charge of her case and began researching new methods for solving old murders.

In 2018, McPherron read an article about a new type of forensic DNA analysis called genetic genealogy. In California, the authorities had just arrested "Golden State Killer" suspect Joseph James DeAngelo after obtaining a familial match by comparing the DNA collected at one of the crime scenes to a commercially available DNA database. Virginia-based Parabon NanoLabs was the facility that analyzed the DNA in the Golden State Killer case, so McPherron called Parabon and asked if they would take a look at the DNA profile collected from Jessica's body.

The field of investigative genetic genealogy is new and powerful. Investigators create genetic profiles from DNA samples gathered at crime scenes. They then upload these profiles to websites such as GEDMatch, where citizens have posted their genetic profiles to learn more about possible relatives and ancestors. If the investigator locates a relative, such as a distant cousin, who matches a suspect's DNA, she searches for all relevant family records, including birth and death certificates. She also studies family connections on social media. She then reverse-engineers a family tree, building backward to a common ancestor, like a great-great-grandparent. Next, the investigator climbs down the family tree until she finds the subsection of the family containing the unknown suspect. Sometimes this process takes hours, but other times, the investigator must work for months to construct the family tree.

When the genealogist finished her analysis of the DNA from the Jessica Baggen case, she sent the report to McPherron. They had a suspect, and his name was Steve Branch, the man accused of raping a teenage girl only months before Jessica was attacked and murdered. Branch had once lived on the road near where searchers found Jessica's body.

Steve Branch now lived in Austin, Arkansas. The Arkansas police were unsuccessful at following and collecting a discarded DNA sample from him, so Alaska investigators flew to Arkansas to confront Branch. He denied killing Baggen and refused to give the detectives a DNA sample. The investigators left Branch's residence to obtain a search warrant for his DNA, and a half hour later, Branch shot and killed himself.

Steve Branch will never be tried and convicted for the murder of Jessica Baggen, but the authorities felt justice was served, and they closed the case.

For Richard Bingham, it was bittersweet news to learn that the authorities had finally found the man who had raped and killed Jessica Baggen. Since his trial and acquittal, Bingham has lived under a cloud of suspicion. He is now in poor health and angry about the events that shaped his life. He feels the state of Alaska should compensate him for the ordeal he endured in Sitka.

In a 2020 interview, Cece Moore, a scientist with Parabon NanoLabs and one of the pioneers of genetic genealogy, said that she believes the real power of this technique will emerge when police use it at the beginning of an investigation. This analysis would narrow their suspect pool and prevent them from arresting an innocent person.

MCCARTHY

McCarthy, snuggled deep in the Wrangell–St. Elias National Park and Preserve, is 406 miles northwest of Sitka, but it takes three and a half days to travel from one town to the other. The trip involves a ferry and a shuttle bus. McCarthy is approximately 120 miles northeast of Cordova and 230 miles east of Anchorage. McCarthy and its sister town of Kennicott (also spelled Kennecott) are located four miles from each other.

The Wrangell–St. Elias National Park and Preserve is the largest national park in the United States, and it encompasses an area the size of West Virginia. Four mountain ranges converge in the park, producing some of the most rugged terrain in the world. The temperature in McCarthy fluctuates from –50°F (–45.5°C) in the winter to 90°F (32.2°C) in the summer.

At the turn of the twentieth century, the richest concentration of copper ever mined was discovered in the mountains above Kennicott. The mine owners developed the town of Kennicott as a place for the miners to live, while McCarthy arose as a place for the miners to play.

By the 1930s, most of the ore was gone, and Kennicott and McCarthy became ghost towns. The railroad track used to transport the ore soon fell into disrepair and became the McCarthy Road. This road begins where the pavement ends in Chitina, sixty-one miles to the west, and by 1983, the road was nearly impassable. Most people in the McCarthy area at that time traveled to the outside world by small aircraft, and once a week, a plane brought mail, groceries, and other supplies to the residents living near McCarthy and Kennicott.

THE MCCARTHY MASSACRE OF 1983

As a crimson stain spread over a bright-white snowbank, survivors knew McCarthy would never be the same again.

In 1983, the McCarthy home of Les and Flo Hegland was the gathering spot where the twenty-two residents of the Kennicott/McCarthy area waited for the weekly mail plane. The Heglands lived near the small airstrip where the plane landed, and not only did they offer their hospitality, but they even built an addition onto their front porch, where they would leave uncollected mail and groceries so nearby residents could drop by at their convenience to pick up their freight. The Heglands owned the only two-way radio in the area strong enough to communicate with the outside world, and they relayed daily weather reports to the Federal Aviation Administration (FAA) office in Cordova.

The Hegland house was more than just a place for residents to sit and wait for the plane to arrive. Other than the mail plane pilot, the Heglands were the McCarthy residents' lone link to civilization. Flo Hegland, fifty-eight, and Les, sixty-four, had lived in McCarthy since 1967 and were considered the unofficial postmasters by area residents. If someone wanted to send a message to a friend or relative, or if a relative needed to contact one of the McCarthy residents with an urgent message, the Heglands sent and received these communications on their side-band radio.

Residents in the McCarthy area were mostly stranded during the long winter of 1983, and they depended upon and looked forward to their Tuesday mail plane. In 1983, McCarthy had no running water, no telephones, and no electricity, except for the power provided by individual generators. The independent souls who called this remote area home had little contact with the outside world, so the weekly gathering to wait for the mail plane was a way to share the latest news.

* * *

On February 28, the night before mail day, in Kennicott, four miles north of the McCarthy airstrip, twenty-nine-year-old Chris Richards played chess with his neighbor, thirty-nine-year-old Louis Hastings. Hastings, an unemployed computer programmer, had moved to Alaska from California in 1980 and had only lived in the Kennicott area for a year. According to Richards, the evening was unremarkable, just a friendly game between two neighbors.

On mail day the following morning, as Richards cooked breakfast, Hastings again appeared at his front door. Richards assumed Hastings was on his way to meet the mail plane, and he pushed open the door and invited him in for tea. Richards then turned his back to the door while he cooked his meal. A moment later, Richards felt something strike his right cheek, shattering his glasses. He immediately ducked and then felt an object hit his head. He turned toward Hastings and saw the other man walking toward him, the barrel of a pistol fitted with a silencer protruding from his gloved hand, ready to fire again.

Richards grabbed Hastings, and they began to struggle while Richards screamed at Hastings to stop shooting. Hastings said, "Look, you're already dead. If you'll just quit fighting, I'll make it easy for you." Richards fumbled for a knife from the sink and stabbed Hastings in the left upper chest and the right leg. Richards then fled the cabin into the waist-deep snow, wearing only socks, one slipper, a T-shirt, and light corduroy pants. The temperature in Kennicott that morning was 10°F (−17.2°C).

Hastings's pistol jammed, and he grabbed the rifle he had stashed outside the door of the cabin. While Hastings fired shots at him, Richards fought his way three-quarters of a mile up a steep hill to an unoccupied tourist lodge, where he found boots, a parka, and snowshoes. Richards continued out the far door of the lodge, but Hastings, who had been following Richards's bloody footprints, thought he was still in the lodge, so he set it on fire.

Richards couldn't manage the snowshoes, so he staggered and then crawled one-tenth of a mile to the southwest to the cabin of Tim and Amy Nash. The Nashes were a young couple who had just gotten married on Christmas Day. After an extended honeymoon, they had only returned to the Kennicott area two weeks earlier. Tim and Amy bandaged Richards's wounds while he told them what had happened.

Since Hastings appeared to be on his way to McCarthy, where area residents would soon gather to meet the mail plane, Richards and the Nashes decided to arm themselves and head to the runway and the Heglands' home to warn the others about Hastings.

Meanwhile, fifty-two-year-old Maxine Edwards had left her husband at home while she crossed the frozen Kennicott River and proceeded to the Heglands' house to await the mail plane.

Back at Kennicott, the Nashes bundled Richards onto a sled and towed it behind their snowmachine as they sped toward McCarthy and the airstrip. When they reached the airstrip, they met Gary Green, a pilot and guide. Green was cleaning off his airplane, and when he heard their story, he told them he had seen Hastings twenty minutes earlier heading toward the Heglands' house. Tim Nash volunteered to check on the Heglands while Green warmed up his plane in preparation to fly Richards to Glennallen, forty minutes away, for medical care. Green said he would contact the troopers and request their assistance.

As Green loaded Richards into the plane, Amy Nash saw her husband limping down the airstrip toward them. He was returning from the Heglands' house, where he'd smelled the acrid aroma of gunsmoke and had seen blood splattered over the interior of the house. Tim believed the Heglands were dead and said that when he'd walked into the kitchen, he saw Hastings standing on the back porch. Nash fired at Hastings and missed, but when Hastings returned fire, he struck Nash in the right leg. The Nashes told Green to go for help, and then they made the fateful decision to stay at the airstrip to warn the others.

Once Green took off, he radioed the incoming mail plane and told the pilot not to land at McCarthy. He explained what was happening and then asked the mail plane pilot to contact the Alaska State Troopers in Glennallen and request their assistance.

Meanwhile, Hastings apparently planned to wait at the Heglands' home and kill his neighbors one by one as they arrived, but once Tim Nash had escaped from the house, Hastings knew he needed to alter his plan and hunt down Nash before he could warn the others.

While Tim and Amy waited in the freezing morning air, Hastings followed a dog sled trail through the thick brush to the airstrip. He crawled up a large mound of plowed snow across the runway from the Nashes and fired ten rounds at the newlyweds, who stood 250 yards away from him. He then walked to within fifty feet of their bodies, fired two more shots, and then continued to approach, firing two final shots into their heads. To hide their bodies in deeper snow, he dragged them to the top of the snowbank across the runway from where they had died.

Soon after Hastings had climbed the snowbank, two more area residents, Harley King and Donna Byram, arrived on King's snowmachine at the north end of the airstrip. Harley and his wife, Jo, had lived on their homestead fifteen miles west of McCarthy since 1966. Jo, a well-known bush pilot and flight instructor, had flown her plane to Anchorage and was waiting for the weather to improve before flying back to McCarthy, so she was not home that fateful day. Harley had agreed to give Donna Byram a ride to the airstrip. Byram, who lived between the Kings' home and McCarthy, planned to fly out on the mail plane.

Byram saw large blotches of blood on the snow-covered airstrip and then saw Hastings standing on the snowbank. When they drew closer, Hastings opened fire on them. Byram was standing on the sled behind the snowmachine, and she saw bullets hit the machine and King. One shot hit Byram in the upper right arm. King drove the snowmachine as fast as he could toward the south, away from Hastings, but one of Hastings's shots broke King's leg, and he soon lost control of the machine. The snowmachine crashed and threw King and Byram onto the runway near the path leading to the Heglands' home.

Byram tried to load King back onto the sled, but Hastings was quickly approaching. King told Byram he couldn't move and urged her to save herself. After a moment's hesitation, Byram fled toward the Heglands' home. As she ran, she heard two shots and knew King was dead. When she reached the Heglands' house, she saw the front door had been kicked in, so she ran to the greenhouse and hid outside. As she huddled, shivering, she heard Hastings's voice grow louder as he said, "Come on out; he's not dead yet." She held her injured arm and fought to stay quiet, certain she was about to die. She heard Hastings's footsteps on the porch and knew he would soon find her, but then he abruptly turned around and sped off on the Nashes' snowmachine.

There were only three Alaska State Troopers within a radius of a hundred miles who were available to respond to the massacre in McCarthy. The troopers knew the situation was dire, and they did not have time to wait for backup. They commandeered an oil company helicopter and ordered the pilot to fly to McCarthy.

Hastings headed west on the McCarthy Road, where the troopers from Glennallen quickly intercepted him by helicopter. Hastings waved to the helicopter, evidently not realizing it was the troopers. He appeared to have seen a chance to get a ride to town and make his escape. When the troopers exited the helicopter, he quickly told them he was Chris Richards and explained that Lou Hastings had gone berserk and was shooting up McCarthy. The troopers knew Richards was already in Glennallen, and Hastings had identification in his pocket. The troopers arrested him without incident.

With Hastings handcuffed and restrained in the helicopter, the troopers continued to McCarthy, where they found the bodies of Tim and Amy Nash and Harley King on the runway. They were all dead from gunshot wounds, with final kill shots to their heads. Inside the Heglands' house, the troopers discovered the bodies of Les and Flo Hegland and their neighbor, Maxine Edwards, stacked in the bedroom. A bloody fur-covered silencer sat on the nightstand beside the bodies.

The troopers found the injured Byram outside the greenhouse and helped her to the helicopter. She was forced to share the ride to Glennallen with the man who had murdered her neighbors and had tried to kill her.

Why did Louis Hastings go on a murderous rampage and kill his neighbors? The reason is nearly as bizarre as the crimes themselves. Hastings was an intelligent computer programmer who had worked at Stanford University in the late 1970s. Still, like many people who move to Alaska, he left the crowded area where he had lived in California with dreams of starting a new life in the unspoiled wilderness of Alaska. At first, he and his wife settled in Anchorage, where he started a computer-service business out of their home, but by 1982, his business and marriage were failing, and he began to spend more and more time at his cabin in Kennicott. Alaska's economy was booming in 1983 due to the construction of the Trans-Alaska Pipeline, which carries oil from Prudhoe Bay south to the port of Valdez on Prince William Sound. The state was flush with money and in the midst of a construction boom. Hastings hated the pipeline and the related development it had created, and he felt the state's newfound prosperity would ruin the lifestyle he had dreamed of when he'd moved to Alaska. It became his mission to destroy the pipeline.

Hastings finally divulged his convoluted scheme to the authorities. He'd planned to arrive in McCarthy before the mail plane and kill anyone who showed up to meet the Tuesday plane. Next, he would kill the mail plane pilot and steal the plane. He then planned to fly to a pump station near the pipeline about eighty miles west of McCarthy. Then, he intended to steal a fuel truck and ram the pipeline while shooting at it. He thought he could badly damage the pipeline, but he hoped the oil would thicken in the cold winter temperatures and not harm the environment. After rupturing the pipeline, he believed the fuel truck would burst into flames and char his body beyond recognition. He hoped people would think he had been murdered in

McCarthy with the other residents, and his family would never know he was a murderer who had committed suicide in the end.

The troopers learned Hastings had never before shot a live animal, so to prepare himself for his rampage, he'd practiced by shooting rabbits. He felt if he could shoot a rabbit, he could shoot a human. The weekend before the massacre, Hastings learned that his wife, who was living in Anchorage, was having an affair. This upsetting news might have been enough to push an already angry man over the edge.

Louis Hastings brutally massacred six people on March 1, 1983, because he believed murdering his neighbors was a necessary first step in his brilliant plan to preserve the Alaskan wilderness. Les and Flo Hegland, Maxine Edwards, Tim and Amy Nash, and Harley King died in the McCarthy massacre, and Chris Richards and Donna Byram were injured. The judge sentenced Louis Hastings to 634 years in prison.

As a sad footnote to this tragic story, Chris Richards, a man the surviving residents of McCarthy considered a hero because his swift actions had saved more people from being killed in the 1983 massacre, died when his Kennicott cabin burned down one week before Christmas in 2001. After his death, many who knew Richards said Hastings had finally claimed his seventh victim. Richards never recovered physically or mentally from the massacre, and in later years, he was plagued by survivor's guilt, depression, and alcoholism. According to his friends, he was trying to give up alcohol and was suffering from hallucinations at the time of his death.

The McCarthy/Kennicott area is now a popular tourist destination. Still, like most remote areas in Alaska, the crowds leave in September, and only a few hardy people choose to live in such a desolate wilderness in the winter. Most of these people cherish their solitude, but they often must depend on each other to survive the long, cold winter. For the folks of the McCarthy area, it was not easy for them to trust their neighbors again after that horrible Tuesday in March 1983, and mail day has never been the same since.

THE HORRIBLE MISDEEDS OF PAPA PILGRIM

Much of this story takes place in McCarthy, and it begins where the last story ended. Chris Richards, one of the survivors of the McCarthy mail day massacre, died when his cabin burned a few days before Christmas in 2001. At almost the exact moment when flames were leaping from Richards's cabin, the Pilgrim clan marched into McCarthy. "Papa" Pilgrim, Country Rose, and their fifteen children made quite a spectacle in the streets of McCarthy.

Alaska's slogan is the "Last Frontier." To some people, this means Alaska is the wild west, a place with less law and order where they can live as they choose. The man who called himself Papa Pilgrim believed moving his family to the wilderness of Alaska would offer him the opportunity to do anything he wanted. Papa Pilgrim was the worst kind of a hypocrite because he hid his crimes behind his religious zeal. Like a charismatic cult leader, Pilgrim could appear charming and persuasive in public, but there was another side to him, and this was the side his family saw all too often.

In most wilderness areas in Alaska, you're likely to find a few people who have chosen to live in such a remote place because they want to escape societal norms and public scrutiny. Most of them are good people who simply don't want to be bothered by the government or be told how to raise their children, or they want to follow their own spiritual beliefs. Alaska does have laws, though. Alaska is not the wild west. Papa Pilgrim might have hidden off the grid in the Alaska wilderness and continued his horrible reign over his family had he not taken on the National Park Service and turned a spotlight on himself and his family.

The strange story of Papa Pilgrim begins much earlier than his arrival in McCarthy. Pilgrim went by his legal name, Robert (Bobby) Hale, when he was in high school. Bobby's father, I. B. Hale, was a college football star who turned down an offer to play for the Washington Redskins and instead joined the FBI. Bobby Hale grew up in an affluent family in Arlington, Texas, where he, his twin brother Billy, and their younger brother, Tommy, attended Arlington Heights High School.

Bobby Hale was known for his violent temper and a love for fighting with his fists. He even trained as a boxer in his youth. At age seventeen, Bobby ran off with his sixteen-year-old high school sweetheart, Kathleen (KK) Connally, the daughter of future Texas governor John Connally. John Connally is perhaps best remembered for riding in the car with President John F. Kennedy in Dallas when Kennedy was assassinated.

Bobby and KK eloped and moved to Tallahassee, Florida, where KK soon learned she was pregnant. Bobby and KK had a tumultuous relationship, and on Monday, April 27, 1959, following an explosive argument, KK spent the night with the landlady of their apartment building. The following morning, KK went to the local police station and asked if they could send her back to her parents in Texas. Before the officers could help her, KK returned to her apartment, where police found her dead a few hours later, the back of her head blown away by a twenty-gauge shotgun.

According to Bobby, he arrived home and found his wife lying on the sofa with a loaded shotgun, threatening to kill herself. He tried to get her to put down the gun, but when she refused, he lunged for the weapon, and it discharged. KK's death was ruled an accident, despite the absence of her prints on the shotgun.

After KK died, Bobby returned to Fort Worth, where he received his GED and attended Texas Christian University for a short while. A few months later, the police caught Bobby and his twin brother breaking into the Los Angeles apartment of Judith Exner, the rumored mistress of JFK. Exner also supposedly had ties to Sam Giancana, a leading figure in the Chicago Mafia. No explanation has ever emerged to suggest why the Hale brothers broke into Exner's apartment. Not long after the break-in, though, the US government awarded one of the largest military contracts in US history to I. B. Hale's new employer, General Dynamics. Some historians wonder if the brothers were trying to find evidence in Exner's apartment about her affair with Kennedy so that they could blackmail the president into awarding General Dynamics the defense contract.

Bobby Hale next wandered from California to Houston and then back to California, where he ran with the same crowd as Charles Manson. At age thirty-three, Bobby, now going by the name Bob Sunstar, met sixteen-year-old Kurina Rose Bresler near a waterfall in the San Bernadino Mountains. He soon began calling his new girl-friend "Country Rose."

Bobby and Rose found a job caretaking a ranch owned by actor Jack Nicholson in a remote section of northern New Mexico. They stayed on the New Mexico ranch for more than twenty years, raising sheep and goats and growing vegetables. Rose gave birth to their first child, Butterfly Sunstar (later renamed Elishaba) in 1975, and every other year, Rose bore another child until she and Bobby eventually had fifteen children.

Bobby Hale experimented with various religions but finally settled on his unique, self-serving form of Christianity. He changed his name to Papa Pilgrim and was not shy about sharing his version of the gospel with anyone who would listen.

The Pilgrim children never watched television, and they had no access to computers. They received no formal education and were naive about the ways of the world. Only Elishaba and the oldest boys learned how to read. Hale destroyed all the family books except the Bible and a copy of *Pilgrim's Progress* and refused to teach the other children how to read or even how to perform simple mathematical calculations. He wanted them to know the Scripture only through his teaching. He did not want them to read the Bible for themselves and then question his interpretation of it.

Papa forced his children to haul his bathwater every night and then allowed them to take baths in his dirty water every three to four days. He bragged that his kids bathed in their undergarments and had never seen a naked body, including their own. Papa demanded total obedience from Rose and his children, and when he felt they'd disobeyed him, he unleashed swift, brutal punishment. He whipped them with a leather strap or his belt and hit them with his fists. As a trained boxer, he delivered severe beatings.

When Bobby and Rose had first moved to the New Mexico ranch, they lived miles from their nearest neighbors, but over time, people began moving closer to the strange backwoods couple whose children never seemed to go to school. Bobby taught his children it was okay to steal from the neighbors if they had something they needed. When neighbors started accusing him of theft and threatened to write a letter to Jack Nicholson asking him to evict the Hale family from the ranch, Papa Pilgrim decided it was time to take his show on the road and move his clan to Alaska. Once in Alaska, he believed he could live in seclusion with his family, preach his gospel, and act as lord of his kingdom. He didn't seem to realize that conditions can be extreme in Alaska, and you often must depend on others to survive.

The Pilgrim family drifted around Alaska for a few years. They lived in Fairbanks and Homer for a short time, but neither town offered Papa the seclusion he desired for his family. He knew as soon as he drove into McCarthy in January 2002 that this was where he wanted to settle. He didn't plan to live in McCarthy itself, but he wanted to live near enough to the small town to get supplies there on the weekly mail plane.

Neil Darish, who was in the process of remodeling the McCarthy Lodge for the summer tourism season, was the first to notice the strange arrival of the Pilgrim family. The temperature hovered at twenty degrees below zero, but most of the Pilgrims huddled together in the open beds of two pickup trucks. When the trucks stopped in front of the lodge, the kids jumped from the beds and looked around excitedly.

A man with long, gray hair, a long beard, a weathered face, and piercing blue eyes climbed from the cab of one of the trucks and introduced himself to Darish as "Pilgrim." Darish invited the family into the lodge's dining room. Pilgrim had come to McCarthy with only ten of his kids. Rose stayed back with the younger children while Papa checked out McCarthy and scouted available property. Papa liked what he saw in McCarthy, and the Pilgrim clan charmed the few residents who'd gathered at the lodge to meet them. The Pilgrim kids grabbed fiddles, guitars, and a mandolin from their trucks and put on an impromptu bluegrass concert for the crowd. The children were cute, shy, and very religious. Most of the residents welcomed the Pilgrims, but some in the group of townspeople saw Papa Pilgrim for the con man he was.

Papa Pilgrim soon returned to McCarthy with Country Rose and the remainder of their fifteen children. They bought an abandoned mine fourteen miles from McCarthy up a mountain and accessible only by the nearly impassable McCarthy–Green Butte Road. Papa called their new home "Hillbilly Heaven."

Hillbilly Heaven could be reached by snowmachine, horse, and even on foot if you didn't mind hiking for a day. Since it was impossible to drive a truck up the road, Pilgrim arranged to have supplies delivered by bush plane or by horse. Soon, though, the freight costs became too expensive, and in the fall of 2002, when the family ran short of funds, the Pilgrims began to secretly use a bulldozer to clear the old road to town. Since the road ran through Wrangell–St. Elias National Park, and park regulations prohibited clearing park land or altering the old road, Pilgrim did his best to hide his illicit actions from the Park Service. The following spring, when park rangers discovered what the Pilgrims had done to the road, they began surveying the damage and prepared a lawsuit against Robert Hale, a.k.a. Papa Pilgrim.

Pilgrim wasted no time preying on the generosity of other Alaskans and asking for their sympathy and support. He posted letters around McCarthy about the unfairness of the Park Service, denying his simple God-fearing family access to their home. He invited a TV news crew from Anchorage so its viewers could see the family's simple lifestyle, and so Papa could talk about how much they needed the old road to haul supplies to their home in Hillbilly Heaven. The charming news piece generated support for the Pilgrims and anger against the Park Service.

The story about the Pilgrims and their simple, godly lifestyle high above McCarthy in Hillbilly Heaven spread to national and even international news organizations. The *Washington Post*, the *Economist*, CNN, and the BBC all did stories on the Pilgrims and their backwoods lifestyle. Zealous reporters uncovered the story of Hale's past, but the Pilgrim patriarch reveled in all the attention and greedily accepted any proffered charity. He pushed his charming children in front of the cameras and never missed an opportunity for his family to perform their gospel tunes for the press.

The residents of McCarthy, who at first had found the Pilgrims charming and welcomed them with open arms, soon began to grow tired of the clan. At the beginning of the 2004 summer tourist season, Pilgrim dressed some of his younger children in ragged outfits and stationed them by the footbridge into McCarthy, where they sold tickets for a bus ride up to the Kennecott Mines. Other local families already provided bus service to the mines, and the residents of McCarthy resented the Pilgrims for stealing the business.

The Pilgrims also set up a squatter's camp down the street from the McCarthy Lodge, where they stayed when they were in town. Not only did they encroach upon the properties of others, but they brought their livestock into the camp, forcing their neighbors to deal with the smell and excrement from the animals. McCarthy residents repeatedly asked the Pilgrims to move their squatter's camp. When the Pilgrims refused to budge, Stevens Harper, a park ranger and a neighbor whose driveway had been partially blocked by the Pilgrims' possessions, approached their camp driving a bulldozer. Two dozen McCarthy residents arrived on the scene to support Harper, and Papa Pilgrim finally moved the camp to a parcel of land he'd recently purchased at the end of the McCarthy Road.

Papa Pilgrim continued to teach his kids that it was okay for them to steal equipment and animals from others, and if the father had a run-in with one of the locals, he often sent Joshua and Jacob, his two oldest sons, to follow or frighten them. When Park Service rangers attempted to climb the road to talk to Pilgrim, some of the oldest kids at first followed the rangers on horseback and then blocked their way when they got close to Hillbilly Heaven.

Papa Pilgrim liked to preach his version of the gospel, and when others disagreed with him, he'd get mad and leave. The people of McCarthy found Papa Pilgrim overbearing and self-righteous, and they were concerned about the welfare of the kids. The older kids often sported large bruises, and people wondered if the bruises had been caused by a rough life outdoors or if their source was more sinister. A few realized that most of the kids couldn't read, and they wondered if the children had ever received formal schooling.

Although the residents of McCarthy worried about the Pilgrim children, most felt it was not their place to interfere in the lives of this devoutly Christian family who seemed well adjusted and happy. No one could know the horrors Country Rose and her children endured at the hands of Papa Pilgrim.

Pilgrim began having sexual relations with his oldest daughter, Elishaba, when she was eighteen years old. Ten years later, she, her father, and her mother often shared the same bed. Hale told his daughter that her mother was old and ugly and no longer excited him. He told Elishaba she needed to get him excited so he could plant his seed in her mother. Elishaba hated having sex with Papa. She knew it wasn't right, but when she told her father she thought their relationship was sinful, Papa told her the Scripture said it was okay for a father to have intimate relations with his oldest daughter. He also pointed out that she was helping her mother have more children.

In 2004, the Pilgrims met another devout Christian family who lived in Palmer, Alaska. The Buckinghams had nine children, and the Pilgrim children were thrilled to meet new friends. At first, even Papa Pilgrim liked the Buckinghams, but then Jim Buckingham noticed the many bruises on Elishaba and suspected her father was physically and sexually abusing her. When Buckingham confronted Pilgrim about his suspicions, Pilgrim grew angry and ordered his family to leave the Buckinghams' home.

While with the Buckinghams, Elishaba told the Buckingham girls that the Bible discouraged marriage. The Buckingham girls, who knew the Bible well, explained to Elishaba that she was misquoting the Bible. Elishaba began to wonder if her father had misquoted the Bible on purpose, and she began to question everything Papa had told her. She mostly wondered if the Bible said it was right for a father and daughter to have sexual relations.

Papa seemed to be losing control of his temper more often. When Jonathan, the youngest child, cried, Papa would set the baby on his lap and pinch his nose and mouth closed until the baby began to turn blue and pass out. This action not only scared Jonathan but also terrified Rose and the other kids, so Papa began to pinch Jonathan's nose and mouth closed to keep the others in line.

In January 2005, Papa took Elishaba and some of the boys down to McCarthy to gather supplies, and they stayed at their shack on the edge of town. That night, Papa argued with the boys over Something Jim Buckingham had told them. He sent the boys out to unload the trucks and then lost his temper with Elishaba when she said he had not been teaching them what the Bible really said. He took off his belt and began whipping her. When the boys heard her scream, they returned to the shack. Elishaba tried to run out the door, but Papa grabbed her by the hair and dragged her back inside the cabin. He told the boys to leave, so they got on their snowmachines and headed up the valley to their home.

Papa beat Elishaba and raped her repeatedly. He kept her locked in the shack for three days, and when he finally took her home, he made her wear a ski mask so the others could not see her bruises and her badly swollen face.

Elishaba's sixteen-year-old sister, Jerusalem, asked Elishaba to remove her ski mask so she could see what Papa had done to her. Elishaba's face was so swollen that Jerusalem barely recognized her sister. Elishaba's brothers were shocked and angry when they saw her face, and they told Papa he was wrong for beating her. Elishaba admitted to her brothers what Papa had been doing to her. She didn't say he had sexually abused her, but she said he had treated her like a wife, only a hundred times worse, and it was as bad as they could imagine.

The older boys confronted their father, and Papa hit Joshua with his fist and broke his nose. The four older boys decided to leave home and told Elishaba she should also consider leaving. After the boys left, Papa declared his sons lost to the devil, and his behavior grew even more erratic as he continued to beat Elishaba and punish the younger kids for small wrongs.

Rose told Elishaba to run away from home, but Elishaba was too terrified about what Papa would do to her if he caught her. Finally, one day when the gasoline supply for the generator was running low, Papa decided to make a quick trip to McCarthy to get more gas, and Elishaba knew this was her chance to make a break for it. She announced to the others that she was leaving, and Jerusalem said she would go with her. Jerusalem was worried that Elishaba did not have the will to keep herself alive, so she wanted to accompany and take care of her sister.

Rose called Joseph in Glennallen, and he said he and the other boys would meet Elishaba and Jerusalem when they arrived in McCarthy and would keep them safe from Papa.

Elishaba and Jerusalem knew they didn't have much time before Papa returned. He planned to hurry to McCarthy, grab the gas, and rush back up the hill because he was afraid Elishaba would escape if he left her alone for too long.

The two young women attempted to start one of the snowmachines, but it wouldn't fire. When they looked at the engine, they realized the spark plug had been removed. They replaced the spark plug, told their family goodbye, and drove a short distance over the snow, but then the fan belt broke. Jerusalem struggled through the deep snow back to the cabin and started a second machine. They only went a short distance on this snowmachine, though, before it ran out of gas, and they saw it had a fuel-line leak.

They were running out of time before Papa returned, and in desperation, they transferred to a third snowmachine. They traveled a short distance and then pulled off the main trail and hid in the trees. Jerusalem had brought white sheets with them, so they covered themselves and the snowmachine with the sheets and remained motionless in the snow. Elishaba couldn't even imagine the magnitude of Papa's rage if he found them, and once he got near the cabin, he would see the stalled snowmachines and know something was wrong.

As they heard Papa's snowmachine coming up the trail, Elishaba prayed and tried to remain calm. When he drove past them, Elishaba told her sister they had to hurry. They had half an hour at best before Papa would be on their tail.

When they arrived in McCarthy, their brothers were not at the meeting place. Elishaba pulled the snowmachine into thick brush, and she and Jerusalem crawled under the boughs of a spruce tree, where they hid from their father and waited for their brothers. They heard Papa on his snowmachine, searching the streets of the town, circling and waiting for any sign of his missing daughters.

Elishaba and Jerusalem stayed under the spruce tree for five days, eating cold cheese and raisins, while the temperature dropped to twenty degrees below zero at night. They didn't dare build a fire, and they had no sleeping bags, so they huddled and waited. They finally decided to sneak down to their town shack and use the phone. They knew they had to be careful because their father could be staying at the cabin. When they arrived at the shack, they quietly searched the surrounding woods, and indeed, Papa had hidden his snowmachine in the brush.

The girls hurried back to their hiding place, and the next day they entered another cabin and used the phone there to call their brothers. The brothers had misunderstood the original rendezvous spot and had been anxiously waiting to hear from their sisters. The brothers rescued Elishaba and Jerusalem, and the girls eventually went to live with the Buckinghams in Palmer.

A few months later, when Elishaba heard that Papa had nearly beaten two-year-old Joseph to death, she knew it was time to report his many sins to the authorities. Bobby Hale heard the troopers were after him, and he managed to hide from them for twelve days but was eventually found and arrested. He stood quietly while the authorities placed the handcuffs on him.

Hale continued to deny the claims made by his wife and children, even after a Palmer grand jury charged him in September 2005 with thirty felony accounts of rape, assault, and incest. He pleaded not guilty to the charges, but a year later, he changed his plea to no contest in exchange for a fourteen-year prison sentence.

At Hale's sentencing hearing in September 2007, his wife and all his children, except the youngest one, addressed the court and scolded their father, asking him why he had done such terrible things to them. They told the judge that they loved their father and were trying not to hold any bitterness against him, but they begged the judge not to let him out of prison.

As fourteen of his fifteen children spoke at the sentencing hearing, spectators cringed when they heard for the first time the depths of horror the Hale family had endured at the hands of their father. Elishaba's statement, when she detailed some of her father's most appalling acts toward her, sickened the crowd. The children confessed that they thought their world was normal until they met the Buckinghams and realized there was another way to live.

Robert Hale died in a prison hospital on May 26, 2008, only eight months into his fourteen-year sentence. He was sixty-seven years old and had been in poor health for many years, with advanced cirrhosis, diabetes, and blood clots. He never apologized to his family nor repented for his evil deeds. In the end, he refused to talk to his family.

Most of the Hale children moved in with the Buckinghams, where they learned to read and write. Joseph and Joshua married the two oldest Buckingham daughters, and Elishaba is also now married.

How do you erase a lifetime of abuse and a childhood where your parents taught you to survive in the wilderness but offered you no advice about how to belong in society and how to treat others? Hopefully, with much support, the Hale children will find their way.

The residents of McCarthy, who had initially found the Hale children sweet and the family charming, were horrified when they learned of the nightmare Papa Pilgrim had created for his family in the cabin on the mountain.

In addition to the fifteen children born to Robert and Rose Hale, Hale fathered three children from previous marriages. Country Rose was Hale's fourth wife and probably not his first abuse victim. KK Connally was sixteen years old when she married Robert Hale, and she died forty-four days later from a shotgun blast to the head. Was the shot self-inflicted, or did Robert Hale murder his young wife? In either case, KK was one of Hale's earliest victims.

Fairbanks and Environs

F airbanks, the second-largest city in Alaska, sits in the center of the state, 360 miles north of Anchorage, and it bears the nickname the "Golden Heart City." Humans have occupied the area around Fairbanks for thousands of years, but a permanent settlement did not exist at the present site of the city until August 26, 1901, when E. T. Barnette established a trading post on the south bank of the Chena River. Barnette originally planned for this trading post to be only temporary, but when prospectors discovered gold near the post, Barnette decided to stay. As the gold stampeders rushed to the area, it quickly grew, and citizens voted to incorporate the city of Fairbanks in 1903.

The economic situation of Fairbanks is closely tied to the booms and busts of the state's mineral and oil resources. In the early 1900s, gold miners flocked to the area, and Fairbanks flourished. The easy-to-reach gold was gone by World War I, however, and Fairbanks struggled. Then, workers completed a railroad from Anchorage to Fairbanks, allowing for the transportation of heavy mining equipment to the area and the exploitation of previously unreachable gold. In the 1940s and 1950s, Fairbanks became a staging area for the building of military depots during World War II and the first decade of the Cold War. In 1968, the massive Prudhoe Bay Oil Field was discovered on Alaska's North Slope, and Fairbanks, the city closest to the oil field, became the headquarters for building the Trans-Alaska Pipeline. During the years of the pipeline construction, the economic and population boom rivaled those during the early years of the gold rush. Now, Fairbanks sees economic upswings and downswings tied to the price of crude oil, but as oil production declines, the city is developing tourism and other industries to diversify its economy.

With all its booms and busts, it's no surprise that Fairbanks has always had a high crime rate. During the oil boom, many compared Fairbanks to a wild-west town with little police presence. The city grew faster than the police force. As with Anchorage, once the criminals began operating outside the city limits, they became the responsibility of the already beleaguered Alaska State Troopers. Today, the violent crime rate in Fairbanks ranks higher than Alaska's average, which, in turn, is the highest in the US per capita.

This section includes crimes that have been committed in and near Fairbanks, including Manley Hot Springs and the town of North Pole.

MURDER AT THE NORTH POLE

After a string of murders of young women near Fairbanks in the late 1970s and early '80s, the abductions and murders mysteriously stopped. Troopers didn't believe the vicious killer had suddenly halted his murder spree, but they feared the predator had moved somewhere else. Unfortunately, at the time, they had no database to track the killer's movements beyond Alaska. Only the deductive reasoning and hard work of seasoned investigators traced the monster to his new hunting grounds, four thousand miles away.

Before the FBI's Combined DNA Index System (CODIS), and before VICAP (the Violent Criminal Apprehension Program), states had no systematic method of sharing the evidence from violent crime scenes. No national database existed, making it difficult for investigators to track vicious predators who crossed state lines.

The North Pole is where Santa and Mrs. Claus live and where busy elves build toys for good girls and boys around the world, or so the legend goes. The city of North Pole, Alaska, is seventeen hundred miles south of the geological North Pole, but the townsfolk take full advantage of the town's moniker. Many streets have holiday names, and stores sell Christmas-themed items year-round. The town's biggest attraction is a large gift shop named Santa Claus House, which boasts the world's largest fiberglass statue of Santa. North Pole sits south of Fairbanks and stretches between Fort Wainwright and Eielson Air Force Base (AFB) and between the Cheena and Tanana Rivers. In the late 1970s and early 1980s, murder shattered the innocence of the town Santa Claus calls home.

Nineteen-year-old Glinda Sodemann vanished from her home in North Pole on August 29, 1979. Glinda was a newlywed and was also the daughter of an Alaska State Trooper. Glinda and her husband had a small baby. According to her husband, when he arrived home on August 29, the baby was in the crib, but Glinda had disappeared. By all accounts, Glinda was happy and had no reason to run away from her home, but investigators found no evidence to suggest foul play.

Two months later, in October, Glinda's decomposed body was found in a gravel pit near Moose Creek on the Richardson Highway, not far from Eielson AFB and twenty-two miles south of Fairbanks. Someone had shot Glinda in the face, and troopers found a .38-caliber pistol cartridge near her body. The medical examiner discovered no evidence to suggest that the murderer had sexually assaulted Glinda, and suspicion fell on Glinda's new husband, who had failed a lie detector test. Even Glinda's father suspected his son-in-law of the crime, but troopers found no evidence to arrest the husband.

On June 11, 1980, eleven-year-old Doris Oehring and her older brother were riding bikes together on the roads in North Pole. Doris cycled ahead of her brother, and when he caught up with her, he saw his sister talking to a strange man standing next to a blue car. The man had propped open the car's hood and appeared to be having engine problems. When Doris's brother pulled alongside her, the man quickly shut the hood, jumped in his car, and sped away. The brother was later able to describe the man to a police sketch artist, and he told the police that he thought the man's blue shirt looked like an Air Force uniform.

Two days after her encounter with the man in the blue car, Doris disappeared, and her bicycle was found hidden in the bushes along Badger Road near her home in North Pole. A witness reported seeing a small blue car tear around the corner at an intersection near Badger Road. The driver had seemed preoccupied and was wrestling with something or someone in the seat next to him. The police believed the attacker hid in the bushes on the side of the road and waited for Doris to ride her bike past his hiding spot. Once she got close, he jumped out of the brush, grabbed her off her bike, and tossed the bike into the nearby ditch.

Because Doris's brother thought the man he'd seen talking to his sister might have been wearing an Air Force uniform, and because the witness described the driver of the speeding car as having a military-style haircut, state troopers asked security at Eielson AFB for a list of blue cars registered to drive on the base. The Air Force handed the troopers a list of 550 names of people who owned registered vehicles that were a possible match for the rough description of the car the troopers had provided them. Investigators were desperate to find Doris, but with no fingerprints or other forensic evidence, they didn't know where to begin.

Since the troopers had not cleared Glinda Sodemann's husband for her murder, they decided to question him about the abduction of Doris Oehring. They gave him another polygraph test, and this time, the examiner found the test results inconclusive. The test results frustrated the troopers. They had no physical evidence pointing to Sodemann, but he could not pass a lie detector test when questioned about the murder of his wife or the abduction of young Doris Oehring. The troopers decided to bring in a polygraph expert to question Sodemann. After ten minutes, the expert left the examining room and told the investigators that Sodemann had an irregular heartbeat, and someone with such a heartbeat could never pass a polygraph. The test results from someone with a heartbeat like Sodemann's would always be classified as inconclusive or failing. Since the troopers had no reason other than his lie detector test results to suspect Sodemann, they had to dismiss him as a suspect in the disappearance of Doris.

On January 31, a little over seven months after someone had snatched Doris Oehring, twenty-year-old Marlene Peters disappeared. Marlene was last seen trying to hitch a ride from Fairbanks to Anchorage to visit her father, who was sick with cancer. The police considered Marlene's disappearance suspicious, but they didn't know if someone had abducted her near Fairbanks or if she had disappeared somewhere else between the two cities. Troopers did not immediately link her case to Doris Oehring or Glinda Sodemann.

Five months after Marlene disappeared, sixteen-year-old Wendy Wilson also vanished. Wendy was last seen hitchhiking, and a witness saw her climb into a white pickup truck in Moose Creek, near Fairbanks. Three days after she disappeared, her body was found near Johnson Road, thirty-two miles south of Fairbanks, near the Trans-Alaska Pipeline. Wendy's killer had strangled her and then obliterated her face with a shotgun blast.

Nine weeks after the discovery of Wendy Wilson's body, Marlene Peters's remains were found. The killer had also dumped Marlene near Johnson Road, only two miles from where he'd left Wendy. He'd also strangled Marlene and then shot her in the face with a shotgun.

In May, two days after the police recovered Marlene Peters's body, they were notified of the disappearance of nineteen-year-old Lori King, last seen walking in Fairbanks.

The Fairbanks police and the Alaska State Troopers now knew they had a serial killer operating in and around North Pole, outside Fairbanks. Soon, the news media labeled the string of murders the "Fairbanks serial murders."

The police, as well as civilian and military volunteers, searched for the bodies of Doris Oehring and Lori King near the Johnson Road area, where the remains of Wendy Wilson and Marlene Peters had been discovered, but they found no sign of either victim.

On September 2, 1981, four airmen on a hunting trip came across the remains of Lori King in a wooded area near a missile site off Johnson Road. Earlier searches had somehow missed this area. The killer had done nothing to hide Lori's body. As with Wendy and Marlene, the killer had strangled Lori and then shot her in the face with a shotgun.

The FBI then joined the case because Lori's body had been found on a federal reservation. Various agencies formed a task force consisting of FBI agents, Alaska State Troopers, the Eielson AFB Office of Special Investigations (OSI), the US Army's Criminal Investigation Division from nearby Fort Wainwright, the Fairbanks Police Department, and the North Pole City Police Department. Investigators now knew they were hunting a dangerous predator who struck frequently, somehow convincing girls and young women to climb into his car. He then murdered the young women and shot them in the face. The bodies of some, but not all, of the women showed signs of sexual assault before they were murdered.

To better understand how to organize an investigation of this magnitude, Alaska State Trooper Investigator Sam Barnard flew to Atlanta, Georgia, where a joint federal and state task force was searching for the serial killer who was murdering young black men in Atlanta. Barnard watched and learned how the Atlanta task force used computer technology to manage and organize the leads in the case. Next, Barnard flew to Quantico, Virginia, where he met with experts at the FBI Behavioral Sciences Division to form a profile of the serial killer operating near Fairbanks.

When Barnard consulted with them, the FBI Behavioral Sciences Division boasted an 85 percent success rate for creating accurate profiles of unknown serial killers. The psychologists in the unit must have seemed like wizards, but humans are not machines, and law enforcement agencies soon learned that while FBI profiles could be a helpful tool, they were only one of many tools and should not be relied upon entirely.

The profilers told Barnard that the Fairbanks serial killer was probably single and lived alone. They said they believed the perpetrator had a hard time holding a job, and even though Doris Oerhing's brother stated he thought the man he'd seen talking to Doris wore an Air Force uniform, experts said they believed the murderer was a civilian. Barnard returned to Fairbanks with the unknown killer's profile, and task force members thought they now had something solid for the foundation of their investigation.

Why did the murderer shoot the women in the face after strangling them? Psychologists suggested that perhaps the killer was repeatedly murdering someone from his past, and he shot his victims in the face to wipe out their identities. Whether accurate or not, this analysis made it no easier for investigators to find the elusive killer.

Troopers Jim McCann and Chris Stockard undertook the massive task of organizing and entering two and a half years' worth of information, tips, and physical evidence into the state computers. Stockard, who had computer training, then developed a program to cross-reference the items in the database, prioritizing valuable leads and suspects.

An investigator on the task force from the Eielson AFB OSI reported that he had identified three people on the base who had acted inappropriately toward women. One of the three men he'd pinpointed was Technical Sergeant Thomas Richard Bunday, a thirty-three-year-old electrical expert. Coworkers said Bunday repeatedly showed disrespect toward women, and one woman who worked with Bunday said he was verbally abusive, and she was afraid of him.

The task force didn't dismiss Bunday as a possible suspect, but he was not high on their list because he did not fit the FBI profile in several ways. The profilers believed the murderer would prove to be a civilian who was single, lived alone, and could not hold a job. Bunday was married, had children, and was enlisted in the military, maintaining a good job as an electrician. The task force identified several suspects who fit the profile better than Bunday, so they considered him a possible but unlikely suspect.

After Lori King's murder on May 16, 1981, the abductions and murders mysteriously stopped. One and a half years later, in November 1982, the task force concluded that the murderer had died, was in prison, in the hospital, or had moved somewhere else. The task force decided they needed to look at military personnel who had transferred outside the state in the past eighteen months. They began scouring the records of recent transfers from Eielson AFB, and they also contacted police agencies near other US Air Force bases around the world and asked them to be on the lookout for and to report any murders similar to the ones perpetrated near Fairbanks.

The list of transferred Air Force personnel included the name Thomas Richard Bunday. Bunday had transferred to Sheppard AFB near Wichita Falls, Texas, and the transfer happened on September 9, 1981, one week after hunters discovered the body of Lori King near Johnson Road. The Wichita Falls police reported they had recently investigated a murder similar to the ones that had occurred near Fairbanks, but the police in Texas believed the woman there had been killed by a drug dealer who also now was dead.

The task force noted Bunday's resemblance to the drawing made from Doris Oehring's brother's description of the man he'd seen talking to his sister. Young Oehring immediately identified a photo of Bunday in a line-up, and he had no trouble picking out a picture of Bunday's car as the vehicle whose driver he had seen talking to his sister two days before her abduction. Troopers interviewed Bunday's Alaska neighbors and coworkers, and most painted an unflattering picture of him. They described him as an unlikeable loner. Bunday had a variety of shotguns and pistols registered in his name.

In January 1983, Trooper Sam Barnard flew to Sheppard AFB and interviewed Richard Bunday. While Bunday agreed to answer Barnard's questions, he refused to take a lie detector test, allow a search of his home, or give samples of his hair. When Barnard told Bunday that Doris Oehring's brother had identified a photo of him as the man he had seen talking to his sister, Bunday didn't respond.

Barnard returned to Fairbanks and said he didn't believe they had solid evidence against Bunday, and since Bunday didn't fit the FBI profile, he felt they should investigate other suspects. Most of the task force, though, felt Bunday was their man, and they believed it was time to take a closer look at him.

On March 7, 1983, McCann and Stockard flew to Texas, where they met with Texas state and federal police, as well as the Air Force OSI. The OSI agreed to place loose surveillance on Bunday.

McCann and Stockard rented two rooms at a local motel for their headquarters. They then called Bunday, identified themselves as Alaska State Troopers, and told Bunday they were investigating a string of murders near Fairbanks. They asked Bunday if he could stop by their motel room so they could talk to him. Bunday willingly spoke to McCann and Stockard and seemed to like the two troopers. The troopers noted that Bunday provided only vague responses to their questions, but he never denied killing the women near North

Pole. At one point, Bunday made the strange comment, "I had trouble with girls in Alaska."

McCann and Stockard invited Bunday to return the following day so they could continue their conversation, and Bunday agreed. This time, the troopers punched harder. They told Bunday they knew he'd killed the women in Alaska, and they knew how and when he had killed them, but they didn't understand why he had killed them. They told him they also knew he had killed a woman in Texas. They knew he was guilty, and they told him he would either spend the rest of his life in an Alaska prison or a cell in Texas, where he was likely to face the death penalty. Bunday said little, but he began to cry by the end of the four-hour interview.

Bunday returned to the motel the following day for another meeting, but he didn't stay this time. Instead, he handed the troopers a note denying he had murdered any women in Alaska. The following day, McCann, Stockard, an FBI agent, an OSI agent, and a representative from the Wichita Falls district attorney's office presented the Bundays with a search warrant and spent twelve hours searching their home and vehicles. They found ammunition consistent with the ammunition used in the Alaska murders, newspaper clippings about the Alaska murders, and surveillance-type photos of young girls.

Bunday agreed to again meet with the troopers at 9:00 a.m. the following day, but instead, he showed up at their motel at 8:00 a.m., an hour early, catching the troopers off guard. Bunday confessed to murdering five women in Alaska, including Doris Oehring, whose body still had not been found. He said he had discarded her body in a remote section of Eielson AFB.

McCann and Stockard felt helpless. They had no authority to arrest someone in Texas, and the Texas police needed a warrant to arrest someone for crimes committed in Alaska. Bunday told the troopers he would voluntarily return to Alaska with them, but they dared not escort him to Alaska until they had the proper paperwork. Without a warrant for his arrest, they could not restrain Bunday. If he suddenly changed his mind during a stopover in Seattle and walked out of the airport, they would have no authority to stop him, and they might never be able to find him again. Bunday promised Mc-Cann and Stockard that he would return to their motel room the following morning once they had the proper warrants.

The following day, the troopers had arrest warrants in hand, but Bunday failed to show up at the agreed-upon time for their meeting. The troopers called Bunday's house, and his wife said Richard was riding his motorcycle, but she expected him to meet her at one o'clock that afternoon at the local H&R Block office to work on their tax return. The OSI surveillance team waited for Bunday outside the H&R Block office, but when Bunday and his wife left the office, the OSI team mistakenly followed her car instead of pursuing Bunday on his motorcycle.

McCann and Stockard waited impatiently for Bunday to arrive at their motel room or for local police to call and say they had Bunday in custody. Dark clouds rolled in over Wichita Falls as they waited, and the skies burst with a heavy downpour.

Bunday sped out of Wichita Falls on his motorcycle, but when it began to rain, he turned around and started back toward town. He stopped under an overpass, pulled McCann's and Stockard's business cards from his wallet, and placed them carefully on a rock. He then continued on his way, driving at a carelessly fast rate of speed in the pouring rain. When he swerved in front of a large dump truck coming toward him in the other lane, the truck driver tried to avoid the collision by turning away from Bunday, but Bunday pursued the truck and crashed into it just behind the cab. Bunday died instantly, and the search for the North Pole serial murderer came to a dramatic end.

Analysis of the forensic evidence found in the Bunday home indicated that some of the hairs collected from Bunday's truck belonged to Wendy Wilson, and the shotgun shells found in his home had been manufactured in the same bunch as the shells used to obliterate the faces of Lori King and Wendy Wilson.

In 1986, three years after Bunday's death and a few months after Doris Oehring should have graduated from high school, Doris's skull was found in a remote section of Eielson AFB.

Although behavioral profiles often prove valuable in identifying a murderer, in this case, the profile provided by the FBI did more harm than good. If not for the misleading psychological profile handed down from the behavioral scientists at Quantico, troopers likely would have identified and captured Bunday much sooner than they did, and possibly even before he left the state of Alaska. This case demonstrates that while a behavioral profile might be helpful, it is only one tool, and nothing beats hours of investigation, careful data collection, solid forensic evidence, and a healthy dose of common sense.

Despite a faulty profile, no DNA database, and no national database to compare similar crimes, the dogged investigation by Alaska State Troopers and other authorities involved in this case caught a vicious predator in the time before DNA evidence became king.

The Homicidal Trooper

Most of us like to believe we can trust the police, but not everyone goes into law enforcement for the greater good. Some enter the police academy because they crave power over others, and what better job than policing to achieve this power? Most police officers are good, and a few are bullies. John Patrick Addis, though, was the worst kind of police officer. He was a monster with a badge.

Born in Flint, Michigan, in 1950, John Patrick Addis loved to hunt and fish. He grew into a big, muscular man with blond hair and green eyes. By all accounts, Addis was talented and brilliant. He played the French horn, piano, and guitar. He excelled at sports and maintained good grades. He did not drink or take drugs, and he ran, exercised, and lifted weights to keep his body in shape.

John liked science and as a young man expressed an interest in studying medicine. He enrolled in college and worked as a lab technician. He married his first wife, Jodi, and the pair initially planned to settle in Michigan and raise their family. For some reason, though, Addis suddenly rejected college and decided he wanted to hunt and fish and live in the wilderness. He gave Jodi little say in the matter, and the couple moved to Sitka, Alaska. Addis began his law enforcement career as the Sitka city dog catcher, but he soon worked up the ranks and joined the Alaska State Troopers in 1974.

Addis was first assigned to Fort Yukon in northern Alaska and transferred to Fairbanks in the mid-1970s. John and Jodi had four children during their eleven-year marriage, and John doted on his kids and spent as much time as possible with them. He was an avid outdoorsman and bush pilot who could survive long periods on his own in the frigid Alaska wilderness. When he lived in Fort Yukon, he loved flying in his Cessna through northern Alaska's Brooks Range.

The Alaska State Troopers patrol vast amounts of sparsely populated territory over challenging terrain, often in adverse weather conditions. It is vital for the troopers to know each other well, to bond, and to have each other's backs in a tense situation. John's fellow officers immediately liked him and embraced him as one of their own.

Alaska State Trooper Sergeant Jim McCann, who appears in many of these stories, worked with John Addis for several years when they were both stationed in Fairbanks, and the two became good friends. When interviewed by author Glenn Puit for his book *Ghost*, McCann remembered Addis as a big, muscular guy with a brilliant mind.

McCann and other fellow troopers noted John's strange lifestyle. Instead of moving to Fairbanks with all its modern comforts, John Addis seemed intent on living the way Alaskans had survived decades earlier. He moved Jodi and their children to a tiny one-room cabin outside Fairbanks. The cabin had a dirt floor, no running water, and only intermittent electricity from a small generator. They had to haul water and use an outhouse, even when the temperature dropped to fifty degrees below zero (–45°C). With no washing machine, Jodi washed their clothes in a tub, scrubbing them on a washboard. Jodi, a registered nurse, could have had a good career, but John did not want her to work. He wanted her to stay home with the kids.

Addis made friends with the other troopers, who described him as sociable and outgoing. John and one or two of his trooper buddies often went flying and hunting together when they were off duty. Fellow troopers considered Addis a brilliant investigator with a strong work ethic and a sharp focus on details. Addis encouraged several of his fellow officers to exercise with him, and they jogged and lifted weights at the trooper barracks. John, an excellent marksman, also spent a great deal of time at the shooting range, and he and McCann helped form a SWAT team for the troopers.

According to McCann, Addis's crime scene investigative skills were his most significant contribution to the troopers. When Addis first joined the Alaska State Troopers, the organization had no crime scene lab, so he and McCann worked to improve their forensic techniques and to develop a police protocol for major homicide investigations. The two troopers read books and took college classes to enhance their skills in collecting evidence. Addis practiced techniques to identify and collect hair and fiber samples, studied blood-spatter evidence, and learned how to read patterns from shotgun "stippling" to determine how far away a gun was from a body when it was fired.

John often took his oldest daughters flying in his plane. To outsiders, the Addis family seemed happy, but years later, Jodi admitted that their family life was not as good as it appeared. When they were alone, John exerted his control over the family and particularly over Jodi, attempting to manage every facet of her life.

Over time, John's fellow troopers noticed chinks in John's armor. He insisted straight-faced to his friends that he often saw tiny humans he called "the thems," and in the early 1980s, his controlling behavior over Jodi became more evident to his colleagues. He called Jodi "Mother" and ordered her around as if he were her boss. Jodi later admitted that John abused her verbally and physically, sometimes choking her until she nearly lost consciousness. She said the abuse began soon after she and John moved to Alaska. In addition to the physical abuse, John would not allow her to drive, work outside the home, or even have friends. He also told her to sever ties with her family because they did not care about her. He wanted her to feel isolated, helpless, and utterly dependent upon him.

In early 1982, not long after the birth of their fourth child, Jodi decided she needed to get away from John, and she filed for divorce. John fought bitterly for custody of their children and told Jodi that if she did not give him custody, he would load the kids in his plane, fly to the Brooks Range, and crash the plane into the side of a mountain. In the end, Jodi won custody of the children, but the court allowed John "liberal" visitation with the kids during the school year and custody for up to six weeks each summer.

Despite her feelings toward her ex-husband, Jodi knew her kids loved their father and wanted to spend time with him. She worried, though, about John having complete control over the kids for six weeks each year. She knew John hated her, and she wondered what he might do.

After Jodi divorced him, John began to withdraw from his friends at work and no longer seemed interested in his job. Those around him believed that once he'd lost control over Jodi and his kids, John began to unravel and lose his grip on his sanity.

A few hopeful signs suggested John was moving forward with his life, however. He met a woman named Sarah, who worked at the Fairbanks office of the US Fish and Wildlife Service. John treated Sarah and her children well, and soon the pair announced they were engaged. They married in December 1982. A short while later, Addis surprised his colleagues when he abruptly quit the state troopers and told them he had decided to return to medical school. He showed everyone a letter of acceptance from the dean of a medical school in Florida, and soon afterward, he and Sarah moved to Florida.

Five months later, Sarah divorced John and returned to Fairbanks. She did not want to talk about what had happened in Florida, but John's former friends believed he had started doing the same things to Sarah that he had done to Jodi. Soon, his friends in Fairbanks learned that John never went to medical school when he moved to Florida. The letter of acceptance was fake.

Sarah revealed that during their brief marriage, John often disappeared for weeks at a time and refused to tell her where he'd gone. She said he was obsessed with having his children live with him, and he told her he planned to steal them. He asked Sarah if she would help him kidnap his kids, but she said no. She refused to help him, and she tried to talk him out of committing a serious crime.

A few months after Sarah left, John Addis began dating a woman named Toni, and a short while later, they married. Toni, a pharmacist in Sarasota, Florida, said Addis swept her off her feet with his romantic gestures and devoted interest in her. In September 1985, the couple had a daughter.

John also told Toni he planned to kidnap his children, and she also said it was a terrible idea and she wanted no part of it. Not long after the birth of their daughter, John began to exert his control over Toni. He wanted to know where she was every minute of the day, and when she went to work, he either followed her or checked her car's odometer to know how far she'd driven during the day. As time wore on, John became physically violent toward Toni. She said he sometimes grabbed her and pinned her down so she couldn't move, and once, he'd pushed her against a wall and lifted her off her feet with his hands around her neck, choking her. She said she loved him, but she also feared him.

One day, Toni was feeding their baby girl when John rushed into the room, ranting and raving. Toni said the expression on his face terrified her; he looked deranged. He stepped on Toni's feet, grabbed her by the hair, pulled her out of her chair, and started shaking her. The baby bottle flew out of her hand, and the baby began crying. After this incident, Toni sought an order of protection, and John soon filed for divorce.

In August 1986, Addis demanded visitation with his children in Alaska. Jodi wanted John to fly to Fairbanks to spend time with the kids, since they would soon start their school year. Addis wanted the kids to fly to Chicago, and then he planned to drive them to Michigan to visit relatives before continuing on to Florida. Jodi took the matter to court, demanding the visitation take place in Alaska, but the judge ordered her to put the children on a plane to visit their father. When it came time for the kids to return to Fairbanks, they weren't on the plane, and Jodi and the authorities could find no sign of John or the kids.

When Jodi learned her kids had never boarded the flight from Chicago to Fairbanks and did not even have tickets for the flight, she knew John had done what she'd always feared he would do. He'd kidnapped their children, and with all he knew and his ability to live off the grid, he would be hard to find. She was terrified, wondering what John might do with the kids, and she remembered when he'd threatened to load the kids in his plane and fly into a mountain. Did he plan to kill their children so she couldn't have them?

Jodi called the police and demanded that they listen to her. Eventually, not only did the Fairbanks police begin to search for John and the children, but they also involved law enforcement in Michigan, where John's family lived and where Jodi suspected John might be hiding the kids. Eventually, the FBI got involved in the search for John Addis and his kids.

Eight long months passed while Jodi waited and worried about where John had taken her children. Finally, someone at a gym in Kalispell, Montana, recognized that the stranger exercising in the gym matched the photo of the guy in the police flyer who had abducted his four children from Alaska. The person called the local police, who rushed to the gym to arrest John Addis.

Minutes later, the authorities located the children locked in a cabin outside Kalispell. The kids were unharmed and healthy. Addis stood trial in Fairbanks for kidnapping his children. A judge sentenced the former state trooper to four years in state prison, with two and a half years suspended. Addis spent only eighteen months in jail for his crime. Still, the prison sentence was a huge downfall for a man who once had been a respected state trooper. John Patrick Addis was now a convicted felon.

Addis left prison in 1988, and due to an interstate parole agreement, he was allowed to move to Fresno, California, where he was required to report to a California parole officer. Addis no longer seemed interested in following the law, though. In Fresno, he met a woman, moved in with her, got engaged, stole her money, and then disappeared, never again reporting to a parole officer. The woman did not report the theft to the police, so the authorities had no reason to look for Addis for the crime. Instead of issuing a warrant on Addis for jumping parole, the state of California simply closed the case. The state of Alaska did issue a statewide absconder warrant, but Addis was never arrested for violating the conditions of his parole.

After leaving Fresno, Addis frequently moved, often working as a fitness instructor at various gyms. He dated numerous women and met many of them at the gyms where he worked. Addis repeated the same pattern in different cities. He'd meet a woman, lavish her with attention, tell her he loved her, promise to marry her, steal her money, and disappear. Addis changed his identity and assumed the name John L. Edwards, a name he borrowed from a man living in Cape Coral, Florida.

In 1995, John Addis, still going by the name John Edwards, moved to Las Vegas and landed a job as a fitness instructor at a World's Gym. One of John's female clients introduced him to her good friend, Joann Albanese. Joann had been divorced for two years and had two daughters. She also had an excellent job with the MGM Grand Resort and probably seemed the perfect mark to John.

Joann and John dated for two months, and their romance quickly blossomed. Tara Rivera, the friend who had introduced Joann to John, initially prided herself on being a good matchmaker, but soon she began to regret bringing John into Joann's life. After only a month of dating, John spent most nights in the house with Joann and her daughters. Joann paid for his food at home, their meals when they went out to dinner, and the gas he put into his pickup. Rivera said John worshipped Joann, but his affection seemed unnatural; it was too much, too fast. Rivera felt that John was obsessing over and controlling her friend.

One evening when Tara and her husband joined John and Joann at a restaurant for dinner, she said she saw John snap. His face contorted with anger over an innocuous comment Tara had made. His eyes bulged, and he pounded his fists on the table to make his point, drawing the attention of other diners. Tara said he looked demented, and he frightened her. When they got home, she told her husband that she thought there was something wrong with John, and she planned to warn her friend and tell her to dump him.

When she approached Joann and expressed her concerns about John, Joann agreed that something was wrong with him. She told her friend that John did not let her out of his sight and would not even let her go to the bathroom without him present. Joann said he was smothering her, and she worried about him living in the same house with her daughters.

On August 18, 1995, Joann called Tara and said she couldn't take it anymore and had decided to end her relationship with John. She planned to take him out to a nice dinner and then tell him it was over between them.

Tara Rivera never heard from Joann Albanese again.

On August 18, 1995, Joann's ex-husband, Tom, picked up their daughters for the weekend. Joann spent the day at work and later talked to her mother on the phone, telling her that she and John were planning to go out to dinner that evening. John asked a coworker to cover his shift at the gym so he could go to dinner with Joann.

On Sunday, August 20, Tom drove his kids back to their mother's home and watched from the car as they safely entered the house. Tom saw Joann's boyfriend's truck parked in the street.

Joann's daughters noticed something was wrong as soon as they entered the house. Usually, when the girls returned home after a weekend with their father, Joann was there to greet them, and when she wasn't home, she would call to let them know she was running late. When the girls entered the house that Sunday afternoon, though, not only was their mother absent, but all the lights were on, and the door to their mother's room was open wide, her bed unmade. Joann always made her bed and locked her bedroom door when she wasn't home. She also made it a point to turn off the lights when she left a room. The girls checked the garage and saw Joann's car was gone. They then looked in their mother's dresser drawers and found both the bracelet Joann wore daily and her purse still in the drawer where she kept these items when she was home. She never left the house without her purse.

The girls called their father and then called the police. At first, the authorities were not concerned about Joann's absence. As the days passed, however, Joann's family convinced the police that Joann would never abandon her daughters without telling them where she was going, and she also would not leave them alone overnight.

Joann's family immediately suspected that Joann's new boyfriend had somehow been involved in her disappearance. Her oldest daughter said Joann and John yelled at each other often, and she described John as creepy. Joann's sister said she never liked John and felt he was only interested in her sister for her money.

Joann's sister asked Detective Hanna with the Las Vegas Police Department if she could look through John's pickup truck. Since

Hanna was busy with what he considered higher-priority cases, he gave Joann's sister permission to look through John's truck. What she found in the truck's camper shell finally convinced the police to take a harder look at John Edwards.

In Edwards's truck, Joann's sister found several IDs from other men, as well as two license plates and tags from Washington and Florida. An envelope in the vehicle bore the name "John Addis." Hanna ran the current plate and tag on the truck and found the tag was not registered to anyone.

Hanna soon discovered that Edwards was not John's last name. When he traced the name "John Addis," he learned that John Patrick Addis was a felon from Alaska who had once been an Alaska State Trooper. Hanna now knew he was trailing not only a dangerous man but also an ex-cop who had the skills to cover his tracks and avoid capture.

On August 23, 1995, a hiker found Joann's gold Honda in a remote part of Little Hell Canyon in Arizona, but the car yielded few clues. Investigators found no body, no bloodstains, and no bodily fluids in the automobile. Detectives believed that if John had killed Joann, he'd most likely dumped her body in the area where he'd left her car. They searched a nearby shallow lake but found nothing. They then combed the wilderness around the lake but again discovered no sign of Joann's body. Even without her body, Detective Hanna now felt certain that John Patrick Addis had murdered Joann Albanese and ditched her car in Little Hell Canyon, only three hours from the Mexican border.

In late 1996, a man who called himself "John Stone" walked into a Gold's Gym in Guadalajara, Mexico. Stone had blond hair and green eyes. He was big and muscular and very friendly. He soon made friends at the gym and dated numerous women. He lived with people he met, and some even gave him money because they felt sorry for him. Stone found work as a tennis instructor and also taught English and gave piano lessons.

Stone began dating twenty-five-year-old Laura Liliana Casillas Padilla, the daughter of an engineer in Guadalajara. Laura Liliana met

Stone at the Gold's Gym, and he charmed his way into her life. She brought him home to meet her family, but her father thought they were just friends because Stone was so much older than his daughter.

In March 1997, a segment about John Patrick Addis and his suspected complicity in the disappearance of Joann Albanese in Las Vegas aired on the *Geraldo* television show. A tipster called the show and reported seeing a man matching the description of Addis at a Gold's Gym in Guadalajara. When the manager of the gym told Stone that a woman had called the gym looking for someone who fit his description, Addis (a.k.a. Stone) decided it was time to leave Guadalajara.

When Laura Liliana Casillas Padilla did not show up for work or contact her family, they began to worry about her. Her sister went to her apartment, but although her belongings were still there, she saw no sign of Laura Liliana. After searching the apartment, her sister found a note on the floor. The note was from Laura Liliana to her family. She told them she loved them, but it was time for her to leave. She said John had proposed to her, and she'd accepted. She told her family she was okay and promised to call them soon.

Laura Liliana's family never heard from her again.

In October 1998, three years after she'd disappeared, a hunter found the remains of Joann Albanese in the mountains near where her car had been found in Little Hell Canyon. Addis had apparently used his remarkable strength to carry Joann's body up a mountain to dispose of it. The authorities did not search the mountains near the canyon because they didn't think a human could carry a body up such a steep incline, especially in the Arizona heat. The discovery of Joann's body left no doubt that John Addis had murdered her before escaping to Mexico. Since her remains were only bones, the medical examiner could not determine the cause of her death.

John Patrick Addis made the FBI's list of the "Top 10 Most Wanted in America." The television show *America's Most Wanted* aired the story of John Patrick Addis and the murder of Joann Albanese eight times between November 1998 and May 2005. Other shows also covered the case and asked the public for information regarding the whereabouts of Addis.

John Patrick Addis and his wife, Laura Liliana, moved to Tuxtla Gutiérrez, in Chiapas, Mexico, sometime in 1997. Chiapas, the southernmost state in Mexico, borders Guatemala to the east. Addis, who now called himself "J. Charles Peterson," worked at a variety of jobs, including tutoring the sons of the police chief. He also worked as a tennis instructor at a local resort. He and Laura Liliana had two children. Although most of their neighbors described Addis as a good father, a few of them noticed that he seemed very controlling over Laura Liliana.

On October 18, 2006, nine years after he and Laura Liliana had fled Guadalajara, their neighbors in Tuxtla Gutiérrez realized they had not seen Addis and his family in several days. When they went to their apartment to check on the residents, they noticed a horrible smell seeping from inside. They called the police, who broke into the home and found Laura Liliana dead on her bed and the bodies of the two children on their beds. The police also found more than twenty syringes near Laura Liliana's body. An autopsy showed that she and her children had died from carbon monoxide poisoning.

The police believed J. Charles Peterson, whose real name they soon learned was John Patrick Addis, had murdered his wife and children and then fled. The Mexican authorities began searching for Addis.

Several weeks later, a maid at a hotel in Guatemala City discovered the body of a man named John Charles Stone, age forty-six, on a bed in a hotel room. The body had been in the hotel room for some time, and an autopsy listed the cause of death as a heart attack. An investigation soon revealed that the dead man was actually John Patrick Addis, a fugitive who'd been wanted since 1995 for murder, kidnapping, and other charges.

Investigators contacted Detective Larry Hanna in Las Vegas with the news, and Hanna wondered if Addis had murdered someone who looked like him to fake his death. A fingerprint match, though, left no doubt. The dead man was John Addis. He had avoided capture and died on his terms, whether from natural causes or suicide. Addis was buried in Guatemala.

John Patrick Addis was a monster who needed to control his world and those around him. He seemed to function well during his years as an Alaska State Trooper in Fairbanks. He managed to cope as long as he kept his wife and kids imprisoned in a one-room cabin. When his wife left him, though, his world began to unravel. After his incarceration for kidnapping his children, Addis constantly moved, leaving a path of destruction in his wake.

The authorities feel that Addis likely killed Joann Albanese because she was strong-willed and feisty and refused to let him manipulate her. Did he murder Laura Liliana and their children because she'd decided to leave him and move back to Guadalajara near her family? His brilliant mind and training in forensic crime scene investigations while he worked for the Alaska State Troopers made Addis a difficult criminal to track and capture. He always managed to stay one step ahead of the authorities.

Massacre at Manley Hot Springs

Manley Hot Springs, located 160 miles west of Fairbanks, marks the end of the road, where civilization meets wilderness. The boat landing in Manley Hot Springs offers the last portage for fishermen, trappers, and wanderers to launch their boats and travel farther up the icy Tanana River. Because the road ends in Manley, residents see their share of drifters and people trying to escape from somewhere or something. When Michael Silka arrived in the tiny village on Monday, May 13, 1984, folks accepted him as another straggler searching for a new life. They should have been terrified. Michael Silka was about to change sleepy Manley Hot Springs forever.

Michael Silka grew up in Hoffman Estates, Illinois, where classmates recalled him as a nonconformist from an early age. Neighbors described his parents as "good people" but stated that Michael was always different. His teachers remembered Silka as a problematic student who often caused trouble. When Silka was still a juvenile and then a young man, police arrested him numerous times for burglary, shoplifting, and unlawful use of a weapon.

Silka loved hunting, fishing, and firearms. A neighbor convinced him to join the Army after he graduated from high school in 1977. In 1981, the Army transferred Silka to Fort Wainwright near Fairbanks, where he began to dream about living in the wilderness of interior Alaska. Silka wanted to subsist and make money selling furs as a trapper. According to Army records, Silka earned an expert marksman rating with the M16 rifle and grenade launcher. While at Fort Wainwright, though, records show that Silka experienced several run-ins with the military police (MPs), including an assault charge and an arrest for discharging a firearm in a barracks.

After the Army discharged him, Silka returned to Illinois and worked at various jobs. He was arrested two separate times on weapons violations and made several court appearances, but on October 26, 1983, he missed a critical hearing, skipped bond, and fled. A warrant for his arrest was issued on December 20, 1983.

Shortly after Christmas in 1983, Silka showed up in Dauphin, Manitoba, Canada, in a brown and white Dodge sedan. He stayed in Dauphin throughout the winter, preparing his vehicle for the drive to Alaska.

In early spring 1984, Silka drove to Alaska. He arrived with a canoe lashed to the top of his sedan and rented a small shack at mile 4.7 of Chena Pump Road on the edge of Fairbanks. Silka chose the most remote shack in the area, where neighbors found him both strange and threatening.

On the afternoon of April 28, a neighbor woman was chopping wood and chatting with her friend, Roger Culp. Silka walked past his two neighbors and suddenly stopped, picked up a large stick, and angrily beat it against the woman's chopping block, sending debris flying into the air. He said, "This is how you do it," and then walked away, leaving the woman and Culp stunned by his violent behavior.

Silka frightened the woman, but his actions angered twenty-eight-year-old Culp, who followed Silka back to his shack. The woman tried to discourage Culp from further interacting with Silka, but he told her he would be back in fifteen minutes. The woman heard gunshots a short while later, and Culp did not return. She was so terrified that she hid in her cabin with a loaded shotgun by her door and stayed there for two days. For unexplained reasons, she did not report Culp's disappearance to the authorities for nine days.

The following day, another neighbor, Wendy Hooker, knocked on Silka's door to confront him about a moose hide she believed he had stolen. She noticed a small pool of blood outside his door, but she assumed he had recently killed a small game animal. When he didn't answer her knock, Wendy walked around his cabin to the back, where she saw a three-by-six-foot mound of freshly turned snow and blood soaking up through the snow in her footprints. Wendy again knocked on his door. No one answered, but she felt certain Silka was inside the cabin. Wendy told her friend Tom about the incident, and he went to Silka's cabin. Silka admitted to him that he had taken Wendy's moose hide and promised to return it.

Wendy and Tom told their friend Don Hopkins about Silka's strange behavior and the blood behind his cabin, and when the trio realized Roger Culp had disappeared, Hopkins called the Alaska State Troopers. Unfortunately, though, the troopers misunderstood what Hopkins was trying to tell them. They thought Hopkins said that both Culp and Silka had disappeared, and he suspected that Culp had killed Silka. They thought Silka was a possible murder victim.

Two troopers warily approached Silka's cabin. They knocked on the door, but when no one answered, they circled to the backyard, where they found the mound of snow but didn't see any blood. They dug into the snow but only found a moose hide. Another hide hung from a nearby tree. The troopers returned to Silka's front door and saw a small amount of blood near the door but not enough to suggest a homicide had recently occurred. They knocked on Silka's door again, and this time, he stuck his head out the door, hiding his right hand. When the man identified himself as Michael Silka, investigators assumed nothing was amiss, since Silka was still alive.

Silka explained that he had been cleaning moose hides for some of his hunter friends, and the hides were the source of the blood on the snow. Since the troopers noted no evidence of a crime and Silka was still alive, they saw no reason to inquire further into the incident. Later, one of the troopers recalled how Silka had kept one of his hands out of sight the entire time they talked to him. Was he holding a gun, and would he have shot them if they'd asked the wrong questions?

Several days later, Culp's female friend finally reported Culp's disappearance to the troopers and told them she'd heard gunshots after Culp had followed Silka back to his cabin. Troopers returned to Silka's shack with a warrant to search the shack and the ground around it, but they found the place abandoned. Silka had disappeared. They spent two days searching the area around the shack and found patches of peat covering bloodstains. They sent samples of the blood to the crime lab in Palmer, and the results confirmed the blood was human.

Silka fled Fairbanks in his battered brown and white 1974 Dodge Monaco filled with hunting gear, guns, and ammunition. He mounted his canoe to the vehicle's roof and drove 160 miles west from Fairbanks down a rutted, muddy road. The road was so bad that the trip would have taken him approximately five hours. He stopped when he got to the end of the road and set up camp near the boat landing in Manley Hot Springs, a tiny town on the banks of the turbulent Tanana River.

Prospector John Karshner founded Manley Hot Springs in 1902 while homesteading near several hot springs. The region quickly grew and became a resort for steamboat passengers and gold miners in the area. The town eventually expanded to five hundred residents, but the population nosedived when mining activity began to decline a decade later. By 1984, just fifty hearty souls called Manley Hot Springs home. The Manley Roadhouse, built in 1903, served as the only restaurant and hotel in the town.

When Michael Silka arrived in Manley on Monday, May 13, 1984, most residents found the twenty-five-year-old man strange and a little scary. Silka told Patricia Lee, who ran the Manley Roadhouse with her husband, Bob, that he could smell clams even when they were covered by six feet of water. Another Manley resident described Silka as okay but odd, and she said he seemed obsessed with a large knife he kept sharpening.

On Thursday, May 17, 1984, six Manley residents visited the Manley Hot Springs boat landing between noon and 2:30 p.m. Joe McVey and Dale Madajski drove to the boat landing to launch McVey's boat. McVey, thirty-eight, a wounded Vietnam veteran, lived with his wife, Alice, across the river from Manley. Madajski, twenty-four, lived nearby with his wife, Kristin. Albert Hagen Jr., twenty-seven, drove to the boat landing with a load of brush to dump into the river. Lyman Klein, thirty-six, Joyce Klein, thirty, and the Kleins' two-year-old son, Marshall, drove to the boat landing on their four-wheeler for a family outing. Joyce was pregnant with the couple's second child.

While no one realized it at first, another area resident also visited the boat landing sometime between noon and 2:30 p.m. Fred Burke, thirty, a trapper, boated from his camp upriver down to the boat landing because he wanted to work on the truck he kept in Manley.

Around 4:00 p.m., Manley resident Sabie Gurtler drove to the boat landing with a carful of children who wanted to watch the mighty Tanana River boil and churn while the winter ice broke apart and sailed down the river. Sabie said she saw a quiet landing, but she noticed that Michael Silka's canoe was half off his car. When Sabie returned to the boat landing two hours later, Silka's canoe was gone.

When Joe McVey failed to return home, his wife drove to the landing and found Joe's boat still there and a six-pack of beer in his truck. Alice immediately began to worry about her husband. When Joe still hadn't returned by noon the next day, Alice called the Alaska State Troopers in Fairbanks. Troopers took her report but thought Joe McVey would probably show up within the next few hours. Gradually, other friends and relatives began to worry about their missing loved ones as well. The relatives gathered and began comparing notes about when they had last seen the missing residents. One person drove to the landing and noticed the strange car. They feared this person could also be missing, so they called the troopers and relayed his license plate number. When the troopers ran the plate, they realized it belonged to Michael Silka—a man wanted for the murder of Roger Culp in Fairbanks.

Now, the troopers were concerned. At least seven people had disappeared, and one of the missing was a suspected murderer. Troopers began arriving in Manley at 2:00 a.m. on Saturday, May 19, and started an aerial search of the river at the break of dawn during the long daylight hours in May. They found splotches of blood and drag marks through the dirt at the boat landing. They also found used cartridge casings, and they feared Silka had shot the missing people and then thrown their bodies into the raging river. Perhaps he'd argued with and then shot McVey and Madajski, the first two of the missing to arrive at the boat landing. As the other victims arrived and saw what he had done, he murdered them to cover his tracks.

By Saturday afternoon, more than fifteen troopers were scouring the Tanana River and its tributaries. The search included boats, two helicopters, and three small airplanes and involved members of the Alaska State Troopers Special Emergency Response Team (SERT). SERT members carry automatic weapons and are trained for high-risk operations. They understood they were chasing a dangerous man who had little to lose. They also knew Silka had been a sharpshooter in the Army and was known to own a variety of firearms.

The left-side doors of the Bell JetRanger helicopters were removed for the search, and two sharpshooters sat in the left-hand front and rear seats, feet on the skids and facing outward. Trooper Troy Duncan sat in the left-rear seat in one of the helicopters, and Trooper Jeff Hall sat in the left-front seat. Both were secured by seat harnesses and held Colt M16A1 rifles equipped with twenty-round magazines. Trooper Captain Don Lawrence took charge of the operation and was in the helicopter with Duncan and Hall. Lawrence hoped to locate Silka and convince him to surrender, but he did not understand the adversary they were about to face.

Not long after the helicopters departed Manley, the troopers saw a woman on the riverbank waving her arms in the air. One of the helicopters landed, and the troopers talked to her. She told them she was worried because her husband, Fred Burke, had gone down the river by boat to Manley on Thursday and had never returned to their cabin. The troopers now knew they were searching for seven missing area residents.

On Saturday afternoon, the helicopter carrying Duncan, Hall, and Lawrence spotted a canoe tied behind Fred Burke's riverboat. The boat was tied to a tree in a slough, and Michael Silka stood on the riverbank near the boat. As the helicopter descended toward Silka, Lawrence used a bullhorn to tell him to surrender. Hall and Duncan saw Silka reach for something in his boat, and then Silka swung his .30-06 Ruger single-shot rifle toward the helicopter and fired. Duncan and Hall returned fire, but Silka's next shot hit Duncan in the face, killing him. Fragments from the bullet hit Lawrence in the face as well, wounding him. Hall returned fire and hit Silka eight times in the legs, body, and head, killing him instantly. According to Hall, the entire firefight lasted two seconds, with twenty-five rounds fired, two dead, and one wounded.

An extensive search ensued to find the missing, but the icy, turbulent Tanana reluctantly releases the dead. By June 23, 1984, the bodies of Fred Burke, Lyman Klein, Dale Madajski, and Larry McVey had been recovered from the river. Burke's wife discovered her husband's body seventy-five miles downstream from the Manley Hot Springs boat landing. The bodies of Albert Hagen Jr., Joyce Klein, and young Marshall Klein were never found. The body of Roger Culp in Fairbanks also was never recovered.

Since the Army had honorably discharged Michael Silka, his father requested to have his ashes buried at the National Cemetery in Sitka. Manley residents were furious when they heard the news, but the military honored the request. His grave is unmarked.

On one day, Manley Hot Springs lost more than 10 percent of its population, but in addition to the seven Manley residents, Roger Culp in Fairbanks, and Trooper Troy Duncan, troopers suspected Silka's rampage might have included other victims. On May 11, 1984, before Silka had arrived in Manley, several witnesses saw two strangers sitting in Silka's car with him. The pair were never seen again, and troopers feared Silka had picked up two hitchhikers and murdered them, possibly burying their bodies in the woods.

No one could explain Silka's violent, deadly behavior. When he reached Alaska, he seemed to unravel, and his actions became increasingly more bizarre until he finally snapped and began his killing spree.

Murder in a College Dorm

A mother feels a bit sad when she sends her daughter to college, but she expects to sit back, breathe a sigh of relief, and watch her blossom. She can't imagine that a monster will snuff out her daughter's life, and she will spend the next thirty years waiting for the authorities to identify her murderer and bring him to justice.

The University of Alaska has three main campuses: the University of Alaska Fairbanks, the University of Alaska Anchorage, and the University of Alaska Southeast. The University of Alaska Fairbanks (UAF) was once the main campus, but now, the Anchorage campus has higher enrollment. As of 2022, over ten thousand students were enrolled at UAF.

While UAF is a small university compared to most state universities in the US, it must have seemed huge to Sophie Sergie when she enrolled there in 1990. Sophie grew up in the tiny Yupik village of Pitkas Point, located near the small town of St. Mary's and 525 miles southwest of Fairbanks. Pitkas Point has a population of only 150 people, but Sophie embraced the move to Fairbanks and the opportunity to get a university education. Sophie was very bright and a rising star. She was majoring in marine biology and was on a full academic scholarship from British Petroleum.

In December 1992, Sophie had braces installed on her teeth, and she took the spring semester off to work and pay for her orthodontic work. She returned to Pitkas Point, where she worked as a teacher's aide, and she took a second job in nearby St. Mary's as a clerk. By all accounts, Sophie was an intelligent, hard-working, respectable young woman.

Sophie periodically returned to Fairbanks to have her braces adjusted, and while there, she stayed on campus in the Bartlett Hall dorm with one of her friends, Shirley Wasuli. If you are not from Alaska, an airplane flight of 525 miles might seem like a long way to travel to the dentist, but remember, this is a big state with only a few cities large enough to support an orthodontist. If you live in a remote town or village, you sometimes must travel a great distance to see a dental or medical specialist.

Sophie's dental appointment was scheduled for Monday, April 26, 1993. She arrived in Fairbanks two days earlier and proceeded to Bartlett Hall to meet Shirley. Bartlett Hall is an eight-story residence hall between Moore and Skarland Halls, two other large residence halls on the upper campus of UAF. The three dormitories are separate buildings, but they share a common lobby called Hess Commons. The central doorway for the three buildings leads into Hess Commons.

For anyone who has lived in a large campus dormitory, you can remember the atmosphere in the dorm at the end of the college semester, especially toward the end of the spring semester, when the air feels warm and the summer break looms. In Fairbanks in late April, the dark winter is a distant memory, and the sun shines late into the night. You can imagine college students standing outdoors, perhaps drinking beer or smoking cigarettes, while other students stagger back to the dorm from the library after a long day of hitting the books.

On Sunday night, April 25, Sophie and Shirley went outside in front of Hess Commons to socialize for a while. Then, they returned to Shirley's second-floor room on an all-female floor of the dorm and watched a movie until a little after midnight. Sophie then left to smoke a cigarette in the shower room, and Shirley departed to spend the night with her boyfriend, allowing Sophie to have the dorm room to herself.

Sophie was last seen alive shortly after midnight in front of Hess Commons, wearing a brightly striped sweater, smoking a cigarette, and chatting with people. A friend snapped a photo of a smiling, radiant Sophie dancing in front of the dorms.

Shirley returned to her dorm room the next day and found the door unlocked and Sophie gone. Shirley told troopers that she was irritated at first to think Sophie would leave her dorm room un-locked. It wasn't until later that she realized Sophie had never slept in the bed. Shirley thought Sophie's absence meant she was taking a long shower, so she left again.

At 2:00 p.m. on Monday, April 26, a janitor ran screaming from the second-floor bathroom of Bartlett Hall. Soon, the residence hall was swarming with police, while rumors flew among the shocked and traumatized residents.

People had been in and out of the bathroom all day, but So-phie's body hadn't been discovered until the janitor opened the door to a private room outfitted with a single tub. Sophie's body was stuffed into the tub. Someone had pulled her pants down around her ankles and then brutally raped her. Sophie's murderer stabbed her several times in the face and then killed her with a gunshot wound to the back of the head. Homicide investigators estimated that Sophie's body had been in the tub for as long as thirteen hours before it was discovered, and they placed the time of her death between 1:00 a.m. and 5:00 a.m. Monday.

Detectives were faced with a nightmare of a crime scene. So-phie had been murdered, or at least her body had been found, in a college dorm with limited security where students and non-students could move freely, not only between floors but also between dorms. The investigation was hampered further because the murder oc-curred toward the end of the spring semester, when students were finishing their classes and leaving the campus for at least the summer and perhaps forever. In 1993, 670 students lived within the Moore, Bartlett, and Skarland dormitory complex. Add to this number the non-residents who might have visited the complex or stayed with friends, just as Sophie had.

Detectives immediately began interviewing Bartlett Hall resi-dents, especially those living on the second floor. They swarmed the building until 9:00 p.m. on the day of the crime, questioning resi-dents and carefully searching the tiled floor of the bathroom where the janitor had found Sophie. They collected fibers, hairs, and other physical evidence, and they collected semen from Sophie's body. In

1993, sophisticated methods for testing DNA had not yet been per-fected, and no national DNA database existed, but crime scene ana-lysts carefully preserved the DNA they found.

In a 2009 interview, Alaska State Trooper Lieutenant Lantz Dahlke recalled the enormity of the situation. He said they tried to talk to everyone who would have been near where Sophie's body was found. Still, it was impossible to segregate the population because anyone could have accessed the floor and the bathroom by taking the elevator or walking up the stairs. No one remembered hearing the crime in progress or the gunshot wound that had killed Sophie. No one recalled seeing Sophie with a man or noticing anything un-usual. In a crowded dormitory where someone should have heard a gunshot, no one remembered hearing anything. Crime Stoppers (an association of dedicated community representatives, the media, and law enforcement) in Fairbanks offered a $20,000 reward for infor-mation leading to the arrest of Sophie's murderer, but no one came forward to claim the reward.

Sophie's death was not an accident. She was brutally raped and murdered. Sophie was what homicide detectives consider a "low-risk" murder victim. She did not have a boyfriend, no one was stalking her, she had no known enemies, she was not promiscuous, and she did not hang out in bars. Investigators said they initially had several promising leads and suspects in the case, but nothing led to an arrest.

In April 1994, Sophie's mother sued the University of Alaska for $4 million, alleging that poor security in Bartlett Hall had led to her daughter's death. Lieutenant Dahlke said the civil suit hampered the criminal investigation because the state was forced to release critical information that law enforcement did not yet want the public to see.

Former trooper investigator Jim McCann (who has featured in several stories so far) said he believed Sophie Sergie happened to be in the wrong place at the wrong time. The murderer could have picked any of the young women in the dorm. According to Mc-Cann, the perpetrator of the crime hated women and enacted his rage on Sophie because she was a convenient victim. McCann said he thought the killer left campus and probably left Fairbanks soon after killing Sophie, and he speculated that the killer was a former or current student.

In 2007, the Alaska State Troopers' Cold Case Unit actively reviewed the Sophie Sergie case. They reinterviewed witnesses and combed through forensic evidence. An independent forensic examiner took a hard look at the case and questioned the long-held supposition that the bathroom was the lone crime scene. He thought it was possible Sophie was killed somewhere else, and then the murderer brought her body to the bathroom and placed her in the tub. Cold case investigator Jim Stogsdill said the authorities were unsure whether Sophie had been murdered in the bathroom or somewhere else. He wouldn't reveal what specific evidence suggested the bathroom might not have been the murder scene.

With the revelation that Sophie might have been killed somewhere else and then moved to the second-floor bathroom, cold case investigators faced the daunting task of tracking down everyone who had lived in Bartlett Hall in 1993, fourteen years earlier. They had official rosters from the university listing the dorm residents in 1993, but where were these people now? They could be anywhere in the state, the country, or the world. To further complicate the task, investigators learned that the students didn't necessarily live in the rooms to which they were assigned. Students often switched rooms during the course of the year.

In the investigation following the murder, the authorities never locked down the dorm, nor did they do a room-by-room search. They believed the bathroom was the murder scene, but if Sophie was murdered somewhere else, then a more thorough examination of the entire dorm soon after her murder could have uncovered evidence of the murder scene and yielded the murder weapon. As it was, the gun that killed Sophie was never found.

Cold case investigators said they thought the killer was a student who lived in one of the three dorms surrounding Hess Commons. He was someone who was familiar with the campus and the dorms and could easily blend in with the other students.

Soon after Sophie's death, Trooper Investigator McCann released a statement saying he believed Sophie's murderer was a current or former student who had returned home for the summer after the spring semester. He urged anyone who noticed frightening or unusual changes in the behavior of someone who had recently returned home from UAF to report the person to the authorities. He said, "The killer thought enough ahead to bring a gun and is likely to have fantasized about committing similar acts. Her killer is someone who uses women to express his anger." McCann was warning the public that Sophie's murderer was a dangerous killer who likely would rape and murder again.

Dave Sperbeck, who was then a forensic psychologist and the director of mental health at the Alaska Department of Corrections, said he believed whoever had forcibly sexually assaulted Sophie had done it before and would do it again. He said, "Some attackers can go some time before striking again, but they always have another in mind."

Despite the convictions of authorities and psychology experts that Sophie was killed by someone who would rape and possibly kill again, officers could not find a match in CODIS (the DNA database that includes profiles taken from convicted felons) to the DNA collected from Sophie's body. Investigators routinely ran the DNA collected at the crime scene through the nation's growing databases of criminal offenders, but no match was ever found.

A few days after Sophie's murder, more than three hundred people gathered in UAF's Constitution Park for a memorial service. Native drummers performed, and Professor James Nageak led the service in Inupiat. An observer noted years later that Sophie's death marked a turning point on the UAF campus. Before Sophie's murder, the campus was wide open and vibrated with youthful energy, but stricter safety measures turned the campus into an armed camp after her death.

In June 2015, due to budgetary shortfalls, the state of Alaska scaled back the Alaska State Troopers' Cold Case Unit, leaving more than a hundred cold cases unsolved. With limited funds to investigate old cases, there seemed little possibility that Sophie's murder would ever be solved, but in February 2019, the Alaska State Troopers held a shocking press conference. The authorities had arrested forty-four-year-old Steven Downs in Lewiston, Maine, for the sexual assault and murder of Sophie Sergie.

Troopers revealed that in 2010, a cold case investigator had attempted to reinterview everyone who had lived in Bartlett Hall when Sophie was murdered. The investigator spoke to a former student named Nicholas Dazer and asked him if he had owned a gun that fired .22-caliber ammunition when he lived in Bartlett Hall. Dazer said he hadn't owned a gun, but he said his roommate, Steven Downs, had an H&R .22-caliber revolver. With little else to go on, the case again went cold.

After the authorities arrested "Golden State Killer" suspect Joseph James DeAngelo in April 2018 by obtaining a familial match by comparing DNA collected at a crime scene to a commercially available DNA database, the Alaska State Troopers decided to try the same thing with DNA collected from Sophie's body in 1993. They even sent the DNA from Sophie's case to Parabon NanoLabs, the same Virginia facility used to analyze the DNA in the Golden State Killer case.

On December 18, 2018, a forensic genealogist submitted a report comparing the suspect's genetic material from the crime scene to that of a likely female relative. The woman whose DNA was considered a familial match to the DNA collected from sperm left at Sophie's crime scene was the aunt of Steven Downs. Downs was an eighteen-year-old college student living at Bartlett Hall when Sophie was murdered. Downs was also Nicholas Dazer's roommate—the one Dazer said had owned the H&R .22-caliber revolver.

Downs was arrested at his home in the city of Lewiston, Maine, and charged with the sexual assault and murder of Sophie Sergie. He denied any involvement in Sophie's rape and murder, despite knowing that a sample of his DNA taken after his arrest matched a sample collected from sperm cells at the crime scene.

Downs was extradited to Alaska, where his trial began in early January 2022 in Anchorage. The jury heard from people in the dorm the night of Sophie's murder. They also listened to a recording of investigators questioning Downs. Downs's roommate told troopers that Downs kept several guns and a large hunting knife in his dorm room, but Downs denied having a gun at the university, and he said he was with his girlfriend the night of Sophie's murder. According to the ex-girlfriend's testimony, Downs left the room several times during the evening.

The jury deliberated for several days but eventually found Steven Downs guilty of first-degree murder and first-degree sexual assault. It took thirty years for Sophie's family to find justice. Of course, nothing can bring back Sophie.

THE YUKON RIVER

This section covers the two villages of Tanana and Ruby, both located on the mighty Yukon River. The Yukon ranks as one of the major rivers in North America and stretches 1,980 miles from British Columbia to the Bering Sea. It is a major transportation route when the river is open, but ice blocks its flow for half the year.

The Koyukon Athabascan village of Tanana sits at the confluence of the Tanana and Yukon Rivers in the interior of Alaska, 130 miles west of Fairbanks. The town has a rich history and was a trading settlement for the Koyukon and Tanana Athabascans long before European contact. No roads lead into the village. Boat travel is possible in the summer, once the rivers thaw, but most transportation into or out of Tanana is by small airplane. Tanana had only 254 residents as of 2020, but it has modern facilities, including a school, a water-treatment plant, and a health center.

About 100 miles southwest of Tanana and 230 miles west of Fairbanks, the town of Ruby is nestled along the southern shoreline of the Yukon River. The residents of Ruby, which had a population of only 166 in 2020, endure an extreme environment and long periods of virtual isolation. For a few weeks in the summer, the temperature soars to 70°F (21°C), but in the winter, the mercury drops to an average of –10°F (–23°C), and at times, it hits below

–38°F (–37°C). There are no roads to Ruby, and boat travel is also impossible when ice fills the river. The flight in a small bush plane to Fairbanks, the nearest city, takes an hour and a half when weather conditions permit.

Established in 1911, the town of Ruby once boasted a population of three thousand and was an important supply depot and port during the Alaska gold rush. The dramatic history of Ruby tells the story of boom and bust as well as any gold rush town anywhere. Prospectors first discovered gold on Ruby Creek in 1906, and to this day, gold still can be found near Ruby. The largest nugget ever found in Alaska, weighing 294 troy ounces (322 ounces), was found near Ruby in 1998.

With the discovery of gold in Ruby Creek in 1906, prospectors and miners flooded the area, dreaming of instant wealth. The town of Ruby grew, with businesses providing supplies and recreation to miners who were far from home and learning to survive in a harsh environment. In 1918, Ruby began to decline when many young miners and prospectors left to fight in World War I. The town lost several businesspeople and their families that same year when they headed south for the winter on the SS *Princess Sophia*, and the steamship grounded on Vanderbilt Reef in Lynn Canal near Juneau. All 343 passengers and crew were lost when stormy seas prevented rescue boats from approaching the vessel before it washed off the reef and sank.

In 1929, a fire destroyed most of the business district of Ruby, and a 1931 flood took out the rest of the buildings on the riverfront. By the end of World War II, Ruby had become a ghost town, until Koyukon Athabascans from the village of Kokrines moved into the town to take advantage of the abandoned houses. Fewer than two hundred people have lived in the village of Ruby ever since.

Tragedy in Tanana

Starting in 2009, a popular *National Geographic* documentary series called *Alaska State Troopers* followed several troopers from different areas of the state as they made their daily rounds. Two of the officers featured on the show were Sergeant Patrick "Scott" Johnson and Gabriel "Gabe" Rich. Both men worked out of the troopers' Fairbanks Rural Service Unit. A camera crew was not with the men on the fateful day of May 1, 2014.

Other than federal officers, the Alaska State Troopers are the most geographically extended group of peace officers in the country, and they have little if any backup. Alaska encompasses one-fifth of the entire landmass of the lower forty-eight states but has only thirteen hundred full-time sworn law enforcement officers to patrol this vast area. Cities and larger towns have local police officers, but they only patrol within the city limits. This leaves three hundred state troopers who are responsible for the rest of the state.

Many Native villages are too small to have a trooper post, so they hire a Village Public Safety Officer (VPSO). VPSOs are state-trained peace officers assigned to carry out basic police tasks in the villages. The Alaska State Troopers manage the VPSO program, which maintains close contact with the troopers, and if a situation escalates, they will call the nearest trooper post and request assistance. Troopers then fly to the village and take command of the case. When the officers arrive in a remote village, they don't know what to expect, and backup is at least one and possibly several hours away from them. They have demanding jobs, and as this story shows, the role of a trooper can be perilous.

Rural Alaska has the worst crime statistics in the country, and Alaska Native communities experience the highest rates of family violence, suicide, and alcohol abuse of any towns in the US. The domestic violence rate in these villages soars ten times above the national average. Physical assault on women peaks at twelve times the national average, and rape in Alaska occurs at three times the national average, the highest rate in the nation. In other words, there's a lot of crime and no actual law enforcement in many small Alaska villages.

Troopers Scott Johnson and Gabe Rich were well known and liked by most Tanana residents. When they arrived in the village on May 1, 2014, to settle a dispute and arrest a man who had been making threats, neither officer likely expected the trip to the village to be anything other than routine.

The events precipitating the troopers' visit to the village began on the evening of Wednesday, April 30, 2014, when fifty-eight-year-old Arvin Kangas confronted a mother and daughter over the sale of a couch. Arvin had sold the pair a sofa for $150, but the women still had not paid him. Arvin became enraged over the matter, and the mother feared he would try to break into her daughter's house and remove the couch. The mother called VPSO Mark Haglin to report the matter, and when Haglin approached Arvin to discuss the situation, Arvin threatened him with a shotgun. Haglin retreated and called the Alaska State Troopers' Fairbanks Rural Service Unit to request trooper support in the village.

The following day at 2:00 p.m., pilot David Keel landed a Cessna Caravan on the dirt-and-gravel airstrip near Tanana. Sergeant Scott Johnson and Trooper Gabe Rich exited the plane alongside Keel. The three men joked and laughed as they crossed the runway to meet VPSO Haglin. At Haglin's office, the troopers filled out the necessary paperwork and then decided Keel should stay at the VPSO office while Haglin and the troopers drove to the Kangas's home to arrest Arvin. Haglin didn't have enough room in his truck for all three men, and since Keel wasn't a trooper, he stayed behind at the office.

The troopers and Haglin approached and talked to Arvin Kangas outside his home, but Arvin began to argue with the men, questioning their authority in the village. Arvin then retreated into his house, where the troopers and Haglin followed him. When Arvin still refused to surrender, Johnson and Rich wrestled him to the floor as they tried to restrain him. The troopers had Arvin pinned beneath them on the floor when Arvin's twenty-year-old son, Nathanial, walked into the room and fired seven shots at the officers with a Ruger Mini-14 semiautomatic rifle. Both men died moments after being shot, although Haglin didn't know this at the time.

Nathanial then pointed the gun at VPSO Haglin. Haglin later said he looked through a mist of red into Nathanial's eyes, dark with hatred, and he thought he was only moments from dying. He turned and fled back to the VPSO office, where Keel still waited.

Haglin raced into the VPSO office and told Keel that Nathanial Kangas had shot both troopers. Keel hurried to Haglin's truck, expecting to see the wounded officers inside the vehicle, and he was incredulous when he didn't see them.

"You left them there?" he asked Haglin.

Haglin said he was scared and thought he was about to be killed, so he ran.

Haglin and Keel called trooper dispatch to report the crime and request assistance. They then headed to the village clinic for medical supplies to treat the troopers (not knowing they had already died) and procure more weapons from physician's assistant Everett Carroll, a retired Army veteran.

When Keel, Haglin, and Carroll approached the Kangas residence, they saw a group of people standing near the house, and Keel said he began to get nervous. He knew most of the people in Tanana were friendly, but a small fragment of the population resented white people and didn't appreciate them meddling in village affairs. Haglin spotted Arvin and Nathanial in the group and pointed them out to Keel, who jumped out of the truck and ordered everyone to get down on the ground. He then checked the people for weapons and told Haglin to watch the bystanders while he and Carroll entered the house.

Inside the house, Keel found a woman, later identified as Arvin's wife, Judy, standing near the bodies of Johnson and Rich. Keel ordered her to raise her arms, and he and Carroll searched the rest of the house to ensure no one else was there. Keel then checked Johnson and Rich for signs of life but determined they were both dead. He kicked a box in a fit of anger, and Judy Arvin asked him why he was so mad.

Keel, Haglin, and Carroll decided to restrain Nathanial Kangas immediately instead of waiting for backup to arrive from Fairbanks. Nathanial did not struggle when they handcuffed him but instead kept apologizing as he was put into Haglin's vehicle.

Trooper Lt. Deputy Commander Brian Wasserman and his SERT (Special Emergency Response Team) unit landed at the Tanana airstrip a few hours after the murders. The troopers' SERT responds to high-risk incidents, including hostage situations, barricaded people, and potentially dangerous warrant executions.

Wasserman and his team felt uneasy about the situation in Tanana because Arvin Kangas had not yet been apprehended, and they knew an antigovernment group lived in Tanana.

At 7:00 p.m., Wasserman received a tip that Arvin Kangas was holed up at a house in Tanana. The SERT unit, wearing camouflage and tactical gear, surrounded the residence while villagers watched. Arvin refused to come out of the house for several hours, but finally, at 10:00 p.m., he peacefully exited the residence and surrendered.

Nathanial Kangas was charged with two counts of first-degree murder. Troopers believed Nathanial and his father, Arvin, had planned to claim that Nathanial had killed the officers in self-defense when Johnson and Rich drew their guns on the father and son. Rich's holster was found unsnapped, and Johnson's weapon was out of its holster on the floor near his body when the troopers arrived to investigate the scene. What Arvin and Nathanial Kangas did not know was that the two slain troopers were wearing audio recorders, which captured the argument between Arvin and the officers, the fatal gunshots, and the aftermath as Arvin and his son manipulated the murder scene and destroyed marijuana plants hidden in the house.

The audio recordings indicated that Nathanial and Arvin left the house after the shootings and were gone for a few minutes while Judy stayed at the crime scene. When Arvin and Nathanial returned, the audio revealed the sounds of them unsnapping two holsters and racking the pistol slides. The two men could also be heard talking about hiding the marijuana plants.

In April 2015, a jury convicted Arvin Kangas on two counts of evidence tampering for manipulating the weapons to make it look as if the troopers had drawn their guns. The judge sentenced him to only eight years in prison. Many people felt Arvin should have been held responsible, at least in part, for the murders of Gabe Rich and Scott Johnson. Not only did he commit the original crime that had brought the troopers to Tanana, but also, the hatred he and his wife had instilled in their son caused Nathanial to despise white people and to fear their authority. Friends and family said Arvin, Judy, and Nathanial Kangas were adamant about Alaska Native rights and wanted to see Alaska's first people reclaim their traditional lands with no intervention from whites. A member of the Tanana council told the authorities that Nathanial's parents brainwashed him with radicalism. Still, he said Arvin was trying to get help for Nathanial, who suffered from mental health issues.

The murder trial for Nathanial Kangas began on May 9, 2016, in Fairbanks. The courtroom was crowded with the victims' families, Alaska State Troopers, and police from other agencies. Forty-five-year-old Scott Johnson had been a trooper since 1993 and left behind a wife and three daughters. Twenty-six-year-old Gabe Rich had joined the troopers in 2011 and was survived by his fiancée and two sons.

During opening statements, prosecutors said Nathanial had ambushed and slaughtered Johnson and Rich. The defense attorney did not deny that Nathanial had shot and killed the troopers but said he did not intend to kill the men. He insisted Nathanial's actions were reactionary.

On the first day of the trial, VPSO Mark Haglin testified that he had watched Nathanial Kangas shoot and kill the two troopers. He said he could see the hatred in the young man's eyes when he pulled the trigger.

Since there was no question that Nathanial had shot the troopers, the central issue in the case became whether his actions were premeditated. On day two of testimony, Trooper Investigator Ramin Dunford said he'd examined the rifle used in these killings and noticed that the rounds in the gun's magazine had been loaded in a specific way. They were arranged with a hard-tip bullet, followed by a soft-tip bullet, followed by another hard-tip bullet. The pattern was repeated throughout the magazine. Dunford testified that hard-tip bullets are designed to penetrate, while soft-tip bullets are designed to mushroom. These rounds had been loaded to do the maximum amount of damage; they were loaded to kill. Dunford supported his point by showing the jury a hole in the supposedly bulletproof vest worn by one of the murdered troopers.

The jury then listened to the audio from the recorders worn by Trooper Rich and Sergeant Johnson. They could hear the troopers talking politely and professionally to an uncooperative Arvin Kangas. Arvin, in return, questioned the troopers' authority. The prosecution showed video footage taken by a villager of Arvin arguing with the officers. Arvin was combative and hostile and told the troopers they were crazy neo-colonialists who were only there to help white people and take his money. The argument then moved to Arvin's porch, where he bellowed and cursed the troopers. Judy soon joined him and also began yelling at the officers. Arvin then declared he was going inside, where the troopers and Haglin followed him. The jury heard a struggle on the audio recording once the men were inside, followed by seven loud shots and then shouts and screams by Arvin, Judy, and Nathanial.

Next, Arvin and Nathanial could be heard leaving the house and then returning several minutes later. The next sounds were of the two men manipulating the troopers' guns, followed by repeated, anguished cries by Nathanial to "God the Creator." He and

Arvin then discussed what to do with the marijuana plants, and then they left the house again. The recording was silent for fifteen minutes, until Keel, the pilot, knocked on the door and ordered Judy to raise her arms.

The prosecution rested its case on Wednesday, May 11, 2016. Nathanial Kangas said he did not wish to testify on his own behalf, and defense attorney Greg Parvin said he had no witnesses to call. In his closing argument, Parvin implored the jury to return a verdict of manslaughter because Nathanial's actions had resulted from impulse, not intent.

The jury began its deliberations on Friday afternoon and then returned Monday at 8:30 a.m. to continue. At 11:30 a.m., they informed the judge that they had reached a verdict.

The jury found Nathanial guilty of two counts of first-degree murder in the shooting deaths of Sergeant Scott Johnson and Trooper Gabe Rich. The jury also returned a "special verdict" for each (meaning a special written finding), since Johnson and Rich were uniformed and were identifiable peace officers engaged in performing their duties when they were killed. Kangas was also found guilty of one count of assault for pointing his loaded rifle at VPSO Haglin after shooting the troopers.

Judge Paul Lyle sentenced Nathanial to two ninety-nine-year terms for the murders and five years for the assault charge. The sentences were to run consecutively, adding up to 203 years in prison with no chance of parole. Nathanial received little solace from learning that he would be eligible to file for a reduction in his sentence after he had served half of it.

When handing down his sentence, Judge Lyle berated Nathanial's parents for indoctrinating their son with distrust and hate for anyone who represented governmental authority.

In June 2014, the Alaska Department of Public Safety decided not to participate in another season of National Geographic's *Alaska State Troopers*. According to trooper spokeswoman Beth Ipsen, the drawback to participating in such a series was that the film crews sometimes presented logistical problems for the troopers, such as when they needed to transport people but had limited space because of the two-person camera teams. The camera crew gave the troopers two more people to worry about whenever situations got tense. Alaska State Troopers have demanding jobs, and requiring them to care for a camera crew, in addition to everything else they do, might have finally seemed too much to ask.

MURDER ON THE YUKON RIVER

When someone brutally murdered the postmistress of Ruby, the Alaska State Troopers believed they had a "locked room" mystery on their hands. They suspected one of the villagers of killing Agnes Wright. After all, there are only two ways into and out of Ruby: either by boat on the Yukon River or by air on a small bush plane. Neither method of transportation is inconspicuous to or from a village where everyone knows everyone else, and a stranger's presence warrants stares and whispers. Since the troopers heard no credible accounts of a stranger in town on the day of the murder, they began with the premise that one of the villagers had committed the crime. But who in this small village hated Agnes Wright enough to beat her savagely and then shoot her?

In 1996, the ice broke up and flowed out of the Yukon River on May 7. Not only can breakup be timed to a specific day, but it can be timed to a specific minute and second, and the citizens of Alaska bet on when breakup will occur on the various major rivers in the state. You can only imagine the excitement the residents of Ruby and other river towns along the Yukon must feel when the river again begins to flow. Their happiness at finally welcoming spring is short-lived, though. Soon after the ice leaves the river, mosquitos hatch in voracious swarms.

In perfect conditions, an isolated village with fewer than two hundred people experiences conflicts between its residents, but in 1996, after a long, icy winter in Ruby, tensions ran high, and tempers occasionally flared. Fights sometimes broke out, and gossip boiled, but why would one of the residents have wanted to kill Agnes Wright, the well-liked postmistress?

On June 20, 1996, around 6:30 p.m., fifteen-year-old Jeansey Esmailka walked to the post office in Ruby to check on her mother,

Agnes Wright, thirty-two. Agnes usually locked the post office door by 5:30 and drove home to her family. When Agnes wasn't home an hour after closing time, Jeansey went to the post office to see what was keeping her. When she arrived, Jeansey found the door unlocked, and when she opened the door, she saw the horrible sight of her mother's lifeless body sprawled on the floor. Someone had beaten, cut, and shot Agnes.

Jeansey summoned help, but lifesaving efforts proved unsuccessful. The VPSO contacted the troopers, who arrived in Ruby later that evening. Trooper Sergeant Jim McCann, featured in several stories so far, headed up a team of troopers and US postal inspectors in the investigation into the murder of Agnes Wright. The murder of a postal employee on duty in the US is a federal offense, punishable by death.

The case stumped McCann. Sadly, most murders in small, remote villages in Alaska are not complicated. Usually, drugs and alcohol fuel the violence, and too often, the murders involve domestic abuse. The murder of Agnes Wright was not so easily resolved, though. Agnes had grown up in Ruby and had borne three children. Although separated from her husband, the pair appeared amicable, and according to him, at least, they were even considering a reconciliation.

McCann and his investigators understood violent crimes. They knew the most likely perpetrator was someone Agnes had known well and perhaps even had loved. McCann believed at least one, and probably several, of the villagers knew or suspected who had murdered Agnes, but McCann quickly became frustrated in his efforts to pry information from the villagers, many of whom did not trust outsiders, especially law enforcement officials.

One witness reported seeing Agnes's estranged husband, Joe, arguing with her at the post office a few days before her murder. Joe would have to pay Agnes child support if they divorced, and Joe admitted he drank too much at times. Investigators interrogated Joe, but they dismissed him as a suspect when he produced an alibi and passed a polygraph test.

Some of the village children told investigators that they had seen a stranger in town during the two days before Agnes's murder. They described the man as white and approximately five foot eight, weighing 160 pounds, with long blond hair tied in a ponytail. They said he carried a brown accordion folder. The children said when they asked him what his name was, he said, "Elvis." The police could find little evidence to support this lead and soon dismissed it.

At first, the villagers did not believe one of their own had murdered Agnes. No one could think of anyone in the village who had ever displayed a tendency for such violence. Several of the residents told McCann that the murderer must have come from outside the village, and they suggested Abram Walter, a twenty-three-year-old trapper who lived with his parents and brothers in a remote cabin near McGrath, seventy miles from Ruby.

Troopers had arrested Walter a few months earlier for burglary, but not long before he was scheduled to appear in court in Bethel, his overturned canoe was found on the river near his home. The canoe was discovered on June 5, and the troopers searched the river for two days but found no trace of him. They determined Walter had drowned, although they knew his remains might never be found.

When one of Agnes Wright's friends suggested Walter as a possible suspect, the trooper questioning her said patiently, "Ma'am, first of all, dead people don't murder. And second of all, if somebody had just walked through the meanest tundra you've ever seen, he's not gonna kill the first person he sees, is he?"

Troopers searched the river and the area around Ruby, but when they found no evidence or possible suspects, they discounted the "stranger" theory. It seemed impossible that a stranger could enter Ruby, kill the postmistress, and then disappear again without anyone seeing him or his boat. Also, why would a stranger kill Agnes Wright? An audit of the post office revealed that only money orders and a money order imprinter were missing from the building. Why would someone steal a bunch of traceable money orders, and why would a robber beat Agnes before shooting her?

Soon, the villagers of Ruby realized the investigators believed that one of their own had murdered Agnes. After the investigators had ruled out Agnes's estranged husband as a suspect, the residents of Ruby began to look at each other differently. Rumors floated, villagers locked their doors, and mothers kept their children inside.

Agnes had been a member of the Ruby City Council, and some questioned if her death could be linked to rumors of corruption on the council. Others whispered about drug traffickers in the town and wondered if she'd caught someone shipping drugs through the postal service. McCann also believed drugs were a possible motive and wondered if Agnes was killed because, in her position as the postmistress, she had become alerted to illegal drug shipments through the US mail.

One of Agnes's friends said that not long before her death, the postmistress was worried about something going on in the village, and she was too afraid even to mention it to anyone else. Villagers kept shotguns beside their doors and began to wonder who among them had murdered Agnes Wright.

It's difficult to imagine a less likely murder victim than Agnes. Neighborhood kids gathered at her house and watched her satellite television. Agnes planned community picnics and games for the children. Her friends described her as cheerful and with a playful spirit, and she never hesitated to volunteer for community projects. Investigators shook their heads. The murder didn't make sense.

After a week and a half of questioning the villagers, McCann and his team of troopers and US postal inspectors needed a break. McCann said he had grown exhausted from repeatedly asking the same people the same questions. He wanted to get out of the village for a while, and he felt the villagers deserved a break from him and his team. He remained convinced that the murderer was still in the village, and he believed the villagers knew more than they were telling him. He wanted to give everyone time to think. He planned to fly back to Ruby in a week or two and begin another round of questioning.

Before McCann could return to Ruby and resume questioning the villagers, something happened to send this investigation in a new direction. On July 16, the post office in the small village of Ester, near Fairbanks, was robbed by a man with a gun. The man demanded blank money order slips and then walked out the door. A money order imprinter had been stolen from the same post office a few days earlier. The village of Ester is 221 miles from Ruby. Still, troopers knew the man who had stolen money orders from the post office in Ester must be the same man who had taken money orders and an imprinter from the post office in Ruby, killing Agnes Wright in the process. The crimes were too similar and strange to have been committed by two different people.

The police discovered a set of keys marked "LeMans" on the ground outside the post office in Ester, and they assumed the thief had dropped them in his haste to get away after the robbery. The keys matched a vehicle that had recently been stolen in a burglary in Nenana, and troopers put out a radio call to be on the lookout for the car. Within hours, a trooper located the stolen Pontiac LeMans and took the driver into custody. The man told the trooper his name was Abram Paul Walter. He was the twenty-three-year-old trapper whom the troopers believed had drowned when his overturned canoe was found on the river.

Walter confessed to staging his death in a canoe accident. He said he then walked several days over the rugged tundra. The night before he killed Agnes Wright, Walter had camped outside Ruby, and he was worried about his girlfriend and her finances. He decided he'd send her a money order the next day, but since he didn't have any money to send her, he embarked upon the crazy plan of stealing money orders and a money order imprinter from the Ruby post office. He didn't know money orders could be traced. He told investigators that he shot Agnes Wright when she tried to wrest the gun from his grip.

While relieved to have Agnes Wright's murderer behind bars, Trooper McCann and his team were surprised to learn the killer's identity since they thought he had drowned in a canoeing accident.

While the troopers had immediately discounted him as a possible suspect for Agnes's murder, the residents of Ruby had not been so quick to exclude him, and for many, Walter remained at the top of their list of suspects. Agnes Wright's father said he'd considered Walter the prime suspect in his daughter's death from the beginning. He said the troopers found Walter's canoe, but they never found him, and he pointed out that Walter was about to go to prison at the time of his disappearance. What better way to escape jail than to stage your own death?

Another villager explained that Walter could have walked from where his canoe was found over the uneven tundra to Ruby within four or five days. The villager told a reporter, "Somebody from LA would probably die out there, but he could do it."

It is impossible to gauge distances in Alaska by looking at a map. If you study a map of the Yukon River, it appears that village after village dot its banks as it winds through western Alaska. Look more closely, though, and you'll realize that large distances separate these small villages. Abram Walter staged his canoeing accident near McGrath and then hiked over the tundra for seventy miles to Ruby. He next surfaced in Nenana, 189 miles from Ruby. Ester, where he robbed the second post office, lies forty-six miles from Nenana and eleven miles from Fairbanks.

How long did it take after Walter's arrest before the villagers of Ruby unlocked their doors and unloaded their firearms? Have they ever been able to trust each other again? Most claimed they knew all along that Agnes was not murdered by one of their own, but between the time Jeansey found her mother's body and the day the troopers finally arrested Abram Walter, the whispers floating on the breeze in the village nestled beside the mighty Yukon River told a different story—one of suspicion and fear.

WESTERN ALASKA

The following section covers the far-flung western Alaskan towns of Nome, Bethel, and Kiana. Nome sits on the southern Seward Peninsula coast on Norton Sound (an inlet of the Bering Sea), just south of the Arctic Circle in northwestern Alaska. As of 2020, the city had a population of 3,700. Residents of Nome enjoy a beautiful view of the Bering Sea, but they also must face the sea's ferocity, especially in the winter. Nome has a subarctic climate with long, cold winters and short, cool summers. The ocean moderates the temperature, so the winters are warmer and the summers cooler than they are in the state's interior.

In 1898, three men ("the Three Lucky Swedes") discovered gold on Anvil Creek near Nome, and the stampede began. By 1899, Nome had a population of about ten thousand, and prospectors discovered gold buried in the sand on the beach for dozens of miles near town. Thousands of people poured into the area with dreams of picking up gold nuggets from the beach and realizing their dreams. Historians estimate that Nome's population rose to twenty thousand by the early 1900s, when a tent city lined the windswept beaches. By 1910, the population had dropped to twenty-six hundred, and by 1934 fewer than fifteen hundred people lived in the city. Gold mining remains an essential source of revenue and employment in Nome, and the city is a hub for the scattered population of northwest Alaska.

Bethel, the southernmost of the three locations, is the largest city on the Kuskokwim River (and in western Alaska). It is both a seaport and a river port. The city sits fifty miles upriver from the Kuskokwim's mouth, where the river flows into Kuskokwim Bay. As of 2020, the town had a population of 6,325, and 67 percent were Yupik. Southwestern Alaska has been home to the Yupik people for thousands of years. Bethel lies inside the Yukon Delta National Wildlife Refuge (NWR), the second-largest wildlife refuge in the United States, after the Arctic NWR, also in Alaska. The area around Bethel is flat and nearly treeless. Bethel has a subarctic climate with long, moderately cold, snowy winters and short, cool summers. The Port of Bethel is the northernmost medium-draft port in the United States, and the Yukon Kuskokwim Correction Center in Bethel is the only detention center in southwestern Alaska. Bethel Regional High School serves grades seven through twelve; in 1997, the setting of the second story below, approximately 450 students attended the school.

Kiana, the northernmost of the three towns, is an Inupiaq (the term "Eskimo" is now considered derogatory) village with approximately three hundred residents located in northwestern Alaska, thirty miles north of the Arctic Circle and fifty-seven miles east of Kotzebue. The village sits near the confluence of the Squirrel and Kobuk Rivers. In late January at the Arctic Circle (the setting of the third story below), the sun rises just before noon and sets in the late afternoon. Extreme cold temperatures hold a grip on Kiana in January, but the folks who call the Arctic tundra home are well adapted to frigid temperatures and limited daylight.

A Betrayal of Trust in Nome

Until a few years ago, the police in Nome often failed to take reports of sexual harassment seriously, especially claims made by Alaska Native women. The Nome Police Department had a serious problem, and it took the murder of a beautiful, nineteen-year-old woman to expose the ugly truth.

Sonya Ivanoff grew up in Unalakleet, Alaska, a small village with approximately seven hundred residents. Unalakleet is located on Norton Sound in the Bering Sea at the mouth of the Unalakleet River. It sits 148 miles southeast of Nome and 395 miles northwest of Anchorage. More than three-quarters of the residents are Native Alaskans, primarily Inuit. Sonya shined brightly in her small village. She was a star on the girls' high school basketball team, and she was also an honor roll student with a friendly, outgoing personality.

After graduating from high school, Sonya and her best friend moved to Nome and shared an apartment. Nome offered more employment opportunities than Unalakleet. Sonya worked in the hospital admissions department at the Norton Sound Health Corporation.

On August 10, 2003, Sonya and her roommate visited friends. A little after midnight, the two roommates went their separate ways. Lam Ngo, A local janitor at a gas station in Nome, saw Sonya walk past the station sometime between 1:00 and 1:15 a.m. A few minutes later, Sonya walked past Florence Habros and Dannite Malywotkuk, standing on the porch of their mother's house. Dannite was a sophomore and an athlete at Nome High School. She recognized Sonya because she'd recently watched her play in a city basketball game and had admired her skill on the court.

Dannite and Florence exchanged greetings with Sonya and then watched her walk down the street. They saw a marked Nome police vehicle slowly follow Sonya and then pull in front of her on West D Street. The driver rolled down the passenger-side window, and Sonya leaned in the window to talk to the driver. She then opened the door and climbed into the vehicle.

Sonya's roommate returned home in the early-morning hours of August 11 and was surprised not to find Sonya at home. She called several friends, but no one remembered seeing Sonya since the previous night. On the morning of August 12, Sonya's roommate called the police, not to report Sonya missing but to find out if Sonya had been arrested and was in jail. Finally, on August 12 at 5:16 p.m., the roommate went to the Nome PD to report her friend missing. She told the police that she had not seen Sonya Ivanoff for forty-one hours.

The roommate described what Sonya was wearing the last time she'd seen her. Sonya's clothing included blue jeans and a pair of Skechers shoes. Sonya usually carried her identification, including her recreation center ID. She kept her apartment keys on a chain around her neck, and she wore a metal band to attach her wallet to her arm.

The search for Sonya Ivanoff began at 8:30 p.m. on August 12. On August 13, retired attorney Jon Larson and his wife, two of the many people who had volunteered to search for Sonya, discovered her body in a clump of bushes near an abandoned gold mine. She had been killed near the side of Dredge Road 5, a little-used road a few minutes outside Nome. Sonya was naked except for a sock on her left foot, and she had blood on her face and bruises on her face, neck, and chest.

On August 15, 2003, Chief Medical Examiner Franc Fallico performed the autopsy on Sonya Ivanoff. Fallico determined that Sonya had died from a .22-caliber bullet wound to the back of her head, and the killer had fired the bullet from a very close range. Fallico found no evidence of sexual assault. The medical examiner and crime scene analysts discovered no trace physical evidence, such as skin scrapings under Sonya's fingernails, foreign hairs, fingerprints, semen, or other DNA evidence on her body. The lack of trace evidence on or near Sonya's corpse alerted law enforcement personnel to the possibility that Sonya's killer had "evidence awareness." In other words, the murderer knew how and where the police would search for forensic clues, and he'd made sure not to leave any incriminating evidence.

Why would anyone kill Sonya Ivanoff? The lovely young athlete had many friends, a good job, and a bright future. Florence Habros said she'd seen Sonya get into a police car. If a policeman had killed Sonya, he would likely have been careful not to leave any incriminating evidence. Were the Nome PD officers looking for one of their own?

Only two police officers, Stan Piscoya and Matthew Owens, were on duty during the early-morning hours of August 11, 2003, when Sonya disappeared. The Nome PD used three Ford Expeditions as patrol vehicles. They had two older Expeditions ("vehicles 321 and 322") and a newer model ("vehicle 983"). Vehicle 983 sported running boards on its sides, and it had a 911 sticker on the back.

On the early morning when Sonya disappeared, Officer Piscoya was driving the newer Expedition (983), while Owens drove one of the older vehicles (322). When the police first asked Florence Habros to describe the police vehicle that had picked up Sonya Ivanoff, Habros said it was the "new" car, and she said it had a 911 sticker on the back. Later, she said the vehicle Sonya entered did not have running boards, indicating that the Expedition in question was one of the older vehicles.

Officer Piscoya said he and Owens were tied up with a midnight domestic violence call for about an hour. When they returned to the police station, Piscoya wrote the domestic violence report, and Owens left the station. Piscoya said he did not see Owens during the 2:00 a.m. bar-closing patrols, but Owens drove him home an hour later at the end of their shifts.

When searchers found Sonya's body, Nome Police Chief Ralph Taylor immediately requested the assistance of the Alaska State Troopers. A few days later, Taylor handed the entire case off to the troopers. At the time, this move seemed curious, because police agencies don't usually invite other law enforcement entities to investigate crimes in their jurisdiction. Before long, though, the reason for Chief Taylor's decision to ask the troopers to investigate the case became apparent, and his move to withdraw the Nome police from the investigation proved wise.

Six weeks after the murder of Sonya Ivanoff, someone stole one of the SUVs from the Nome PD's lot. Ninety minutes later, Officer Matthew Owens found the vehicle in a gravel pit. Owens claimed someone had fired shots at him with the vehicle's shotgun. The Nome police and the Alaska State Troopers searched the area but did not find a suspect. The Nome police generally locked their vehicles after parking them in the police lot, but they left keys in the lock on the gun case. If someone managed to break into a vehicle, the thief would have easy access to the gun in the SUV. The police towed the Expedition back to the station and examined the vehicle, searching for any evidence that might lead them to the thief. The culprit had smashed in one of the windows in the SUV, but the crime scene techs found no incriminating fingerprints in the vehicle. They did find Sonya's recreation center ID, a card she almost certainly had with her the night she disappeared, and an envelope containing a typed note. It read:

> Pigs. I hate cops. I hate every one of you. Sonya was just a person in the wrong place at the wrong time. I do not know her. As you can see it was easy for me to take your pig car keys right there. It was not her fault. She thought I was a pig and shit just happened. She was just a person. And I wanted to see if I could that night. Every one of you should be more careful. I watch every move you make. You leave me alone and I will leave you alone. I will also shoot you in the head if you get close.

After the vehicle's theft and the discovery of the note, Alaska State Trooper Investigation Sargent Randy McPherron (featured in two earlier stories) focused the investigation on twenty-nine-year-old

Matthew Owens. The troopers believed Owens had staged the stolen vehicle and threatening note to divert suspicion for the murder of Sonya Ivanoff away from himself.

On October 25, 2003, the troopers arrested Matthew Owens at his residence and charged him with the murder of Sonya Ivanoff. They took him into custody sooner than they had planned because they feared he was about to leave town. Owens went to the bank twice on October 24, and they heard that one of his relatives had called the airlines twice, asking for flight information. They thought Owens was a flight risk, so they arrested him before he could disappear.

The grand jury indicted Owens for first-degree murder, tampering with evidence, and official misconduct. The charge of tampering with evidence was related to the police vehicle theft.

Nearly twenty witnesses testified before the grand jury, including the Nome police chief and five police officers. Florence Habros testified about seeing Sonya get into a police car on the night she'd vanished. Perhaps the most interesting witness, though, was Matthew Owens's estranged wife, Trinh. According to the documents filed when the troopers arrested Owens, he'd called his wife at work forty-five minutes before Sonya Ivanoff was reported missing and asked her if she could take their son. He said he needed to go into work because a girl was missing, and "it didn't look good." He told Trinh the name of the missing girl and offered her a physical description. Then, he told Trinh to keep the information quiet.

Owens's defense attorney, James McComas, filed a motion for a change of venue for the trial, asking Judge Ben Esch to move it to either Fairbanks or Anchorage. McComas said he believed the publicity and gossip surrounding the murder of Sonya Ivanoff had tainted the jury pool in Nome. Judge Esch refused to move the trial.

Nearly a year and a half after the murder of Sonya Ivanoff, the case against her accused killer, Matthew Owens, finally went to trial. The trial began on Tuesday, January 18, 2005.

Prosecutor Richard Svobodny and his team had no forensic evidence to support their case, so Svobodny sought to turn this lack of trace evidence, fingerprints, and DNA to his advantage. He attempted to plant the idea in the jurors' minds that the killer had evidence awareness. He knew what types of things the police would search for, and he knew how not to leave this evidence. A police officer would have evidence awareness, so the lack of fibers, fingerprints, and DNA pointed toward a policeman. When taken with all the other circumstantial testimony, Svobodny maintained that Matthew Owens was the only viable suspect in the murder of Sonya Ivanoff. Owens was on duty when Sonya disappeared. Florence Habros and her sister saw Sonya climb into a police vehicle. Officer Piscoya testified that he did not know where Owens was for more than two hours during their shifts on the night in question. Owens's estranged wife said he had told her a girl was missing even before Sonya's roommate contacted the police to report her missing friend. No one single thing pointed at Matthew Owens, but Svobodny hoped the jurors would consider the totality of the evidence and find Matthew Owens guilty of the murder of Sonya Ivanoff.

The bullet that killed Sonya had a rare rifling pattern of "lands and grooves," and troopers found a .22-caliber pistol with a similar rifling pattern in the police station evidence room in an area Owens could have accessed. On the stand, though, a firearms expert could not definitively match the bullet to the .22 pistol.

The state also presented evidence showing that Owens had driven to Coffee Creek, seventy-five miles from Nome, not long after Sonya's murder, and a witness saw him burning items in a pit. When troopers searched the area, they found grommets from a pair of Tilt jeans, eyelets from Skechers shoes, the underwire and other metal parts from a bra, four keys on a ring, and various zippers. Sonya was last seen wearing jeans and Skechers shoes, and her roommate said Sonya owned a pair of Tilt jeans. One of the keys the troopers found in the pit was similar to a key for Sonya's apartment. A replica of the key fit the lock to Sonya's apartment door but did not open it. The troopers believed the key they found in the firepit was the key to Sonya's apartment, but the heat of the fire had warped it, so it would no longer open the door.

Defense Attorney James McComas told the jury that Matthew Owens did not know Sonya Ivanoff and had no reason to murder her. He pointed out the lack of hard evidence presented by the prosecution and suggested the actual killer was Sonya's ex-boyfriend. Matthew Owens took the stand in his own defense and clearly stated that he did not kill Sonya Ivanoff.

The jury deliberated for five days but could not reach a verdict, and on February 28, 2005, Judge Esch declared a mistrial. When interviewed, the jury foreman said the majority of the jurors had voted in favor of conviction, but the circumstantial nature of the case made it difficult for some of them to find Owens guilty beyond a reasonable doubt.

James McComas again requested a change of venue for the second trial of his client, Matthew Owens. McComas wanted the trial moved to Anchorage or Fairbanks, but Esch instead moved it to Kotzebue, a town of 3,200 people located 184 miles northeast of Nome. Judge Esch said a jury from Kotzebue would be drawn from a community similar to Nome, where the crime had occurred.

The second trial began on October 17, 2005. The prosecution presented much the same case it had in the first trial. In his closing argument, McComas told the jury that the state offered nothing more than "could have," "would have," and "might have." McComas said, "The state didn't even come close to prove without reasonable doubt that Matt Owens is guilty."

The jury did not agree with McComas. After deliberating for three days, the jury found Matthew Owens guilty of the first-degree murder of Sonya Ivanoff. Jurors also found Owens guilty of evidence tampering. Judge Esch sentenced Owens to ninety-nine years in prison. Owens's attempt to appeal his conviction failed.

In late 2005, Sonya Ivanoff's family settled a wrongful death suit against the city of Nome. The complaint filed by the Ivanoff family said the city should have known Owens would be a danger to the women living in Nome. In 1997, then police chief Milton Haken had refused to hire Owens, citing his lack of character. Despite knowing about Haken's assessment of Owens, though, a new police chief hired Owens in 2000.

The murder of Sonya Ivanoff by a Nome policeman finally forced officials to listen to the cries of Alaska Native women in Nome, who claimed the police repeatedly ignored their reports of sexual assault. Nome hired Robert Estes, a retired police chief from Virginia, who brought in two cold case detectives to sift through a decade's worth of sexual assault reports. What they found shocked them. Time after time, the reports showed that rapes and other sexual crimes often went uninvestigated in Nome. Sometimes, the police never even bothered to interview the victim or suspect.

Police Chief Estes announced that he and his staff planned to review 460 sexual assault cases going back almost a decade and a half. The Nome City Council seemed less than enthusiastic about this idea, though, since they did not want to dredge up old cases. They only wanted to look forward. Finally, Robert Estes felt defeated. He did not believe he could accomplish the job he was hired to do, so he resigned and returned to Virginia.

Robert Estes might think he had accomplished nothing in Nome, but he shined a bright light on the ugly problem of sexual abuse of Alaska Native women. The new Nome city manager has promised to hire additional detectives and continue the cold case review started by Estes and his group.

We will never know why Sonya Ivanoff climbed into Matthew Owens's police cruiser. Did he offer her a ride home? Did she know him? Sonya was not drunk or impaired when she accepted a ride from him. Whatever reason Sonya had for getting into his car, she likely felt safe. We might not always like the police, but most of the time, we trust them. Sonya Ivanoff paid with her life because she trusted the police.

The Bethel School Shooting

Before Santa Fe, before Marjory Stoneman Douglas, before Sandy Hook, and even before Columbine, there was Bethel Regional High School in Bethel, Alaska. On February 19, 1997, Evan Ramsey loaded a Mossberg 500 twelve-gauge shotgun, hid the gun in his pants, and rode the school bus to Bethel Regional High School, where he attended classes. What happened next would tear apart the small town of Bethel, and as with all the school shootings to follow, students and parents would be left asking, "Why?"

Evan Ramsey had the worst of childhoods. When he was five years old, his father, Don, earned the nickname "Rambo of Alaska" when he stormed the *Anchorage Times* office. Don Ramsey was furious with the newspaper for refusing to publish his political-attack letter. He entered the newspaper office armed with an AR 180-223 semiautomatic assault rifle and 180 rounds of ammo, plus a .44 Magnum handgun with thirty rounds of ammunition. Ramsey also carried smoke grenades into the building, but at the last moment, he changed his mind and did not go through with the attack. He surrendered before he hurt anyone. The elder Ramsey spent ten years in prison for his planned attack. He was released in February 1997, just two weeks before his son entered Bethel Regional High School armed with a shotgun.

Not long after Don's arrest, someone set the Ramseys' house on fire, and the family had to find another place in Anchorage to live. Evan Ramsey was the middle of three boys, and their mother, who already had a drinking problem, descended further into alcoholism and could not support her children. When Evan was seven years old, the Department of Youth and Family Services removed him and his two brothers from their mother's custody and placed them in foster care. Evan and his younger brother, William, were separated from their older brother, John. Between 1988 and 1991, Evan lived in eleven foster homes.

According to Evan and William, they were abused by several of their foster parents. William later said that some of their foster brothers paid other kids to beat Evan while they watched. Evan suffered from depression, and at age ten, he attempted suicide.

Around the same time, Evan and William moved to Bethel with their guardian. In addition to being depressed, Evan struggled academically and had an explosive temper. Not long before the shootings, Sue Hare, the Lower Kuskokwim School District superintendent, became Evan's guardian. Evan seemed to do much better in his new home, but he struggled to cope with the endless teasing at school. Kids referred to him as "retard," "spaz," or "brain dead." Evan hated it the most when his classmates called him "Screech," after a geeky character on the TV series *Saved by the Bell*. Evan didn't know how to deal with the bullying and harassment, and he quietly drew up a hit list of kids he wanted to kill.

Evan Ramsey was not the most popular kid attending Bethel Regional High School, but he was also not an outcast. Some of the kids made fun of him and called him names, but he had a few close friends, and they spent hours playing the computer game *Doom*. Many concerned parents were worried about the violence portrayed in *Doom*, where the characters stalk, shoot, and kill each other. Some adults believed *Doom* was not appropriate for teenagers. The Bethel school shooting would not be the only time *Doom* received some of the blame for teenage gun violence. Dylan Klebold and Eric Harris, the two suspects in the Columbine school shooting, enjoyed playing *Doom*, as did Michael Carneal, the shooter in West Paducah, Kentucky, and Andy Williams, the gunman at Santana High School in Santee, California.

Whether Evan got the idea for shooting his fellow students from a video game or his father's actions a decade earlier remains unclear. Both the game and his father's violent activities probably factored into the creation of Evan's plan. Perhaps the terrible idea would have withered away as nothing more than a teenage fantasy if not for the urging of his two friends, James Randall and Mathew Charles. The twelve-gauge pump-action shotgun Evan took from his foster mother's home resembled a gun often used by the characters in *Doom*, but Evan had no idea how to load or shoot the gun. James Randall showed Evan how to load and fire the weapon, and Matthew Charles encouraged Evan, telling him he would be famous for carrying through with something other kids only dreamed of doing.

Evan's friends helped him compile a hit list of the teachers they hated and the students who teased them. Evan put a ninth-grade boy and girl at the top of his list because he said they'd spat on him and called him stupid. When the time came for Evan to execute his plan, he did not see the kids he wanted to shoot. He decided instead to shoot those who were there.

A few days before the attack, Ramsey and his friends had told their classmates something big was about to happen. Rather than telling an adult that Evan Ramsey planned to bring a gun to school, some of the kids took cameras with them on the morning of the shooting spree, and several students gathered in the library on a mezzanine overlooking the lobby, where they had front-row seats to the carnage.

On Wednesday, February 19, 1997, Evan Ramsey stuffed the Mossberg twelve-gauge shotgun down his pant leg to hide it. He rode the school bus to the high school and walked into the school's student commons area, where he pulled the gun from his pants and opened fire. He shot fifteen-year-old Josh Palacios in the abdomen and wounded two other students. Josh was a popular student and a star basketball player.

Reyne Athanas, an art teacher, was sitting in the teachers' lounge when she heard a popping sound, and she initially thought someone was setting off firecrackers. She walked down the hall toward the loud noises and encountered a stream of kids fleeing toward her, screaming, "He's got a gun! He's got a gun!" Athanas hurried toward the commons and saw Josh Palacios sprawled on the floor, dying. She knelt beside Josh, and when she looked up, she saw Evan Ramsey pointing his shotgun directly at her.

Athanas told Evan to put down the gun, but he refused. She saw rage on his young face and said he looked out of control. For some reason, Ramsey decided not to shoot Athanas. He left the area but returned a few minutes later, and this time, without hesitation, he shot and killed the fifty-year-old principal, Ron Edwards. Ron's wife, a substitute teacher, was at the school that day, and as Ron lay dying on the floor, she cradled her husband in her arms.

Next, Ramsey raised the barrel of the gun to his chin as if planning to commit suicide. He held the weapon there for several moments but did not pull the trigger. Finally, he threw the gun down and yelled, "I don't want to die!" Ramsey quietly surrendered to the police, leaving two dead, two wounded, and a deep scar on the town on the tundra of southwestern Alaska.

After his arrest, Ramsey claimed he did not understand that his actions would kill anyone. He thought he would just scare his bullies into leaving him alone. Prosecutors debated whether to try Ramsey as an adult or a juvenile but finally decided to try him as an adult. The judge moved his trial to Anchorage.

On December 2, 1998, a jury found Ramsey guilty of two counts of first-degree murder, three counts of first-degree attempted murder, and fifteen counts of third-degree assault. Judge Mark Isaac Wood sentenced Ramsey to 210 years in prison, but his sentence was reduced to two ninety-nine-year terms on appeal. Evan Ramsey will be eligible for parole in 2066, when he'll be eighty-five years old.

The judge called teacher Reyne Athanas a hero who tried to stop Evan three times during his rampage. Athanas said she was mad at Evan for putting her through the ordeal, and she said, "I'm mad at all those other boys and girls who didn't come forward and say anything." She said she saw ten to fifteen kids lined up in the library, watching the show below them in the commons. Athanas said she believed at least some of those kids knew Ramsey had planned to bring a gun to school to shoot students and teachers, but none of them came forward to report the plan.

Ramsey was initially incarcerated at Spring Creek Correctional Center in Seward, but he was later transferred between facilities. He resided at the Goose Creek Correctional Center between Anchorage and Wasilla for a while and then was moved to the Wildwood Correctional Center in Kenai.

Matthew Charles, the boy who had convinced Ramsey he would live in infamy if he opened fire at the school, pleaded guilty to criminally negligent homicide. James Randall, who had shown Evan how to load and fire the shotgun, was convicted of second-degree murder. Since the court tried both boys as juveniles, they could only be held until their nineteenth birthdays.

Ramsey first told the police that he didn't think his actions would kill anyone. Did he think he was playing a video game, and the dead and dying would get up and walk away once the game was over? Ramsey also said, "My main objective of going into the high school was to check out. To commit suicide." These two statements contradict each other, and he couldn't very well have it both ways. If he knew he could kill himself with his gun, he also knew he could kill others.

Prosecutor Renee Erb placed the blame for the murders at Bethel Regional High School squarely on Evan Ramsey's shoulders. She said Ramsey was a bad person. According to Erb, "There are some people in this world that are no good. Nobody really knows where they come from or why. But they've always been with us, and it may be that they always are." Erb said she believed Evan had killed those at the school because he desired fame, and she pointed out that he had planned the crime ahead of time.

A psychiatrist named John Smith, who examined Evan a few months after his rampage, was not as harsh in his assessment of Ramsey. He noted Evan's history of depression, including his suicide attempt when he was only ten. By the time of the murders, Evan was using marijuana, getting poor grades, and struggling to control his explosive temper. Smith also pointed out that Evan had not planned the violence alone but did so with the help and encouragement of his two friends. The night before the attack, Evan stayed awake all night and didn't dare back down from his plan for fear of disappointing his friends. Dr. Smith said, "The tragedy of everyone in Bethel, particularly the young man and the principal who were killed and their families, is that Evan was not recognized as needing as much help as he did."

Ramsey later said he felt good in the hours after the killings and believed he had solved his problems. He said, "Through my crime, I released hate and pain." He added, "There were a couple of people I wanted to kill. There were two people I hated, hate in the way Hitler hated the Jews." When Ramsey arrived at the school and didn't see his intended targets, he shot those who were there instead. Ramsey said he didn't think about what would happen to him after his rampage. He said all he cared about was, "What is it going to take to get rid of this problem now?"

Not long after his sentencing hearing, Ramsey apparently realized that his actions would not bring him lasting fame. He said, "I'm dead to the world. In a few months, nobody will remember me. There will be other people that will commit other offenses, and I'll be considered yesterday's news." Ramsey said he didn't know why he'd let the teasing bother him so much. He said living in prison was much worse than living with his rage.

In a 2001 interview, four years after the shooting, Evan Ramsey seemed to understand the hopelessness of his future. He told the reporter that he knew he would never leave prison. He blamed the school bullies, his parents, the foster care system, and the teachers who wouldn't listen to him for making him believe the only way to solve his problems was to shoot people. When asked if he had a message for troubled teenagers contemplating a similarly desperate act, he said, "I would tell them the situation they're in now is not half as bad as the situation they're going to be in if they do something similar to what I did. It will only get worse."

In 2007, ten years after Evan Ramsey walked into Bethel Regional High School with a gun and began shooting, CNN reporter Anderson Cooper interviewed Ramsey in prison. Cooper asked Ramsey how long he had spent plotting the attack. Ramsey said he'd planned what he would do for two weeks. Cooper asked him why he'd taken the gun to school, and Ramsey said he'd felt he had to do something drastic to stop the other kids from picking on him. According to him, other kids had beaten him up, spit on him, thrown things at him, and called him names. Ramsey said he had a list of people he wanted to shoot, but he claimed he did not understand how the world worked. He thought life was like a video game and believed that if he shot people, they would fall, but later, they would be able to get up and leave. He said he didn't understand that a person would bleed to death and die if he shot them. In the video game *Doom*, he said, you have to shoot something eight or nine times before it dies, and he thought the same concept applied in real life. Anderson Cooper said he thought most people would have a hard time believing that Ramsey did not understand dead is dead.

Cooper asked Evan Ramsey what it felt like to pull the trigger, and Ramsey said he felt relieved. He believed he was scaring people, and they would stop picking on him. Ramsey said he wished an adult would have sat down with him and explained that the name-calling and other abuse would pass. His sixteen-year-old brain did not know how to deal with the situation, and he badly needed guidance. There is no indication Ramsey ever asked an adult for help, and Evan Ramsey had passed through so many foster homes that none of the adults in his life knew him well enough to understand his psychological struggles.

A 2017 news report covered the twentieth anniversary of the Bethel school shooting. Reporter Rhonda McBride talked to thirty-six-year-old Evan Ramsey at the Goose Creek Correctional Center, a ninety-minute drive from Anchorage. McBride noted the gray streaks now running through Ramsey's black hair.

When McBride asked Ramsey his thoughts on the shooting, he said a curious thing: "There's a part of me that will always be sad for what I did, but the small amount of sorrow that I have, others feel more." Ramsey said he wished that he had known when he was sixteen that his high school years would pass quickly and the frustrations and bullying would end.

Claudia Palacios, the mother of Josh Palacios, the popular teenager Ramsey killed, continued to suffer the sharp pain of losing her son. After the school shooting, Claudia moved away from Bethel, and although she eventually returned, she could not bring herself to go to the high school to see the memorial for Josh and Principal Ron Edwards. Claudia eventually forgave Evan Ramsey, but she would never forget what he had done. Mrs. Palacios fostered many children over the years, and she wished she could have fostered Evan Ramsey. She said if she had fostered him, maybe he wouldn't have brought a gun to school.

Evan had severe anger issues and did not know how to deal with bullies. Despite his inability to stand up to the kids in high school, though, Ramsey quickly learned how to survive in prison. When an inmate accused Ramsey of cheating at a card game, Evan attacked him with a sock filled with batteries. He said other inmates had told him he would have to get into a fight to prove he was not a cheater and to make sure the other inmates left him alone. If only someone had helped Evan learn how to stand up to or ignore bullies in high school, perhaps he would not have murdered Josh Palacios and Ron Edwards.

If the court had tried Evan Ramsey as a juvenile, would he have become a repeat offender once he returned to society? Some of his statements to reporters over the years make you wonder. Ramsey regretted his actions on February 19, 1997, but he expressed little remorse for his victims. He mainly felt sorry for himself because his actions had landed him in prison for the rest of his life. His lack of empathy for other humans and his explosive temper made him a potentially dangerous person.

Was Evan Ramsey confused when he opened fire on his classmates and teachers? Some reports describe him as mentally slow or developmentally challenged, but when quoted, he always sounds articulate and has an extensive vocabulary. He made poor grades in school, but grades do not always reflect intelligence. Evan Ramsey knew what he was doing when he walked into his high school with a loaded shotgun. He knew those he shot would not get up and walk away when "the game was over."

MURDER NORTH OF THE ARCTIC CIRCLE

Most people imagine snow, ice, and bitter cold when they think of Alaska in January, but Alaska is a big place. The temperature in Southeast Alaska, for instance, averages above freezing in late January. The weather above the Arctic Circle, though, matches many people's imaginations. The following story provides a feel for Alaska at its coldest. This brutal crime occurred north of the Arctic Circle in January, with the temperature hovering at –50°F (–45°C), when someone shot three men on a caribou-hunting expedition and left them to die in their tent.

Frigid temperatures, a clash of cultures, and a language barrier all played a part in this crime, but the primary cause, sadly, was something we often see in all cultures. A father gave his son a gift he believed would make him more of a man and help him find his way in the world. Unfortunately, the father did not understand his son and his problems, and his well-meaning present ended up causing his son great harm. The gift also ended the lives of three good men.

On January 25, 1970, a pilot flying a local physician on a wolf-hunting trip buzzed low over the Kobuk River and was surprised to spot a man holding his hands above his head. The man was standing in the middle of the frozen tundra, miles from any habitation. When the Cessna flew over him, the man collapsed onto the snow, and the pilot landed the plane on its skis near him.

The pilot and doctor soon realized the young man was little more than a teenager, and blood spattered his clothing. He got to his feet and could barely walk as he stumbled toward the plane. The physician helped him into the back of the aircraft, and the young man told the doctor and pilot that he had been a member of a hunting party of four men. Someone had murdered the other men, but he'd managed to escape. He explained that the other men's bodies were miles away at their camp on the Kobuk River. He said he'd left them there and walked all night, trying to get back to Kiana. After telling his story, the young man lost consciousness.

The pilot flew the young man back to Kiana, where he was taken to a local clinic. The pilot then radioed Alaska State Trooper Bob Boatright in Kotzebue and told him the story his passenger had just relayed. Next, the pilot flew back up the Kobuk River toward the hunters' camp. He circled the camp and saw one body sprawled on the ground outside the tent, but he could see no sign of life in the camp. Since the sun was dropping below the horizon, he returned to Kiana for the night.

By the time Trooper Boatright and Kotzebue Chief of Police William Stevens arrived in Kiana, it was too dark to travel to the hunting camp, so instead, they went to the clinic to check on the patient. The young Caucasian man was now conscious, and his condition had improved. He told the officers he was nineteen years old, and his name was Norman Leroy "Butch" Johnson. His father was a foreman for the Alaskan Housing Authority and was responsible for building houses in small, remote communities.

Butch said his father had given him a new rifle for Christmas and had arranged for him to go on a caribou-hunting trip with three Inupiat men from the village of Kiana, where his father currently worked. Butch's hunting companions were Freddie Jackson, Oscar Henry, and Clarence Arnold, all from Kiana. Butch told the officers that a stranger had stopped by the hunting camp the previous night and had murdered his fellow hunters.

The next morning, Boatright and Stevens flew up to the hunting camp, where they found an eight-by-ten-foot tent fifty yards from the north side of the Kobuk River. Two snowmachines with gear sleds attached were parked at the campsite. They saw rifles and shell casings near the tent and several gutted caribou strung up nearby.

The body of Frederick Jackson lay sprawled on his stomach in front of the tent. Someone had shot him several times. Bloodstains led from his body to the tent's interior, indicating that he had been shot in the tent and had stumbled outside, where he fell. The officers found the body of Clarence Arnold face-down on the floor inside the tent. The killer had also shot him numerous times. Oscar Henry's body lay toward the rear of the tent, his hands grasping his pants as if he had been pulling them up when attacked. In addition to shooting him, the killer had also repeatedly hit Henry in the head with a heavy object.

Multiple bullet holes pierced the tent and the objects inside it. From the changing trajectory of the bullets entering the tent, the officers concluded that the killer had walked around its outside perimeter while shooting at it. Numerous boot tracks surrounding the exterior of the tent supported this hypothesis. Officers found shell casings from several rifles both inside and outside the tent.

When Trooper Boatright and Chief Stevens returned to Kiana, they found tensions high in the community. Someone had murdered three well-respected men from the village, and the residents believed the young white man in the hunting party must have been responsible for their deaths. Boatright called the Fairbanks Trooper Post and requested the help of Trooper Lorry Schuerch. In addition to being the first *Inupiat* ever to become an Alaska State Trooper, Schuerch was also a former resident of the village of Kiana. Boatright felt Schuerch would be a valuable asset to the investigation, and he could communicate with the villagers in a way other law enforcement officers could not.

With Butch's father present, Boatright and Stevens interviewed the teen again. Butch said he'd left Kiana on the morning of January 23, riding on the sled behind Freddie Jackson's snowmachine. When they arrived at the hunting camp, Clarence Arnold and Oscar Henry were already there and had set up the tent. The next morning, the older men spotted a small caribou herd a few miles from their tent, and they sped toward it on their snowmachines. Butch once again rode on the sled behind Freddie's snowmachine, but as they crossed over rough terrain, he could not hold on and was tossed out of the sled. The men feared that if they stopped to pick up Butch, they would lose sight of the caribou herd and their chance to supply their village with fresh meat, so they continued toward the caribou herd, planning to return for Butch after they'd shot the caribou.

Butch was furious with his fellow hunters for leaving him alone on the tundra, and he wondered if they planned to return for him. Slowly, he began to follow the sleds on foot. Butch told the troopers that by the time he'd caught up with the Inupiat, they had already shot the caribou and were dressing the animals. He said that after they'd returned to their tent for the evening, another Inupiaq man, Clarence Wood, drove up to their camp on his snowmachine and stayed for dinner. The men spoke in Inupiaq, so Butch did not understand what they were saying, but he said it sounded like a friendly conversation.

After dinner, Wood left, and Butch said the men were crawling into their sleeping bags when they heard a snowmachine approach their tent and stop. According to Butch, the other men went outside the tent to greet the newcomer, and a fight ensued. He said the stranger started his snowmachine and began to drive away but then returned. Meanwhile, the hunters were getting ready for bed when the stranger started shooting at the tent. Butch said he slipped out of his bag, crept under the rear tent flap, and hid in the brush while the stranger continued to shoot at the tent. Finally, the man stopped shooting, got on his snowmachine, and departed.

After the stranger left, Butch said he went into the tent, where he found his three fellow hunters dead. He grabbed his gear and attempted to start one of the snowmachines, but the engine wouldn't fire in the frigid temperatures, so he began hiking toward Kiana with the temperature dipping to –50°F (–45°C). He had walked more than thirty-eight miles before the airplane stopped for him. Butch told the troopers that he did not shoot his fellow hunters, but he could identify the man who had.

As tensions grew in Kiana, animosity toward the few white residents increased. When Trooper Schuerch arrived, he calmed the villagers and promised them that the troopers would find and arrest the person who had murdered their friends. Trooper Boatright told Butch and his father to leave the village immediately and fly to Anchorage, where troopers would meet them for further questioning.

Troopers located and interviewed Clarence Wood, the man who had stopped by the hunting camp and stayed for dinner the night of the murders. Wood told the troopers that Butch had barely spoken a word while he was at the camp, and the other men said the boy had fallen off the sled and then had to walk ten miles to the site of the hunt. They said Butch was unhappy about being left alone and was upset at not being included in the hunt. Wood said he'd left the camp immediately after dinner and knew nothing about the murders.

When Butch and his father arrived in Anchorage, they were interviewed by Trooper Sergeant Tom Anderson, Corporal Dean Bivins, and Sergeant Bill Nix. Nix wasted no time with small talk. He assumed an aggressive posture and called Butch a liar. He said another Inupiaq did not shoot the men, and he told Butch it was time to tell the truth. It took troopers less than two minutes to break Butch. He admitted he'd killed Freddie, Clarence, and Oscar. After everyone had gone to bed, he got up to urinate, picked up a rifle, and fired it seven times into the tent. Then, he picked up Freddie's rifle and fired it until it was empty. He said someone came out of the tent, and he grabbed another gun and shot him. He then went inside and got his clothes. He tried to start one of the snowmachines, but it was dead, so he grabbed a rifle and started walking. Butch said he didn't know why he'd killed the men; he'd felt no animosity toward them.

When the troopers reconstructed the murder scene, they determined that the events had happened in a slightly different manner than Butch had claimed. They found evidence indicating Butch had headed down the trail, not realizing two of the men in the camp were still alive. When he heard Freddie Jackson try to start a snowmachine, he ran back to the camp and shot him. Then, he went into the tent and saw Oscar Henry still alive, so he beat him in the head with the butt of the gun until he died. Butch then buried the bloody gun in the snow, where troopers retrieved it.

Butch Johnson was tried in Anchorage in January 1971, one year after the murders. Psychiatrist J. Ray Langdon testified on Johnson's behalf and said Butch had suffered a psychotic lapse and was divorced from reality at the time of the shootings. Butch admitted he was disturbed as he watched the Inupiat butcher the caribou, and he felt disgusted when one of the men slit open a female caribou, exposing an unborn calf inside her. Langdon and psychiatrist Barbara Ure testified that Butch had suffered a psychotic break when confronted by the freezing weather, the language barrier with the Inupiat (who often spoke in their native Inupiaq), and the blood and carnage of the caribou hunt. Dr. Ure said, "He was already insecure as to who he was. Having lost contact with his culture and his geography, he felt displaced. He had absolutely no preparation for this caribou hunt."

Butch was indeed a troubled young man. He had been diagnosed with latent schizophrenia, which may present itself as a paranoid or persecution psychosis if exacerbated. Butch had a low IQ, struggled in school, and could not hold a job. He suffered from low self-esteem, and his father believed that a wilderness hunting trip might improve his self-confidence.

Butch Johnson's plea of temporary insanity was denied, and he was found guilty of three counts of second-degree murder. The judge sentenced him to life in prison but ordered psychiatric treatment for him; no date was set for when Butch would be eligible for parole.

Johnson served most of his time in California to receive psychiatric treatment, and to the dismay of the residents of Kiana and the Alaska State Troopers, he was released on parole after serving only four years in prison.

Butch Johnson's father had undoubtedly believed he was helping his son by giving him a rifle and arranging a hunting trip in the Arctic wilderness. Still, he had to know about his son's psychological problems and should have known his issues could not so easily be remedied. Sending his withdrawn son on his first hunt in frigid weather with men who spoke a language and observed customs foreign to Butch was not only poor judgment but could also be considered criminal. Freddie Jackson, Oscar Henry, and Clarence Arnold agreed as a favor to Mr. Johnson to take his son hunting with them, and as repayment for their generosity, Butch murdered them.

THE MATANUSKA-SUSITNA VALLEY

The Matanuska-Susitna Valley (or Mat-Su region) encompasses a wide swath of south-central Alaska south of the Alaska Range. It begins about thirty-five miles north of Anchorage and includes the valleys of the Matanuska, Knik, and Susitna Rivers. The Mat-Su region is one of the fastest-growing areas of Alaska, and it includes the towns of Palmer, Wasilla, Big Lake, Houston, Willow, Sutton, and Talkeetna. This section includes two murders in Wasilla, one in Palmer, and one in Chulitna, a designated wilderness area forty miles north of the small town of Talkeetna.

Palmer, located forty-two miles northeast of Anchorage, is the borough seat of the Matanuska-Susitna Borough. Palmer had a 2020 population of approximately 5,900. In the late nineteenth century, the Matanuska coalfields north of Palmer caught the interest of US investors, who constructed a railroad from the coalfields to the port of Seward. Much of this coal was used to fuel battleships during World War I. Once the war ended, the government opened land around the Palmer area for homesteading. The rich, fertile soil in the Matanuska Valley and the availability of the railroad to transport farmed goods to the coast attracted farmers to the area, and soon Palmer began to grow.

Farming still occurs in the Matanuska Valley, but the high cost of fuel and transportation and competition with the worldwide food supply have made farms less viable. Some mining still takes place in the region, but many people simply choose to live in Palmer and work in Anchorage.

The town of Wasilla sits forty-three miles northeast of Anchorage, hugging the northern point of Cook Inlet. Wasilla primarily developed as a mining and agricultural center, but in the 1970s, it became a bedroom community for Anchorage and workers on Alaska's North Slope oil fields. Nearly 11,000 people lived in Wasilla as of 2020, but in 1993, the population was less than 5,000.

The small town of Talkeetna, seventy-seven miles north of Anchorage, sits at the confluence of the Susitna, Chulitna, and Talkeetna Rivers. The town arose in 1916, when developers chose the area as the district headquarters for the Alaska Railroad. It also served as a base for gold miners in the region. Today, Talkeetna serves as the gateway to Denali National Park, and tourism is vital to its economy. The town had only 1,055 permanent residents as of 2020, but during the summer months, the population swells as visitors flock to this unusual town to fish, raft, go flightseeing, or shop for arts and crafts from local artists.

THE MACHETE KILLER

W e've all seen the horror movie where a stranger towers over his unsuspecting victim while she sleeps, and she awakes just in time to see him swing the machete toward her head. Imagine if this was no horror movie but a terrible, true event, happening as you struggled to clear your mind from sleep and attempted to focus on your survival instincts. Now, what if you knew the maniac wielding the machete, and he was someone close to you? Could you fathom anything so horrible? Elann Moren had no choice; she had to grapple with the situation and spring into action. In one moment, her beautiful, new life became a horrible nightmare.

On Saturday, December 1, 2007, Christopher (Chris) Erin Rogers Sr., fifty-one, and his fifty-five-year-old girlfriend, Elann Moren, threw a party in their Palmer home to celebrate the first anniversary of their relationship. Rogers's twenty-eight-year-old son, Christopher Erin Rogers Jr. (Erin), helped Elann buy groceries and prepare his favorite meal, homemade pizza, for the occasion. During the celebration, Elann and Chris discussed their planned wedding scheduled for June 21, the summer solstice, and Erin volunteered to oversee the flower arrangements for the wedding. Amid the frivolity sat Chris's dog, Bear, a half English mastiff and half wolf mix, weighing 150 pounds. Bear was very loyal to Chris and never left his side.

After the party ended, Elann and Chris retired to their bedroom. Elann said she heard Erin in the living room watching TV, and she listened as he went in and out of the house several times. She assumed he was smoking cigarettes outdoors and then returning indoors to watch television. When she awoke at 4:20 a.m. and still heard the TV, she considered telling Erin to turn it off and go to bed.

A few minutes later, Elann froze as a shadowy figure walked into their bedroom. It was too dark to make out the person's features, but she could see that the person held something long and slender in his hand. She thought the object was a stick, and when the shadow began hitting Chris with it, she reached over to grab the offending object and stop the beating. After two of her fingertips fell from her hand, she realized the attacker was gripping a machete, not a stick. As her mind raced to find a rational explanation for this nightmare, she briefly wondered if this intruder had also attacked Erin. In a flash of horror, though, she realized the man hitting Chris repeatedly with the machete was Erin. When Elann asked Erin why he was hurting his father, Erin said, "You made me do it." Elann thought that Chris must have been dead, but a moment later, Chris rose out of bed in one burst, grabbed Erin, and carried him into the kitchen, where Chris collapsed and died.

Meanwhile, Elann hurried to the bathroom. She shut the door but couldn't lock it with her mutilated fingers and blood-slick hands. Erin had also whacked off part of her elbow and inflicted a deep wound on her leg. She huddled in the bathroom, terrified and unsure of how to save herself. A moment later, Erin burst through the door and again began striking her with the machete. Elann told him, "We're dead. You've killed us. You can stop now." Erin paused his relentless attack for a moment, and Elann thought her words had penetrated his deranged mind. Soon, though, she realized it wasn't her words but Bear, Chris's huge dog, that had stopped Erin. Bear gripped Erin's pants in his teeth and pulled him away from Elann.

Bear viciously chased Erin out of the house, and Erin jumped in his father's pickup and sped away. Meanwhile, Elann managed to lock the bathroom door with her teeth and dial 911 by tapping her engagement ring against the keypad on the phone. She told the 911 operator, "We're dying here. He started chopping us up. My arm is barely on my body. Please help us." The 911 operator told Elann to remain on the line, but she said she couldn't because she was passing out.

When the troopers arrived at Chris and Elann's home, they found pools of blood on the floor and crimson splattered across the walls. Elann was barely alive, but she told investigators it was Erin who had attacked them, and she told the police that if Erin had left the premises in Chris's truck, he was now armed with more than a machete. Before their dinner party the previous evening, Chris had decided it would be safer to place his .357 Magnum revolver under the seat of his truck instead of leaving it in the house. Erin now had a gun, and no one knew where he would go next.

The troopers found bloody paw prints in the snow outside the cabin, and when they followed them, they discovered Bear whining in pain. Erin had hit the dog with the machete, and Bear was missing a canine tooth and had a six-inch gash in his chin.

By Sunday morning, the Anchorage police had learned about the domestic crime in Palmer and were aware that troopers were still searching for the assailant. They knew to be on the lookout for the missing vehicle, but they did not understand the brutality of the Palmer crime nor the unhinged man who had committed it. They also had no idea the vicious killer had driven to Anchorage with a gun and was looking for his next victim.

Troopers checked to see if Erin Rogers had a police record, and what they discovered worried them even more. Rogers was a habitual offender who twice had been caught stealing. He also had started two forest fires in the Anchorage suburb of Eagle River. The police had arrested him for domestic violence, and he had two DUIs. After each conviction, the judge had given Rogers probation and another chance. After the last DUI, four months earlier, Chris and Elann had agreed to allow Erin to live with them and had promised to supervise him in their home while he served his probation. Neighbors said Erin seemed to be doing well and helped around the house with construction, painting, and yard work.

Erin Rogers drove from Palmer to Anchorage, where he abandoned his father's truck at a gas station. Then, taking his father's gun and ammunition, he walked into a residential neighborhood. Around 7:00 a.m. Sunday, Erin spotted twenty-seven-year-old Jason

Wenger warming up his Ford Bronco in his driveway. Wenger was sitting in his vehicle with the radio playing, probably oblivious to his surroundings, when Erin walked up to the driver's side window and shot him eight times. After Wenger's body fell against the accelerator, Erin panicked and ran away, afraid neighbors would hear the revving engine and come to investigate. It was not until 10:30 a.m. that a neighbor walking his dog discovered Wenger's body.

Wenger's murder initially stumped the authorities. Who would want to kill this young college student on his way to church? The crime made no sense. Jason Wenger worked with developmentally disabled folks and had a big heart. He was well liked and did not seem to have any enemies.

After murdering Wenger, Rogers crawled into the woods and took a short nap. He then walked to a nearby convenience store and bought beer and cigarettes. Erin later told the authorities that he no longer worried about being apprehended at this point. He "just wanted to kill a few more people along the way."

After resting, Rogers began to wander through the woods. He saw Elizabeth Rumsey walking down a bike trail while talking on her phone. Elizabeth, a law clerk for the Alaska Supreme Court, had been helping with an event at a local theater and now was headed home. Erin approached her and asked her if she knew what time it was. Erin's appearance frightened Elizabeth, and she began to walk faster. When she was within a block of her home, Erin opened fire, shooting her three times. As she fell to the ground, she lost her grip on her phone, but she called out to her friend and told her she had been shot. Residents heard the gunshots and called the police. Elizabeth Rumsey was rushed to the hospital at 7:20 p.m. Despite her serious injuries, she survived the attack. Erin Rogers later said he'd shot Elizabeth because she seemed nervous, and he feared she'd recognized him.

The random shootings in the city confused the police, and neither the Anchorage nor the Palmer authorities realized they were hunting the same person. After the murder of Jason Wenger and the shooting of Elizabeth Rumsey, the Anchorage police remained on high alert.

At 7:00 a.m. on Monday, December 3, architect Tamas Deak started his Jeep Cherokee in his driveway, planning to let the vehicle warm up while he returned to the warmth of his house for a few minutes. When Deak stepped out of the Jeep, Erin Rogers, who had been hiding nearby, began firing at him. Six of Erin's shots hit Deak, and then Erin bashed him in the head with the butt of his revolver, knocking Deak to the ground. Erin jumped in the Jeep and sped down the road. Deak tried to call to his wife, but one of the bullets had punctured a lung, and he couldn't draw enough breath to speak above a whisper. His wife had heard the gunshots but dismissed them as fireworks. Despite his critical injuries, Tamas Deak managed to withdraw his cell phone from his pocket and dial 911. Help arrived within minutes. Deak described his assailant as very thin, bearded, and dressed in a dark-blue jumpsuit with a hood.

Now with Deak's description, the police finally understood that they and the troopers in Palmer were chasing the same man. They quickly pooled their resources and began searching for Erin Rogers, driving Tamas Deak's Jeep Cherokee.

Approximately a half hour later, the police spotted Deak's stolen Jeep, and after a brief pursuit, officers rammed the vehicle, pinning it between a utility pole and a tree. Rogers attempted to shoot the officers, but his gun jammed, and the police arrested him without further incident. Once he was in custody, Rogers confessed to killing his father and Jason Wenger as well as wounding Elann Moren, Elizabeth Rumsey, and Tamas Deak.

What caused Erin Rogers to embark upon his murderous rampage? Elann Moren told troopers she believed Erin might have taken some of her prescription medication before he began his murder spree. Erin told the police he had attacked his father and Elann because he was angry with them and believed they thought poorly of him. He also told troopers that the machete attack required too much energy, and he would have preferred to shoot them if he could have found his father's gun.

Rogers stood trial in both Anchorage and Palmer. For the Palmer portion of his crimes, prosecutors charged him with the murder of his father, Christopher Rogers Sr., the attempted murder of Elann Moren, animal cruelty for hacking Bear with the machete when Bear pulled him away from Elann, and several other offenses. In Anchorage, the charges included the murder of college student Jason Wenger, the attempted murders of law clerk Elizabeth Rumsey and architect Tamas Deak, robbery, and assault. Rogers was found guilty on all charges.

In November 2009, an Anchorage judge sentenced Rogers to 309 years in prison, and in January 2010, a Palmer judge handed down a sentence for an additional 189 years in prison. Rogers appeared at the Palmer sentencing with a long beard and a shaved head and eyebrows. His eyes remained downcast during the proceeding. When asked if he had anything to say, he told the court he was sorry for what he'd done and regretted that his actions had affected so many people. "I wish I could die today," Rogers said. "I do hope that capital punishment is passed in Alaska and that I'm eligible for that. Because thinking about my crime and what happened, every day tears me apart more than people believe."

Rogers appealed his Anchorage and Palmer convictions but lost both appeals.

Bear, the dog who'd pulled Rogers off Elann Moren and then chased him away from the house, received local and national citations as a hero. Sadly, though, Bear died a year and a half after surviving his wounds from the machete attack. He was ten years old when he died from cancer in Elann's arms. Elann said she believed Bear had not only saved her life but possibly also the lives of their neighbors in Palmer.

DEADLY PASSION

What would you do for love? What if someone stood between you and your heart's desire, and the person in the middle was your true love's estranged spouse? What if the woman you loved and her spouse tried to rekindle the flames of their damaged marriage, and you had to think of them together? Would you accept defeat and quietly walk away, or would you take a more proactive approach? Jim Wheeler decided the best path to his true love's heart was to blow up her husband's truck with her husband in it.

On October 18, 1993, a bomb exploded in Robert "Hank" Dawson's pickup moments after he'd entered the gates of the Alcantra Armory in Wasilla, where he worked. Dawson, a fifty-year-old National Guardsman, died instantly from the blast. The Alaska State Troopers, the FBI, and the Bureau of Alcohol, Tobacco, and Firearms (ATF) quickly began investigating the explosion, and they soon discovered remnants of a bomb and a radio receiver in Dawson's demolished truck. The authorities knew someone had planted a bomb in the truck and then detonated it with a remote-controlled device when he drove through the gates of the armory.

Who hated Hank Dawson enough to obliterate him with a bomb? Calls soon flooded trooper headquarters, and most of the callers suggested that the authorities put James Wheeler at the top of their suspect list.

James Wheeler, sixty-two, moved to Alaska in 1952 while in the Air Force. In 1956, he began serving as a law enforcement officer in the Alaska Territorial Guard. His original role in the Guard was to enforce Fish and Game regulations during the era before Alaska became a state. Wheeler retired from the Guard in 1972, and after working as a security guard for a few years, he became an expediter for the Anchorage street department. Esther, his wife, worked as a secretary at Elmendorf Air Force Base, and the couple lived near Cheney Lake in Anchorage until they retired in 1988. Wheeler's son, Gary, became an investigator with the Alaska State Troopers.

Once Esther and Jim retired, Esther insisted on moving south to Sequim, Washington. Soon after the move to Sequim, Esther learned she had cancer, and she died two years later. Esther's death hit Jim hard, and he decided to move back to Alaska, where he would be closer to his son. He bought a house in Wasilla on Goldendale Drive, and his neighbors across the street were Hank Dawson and his eighth wife, thirty-year-old Terri.

According to neighbors, Wheeler became good friends with the Dawsons and was a frequent dinner guest at their house. Hank and Terri Dawson suffered marital problems in the summer of 1993, and Hank temporarily moved out of the house to live in Anchorage. After Hank walked out on her, Terri immediately called her neighbor, Jim Wheeler, to cry on his shoulder. Perhaps Terri considered her relationship with Jim platonic, but friends said Jim fell hard for Terri. Jim apparently could not keep his emotions to himself because he told anyone who would listen that he was in love with Terri Dawson.

Meanwhile, Terri and Hank decided to work on their marriage, and Hank moved back into their Wasilla home over the 1993 Labor Day weekend. By this time, Jim Wheeler's feelings for Terri had grown into an obsession, and he told several people that he could not stand to think of Terri and Hank in bed together. Hank died in the explosion only four weeks after he'd returned to live with Terri in Wasilla.

When the troopers listened to accounts of Wheeler's obsession with Terri Dawson, they believed they had a viable suspect for the murder of Hank Dawson. Investigators convinced one of Jim's friends to call Wheeler and record their conversation. They hoped he would incriminate himself during the call, and they weren't disappointed. While talking to his friend, Wheeler admitted that he had paid someone to kill Hank Dawson. He said he was in love with Terri and could not stand to think of her in bed with her husband. But

Wheeler refused to tell his friend the name of the person who had planted and detonated the bomb.

On November 9, 1993, troopers arrested James Wheeler as he ate lunch at the Windbreak Café in Wasilla. Wheeler hired John Murtagh, a highly regarded defense attorney, and said nothing to investigators.

At first, troopers didn't know if they should believe Wheeler's claim that he'd hired someone to murder Dawson. Was he telling the truth, or was he trying to pin Dawson's murder on someone else?

The authorities strung crime scene tape around Wheeler's house and began combing through everything in the residence, and soon, a possible suspect emerged as someone who might, for the right price, build and explode a bomb. Jim Wheeler's former mining buddy, Ronald Geiger, had extensive experience with explosives, and, according to acquaintances, he needed money. One man stepped forward to say he saw Geiger make a large purchase using $100 bills the day after the explosion. Ten days after the murder of Hank Dawson, Geiger left Alaska and moved to Everett, Washington.

Troopers wanted to collect more evidence against Geiger before they questioned him. The fifty-eight-year-old had few friends in Wasilla, and those who knew him described him as an unlikeable character. Until recently, though, he'd lived with his girlfriend, Wilma "Fay" Badal, who'd also moved from Alaska soon after the explosion. Troopers located her in California and flew there to question her.

According to Fay Badal, in October 1993, Geiger had worked for a man he referred to only as "Jim." Badal didn't know Jim's last name, and she said Geiger would not tell her what he was doing for him. Geiger never used his home phone to contact Jim. Anytime he wanted to talk to him, he left the house and used a payphone. When troopers asked Badal if Geiger had mentioned any details about Jim, she said Geiger had told her Jim was a widower with a blind poodle. The investigators knew Jim Wheeler owned a nearly blind poodle. Badal also said that Geiger, who never seemed to have money, suddenly had wads of $100 bills. Although circumstantial evidence was mounting against Ronald Geiger as the hit man, the troopers knew they'd need a confession from him to build a solid case against him.

In early March 1994, police in Washington arrested Ronald Earl Geiger and incarcerated him in the Snohomish County Jail in Everett. Alaska State Troopers flew to Washington to question Geiger. Under interrogation, Geiger admitted that Jim Wheeler had paid him $15,000 to build a bomb, place it in Dawson's pickup, and ignite it remotely with a radio-controlled device.

Papers filed in the Palmer District Court charged Geiger with first-degree murder in the killing of Hank Dawson. Still, despite his confession to the Alaska State Troopers who had questioned him in Washington, Ron Geiger pleaded not guilty.

Terri Dawson, Hank's widow and the central figure in this tangled web, filed a civil suit against James Wheeler, seeking $1.6 million from him to compensate her and her young son for their loss. She said Wheeler "has caused us incalculable grief and suffering to satisfy his warped desires." She claimed Wheeler had developed an obsessive romantic fixation on her, while she'd only considered him a friend. She said she had never had sexual relations with Jim Wheeler, but Wheeler's lawyer, John Murtagh, said Terri was lying. According to Murtagh, Terri Dawson told law enforcement officers that she and Mr. Wheeler did have a sexual relationship, and she said things got steamy several times.

Terri Dawson finally admitted in court that she and Wheeler had engaged in sexual contact on four occasions but said it was limited to fondling. Wheeler insisted they'd had sexual intercourse. Regardless of how Terri regarded her relationship with Wheeler, Jim Wheeler had fallen in love with Terri Dawson and could not stand the thought of her with someone else. Wheeler said Terri reminded him of his late wife, and when Hank moved out of the house, Wheeler had helped Terri with chores and often invited her over for dinner. When Wheeler took a quick trip to Seattle, Terri accompanied him. Neighbors said the two became constant companions during the summer of 1993.

In October 1994, James Wheeler went on trial for the murder of Hank Dawson. Wheeler testified in his own defense for nearly four hours. He didn't deny his feelings for Terri Dawson, but he said he did not murder her husband. Wheeler said he had no reason to kill Dawson because he knew Hank would eventually leave Terri. Hank Dawson had divorced seven previous wives, and Wheeler said he believed it was only a matter of time before he divorced Terri, too. According to Wheeler, Hank had told him numerous times that he could care less about Terri and had no use for sex with her. Wheeler said Terri had also confided in him about her troubled marriage, and the night Hank moved out of their house, Terri called Wheeler in tears. Wheeler said his intimate relationship with Terri began the following day, and the affair lasted until Labor Day weekend, when Hank moved home.

When District Attorney Ken Goldman asked Wheeler if he would like to get back together with Terri, Wheeler said, "If she'll have anything to do with me, yes." Terri's civil lawsuit against him apparently had not diminished Wheeler's feelings for her.

The jury deliberated for only two hours before finding James Wheeler guilty of first-degree murder. The court sentenced him to ninety-nine years in prison.

The road to justice for Ron Geiger, the man who had built, planted, and exploded the bomb, proved rockier. The state of Alaska initially charged Geiger with the first-degree murder of Hank Dawson. When Alaska State Troopers interviewed Geiger at the Snohomish County Jail in Washington, he'd confessed to planting and igniting the bomb that killed Hank Dawson. Still, he later pleaded not guilty to the crime. Unfortunately, Superior Court Judge Beverly Cutler threw out Geiger's confession because the troopers did not tape the first ninety-five minutes of the original two-and-a-half-hour interview when he confessed to the crime.

According to Alaska law, officers must tape-record interrogations of people in police custody, but as long as those who are being interrogated know they are talking to a police officer, the officer does not need to tell them they are being recorded. The law differs in Washington State, where the police must ask the suspect's permission to record the interview.

District Attorney Ken Goldman said the troopers had been afraid Geiger would refuse to talk if he knew they were recording him, so they'd followed Washington law and did not tape him for the first hour and a half of his interview. They then turned on the tape recorder for the remainder of their interrogation. Judge Cutler said there was nothing she could do. Since the troopers had not taped the entire interview with Ronald Geiger, she had no choice but to rule his confession inadmissible in court.

Goldman knew the state's case against Ronald Geiger rested on shaky ground without the interview. Without Geiger's confession, Goldman only had circumstantial evidence, including Geiger's former girlfriend's testimony. Fay Badal not only claimed Geiger had worked with a man named Jim on a secretive project, but she also admitted she'd once heard Geiger on the telephone discussing explosives with Jim. Goldman also had the testimony of the man who had seen Geiger make a large purchase with $100 bills the day after the explosion. These scattered pieces of information meant little, though, without Geiger's confession.

After the Alaska Supreme Court refused to review Judge Cutler's decision concerning the admissibility of Geiger's confession, Goldman contacted federal prosecutors and asked them to take up the murder case against Ronald Geiger. Federal law does not require officers to tape the entire interrogation of a suspect, so Geiger's confession would be admissible in federal court.

Because Hank Dawson had leased the truck destroyed by the bomb, Ford Motor Company, not Hank Dawson, had owned the pickup, and an out-of-state company had insured it. The federal prosecutor maintained that the truck's destruction affected interstate commerce, making this a federal crime. According to federal law:

> Whoever maliciously damages or destroys, or attempts to damage or destroy, by means of fire or explosive, any building, vehicle, or any other real or personal property used in interstate or foreign commerce or in any activity affecting interstate commerce and if death results to any person, [the

perpetrator] shall be subject to imprisonment for any term of
years or to the death penalty or to life imprisonment.

In other words, if Hank Dawson had owned the truck destroyed by
the bomb, then the US federal government would have had no jurisdiction in this case. Since he leased and insured the vehicle from out-
of-state companies, its destruction affected interstate commerce, allowing the federal government to bring a lawsuit against Ron Geiger.

US Attorney Robert Bundy charged Ron Geiger with five
felony counts in connection with the death of Hank Dawson.
These included illegally making a bomb, possessing a bomb, and
using a bomb to commit a violent crime. The court also charged
Geiger with maliciously destroying Dawson's truck and affecting
interstate commerce.

Ronald Geiger was convicted in federal court of malicious destruction of a vehicle used in and affecting interstate commerce, using and carrying a firearm connected with a crime of violence, and
possession of a destructive device. The judge sentenced him to life
imprisonment, plus a term of thirty years. Geiger appealed the verdict and questioned the federal court's jurisdiction, but the appeals
court did not overturn his conviction.

While Jim Wheeler and Ron Geiger had carefully plotted their
plan to murder Hank Dawson, did they not see that they would
quickly emerge as the crime's logical perpetrators? What happened
in Wasilla in 1993 to cause Jim Wheeler, who up until then was a
law-abiding citizen, to hire a hitman to kill his neighbor? James
Wheeler would tell you he murdered for love, but the truth is that
three of the oldest and most common criminal motives spawned the
murder of Hank Dawson: sex, jealousy, and greed.

THE KIDNAPPING AND MURDER OF AMY SUE PATRICK

We can never know another person's thoughts and motivations. Most killers have a reason to commit murder; whether for revenge, jealousy, or money, they understand why they killed their victim. Kyung Yoon, however, said he did not know why he killed eighteen-year-old Amy Sue Patrick. He claimed he murdered her on the spur of the moment, but some evidence suggests the crime was premeditated. Events in this case took a bizarre twist when the troopers arrested Yoon and hauled him to prison.

Friends and relatives describe blonde-haired, blue-eyed Amy Sue Patrick as a good girl who was quickly growing into a responsible young woman. According to her parents and her boss, Amy Sue was honest and trustworthy. She never missed work, and she arrived on time for her shift as a waitress at the Country Kitchen restaurant in Wasilla. According to her father, Amy Sue always called when she was running late, and she made sure her family did not worry about her. Amy kept her bedroom tidy and always had a neat, clean car. She played by the rules and never exhibited erratic behavior. Her father said Amy Sue was not "prone to do anything wild." She was not a young woman who would run away from her responsibilities.

Amy Sue had just graduated from Wasilla High School a few months earlier, and she looked forward to attending college and majoring in education. She wanted to teach children. Her long-term plan was to work as a teacher in a remote Alaska community for five years and then return to Wasilla to live near her parents and five siblings. Still, no one lives a perfect life, and her quote in her senior yearbook suggested her life was not always rosy. "Life is hard, and then you die," Amy wrote. Her friends and family would wonder if Amy could see her future.

Amy Sue had a boyfriend named Bob Marhenka, and according to her friends and relatives, Amy Sue seemed happy and content. Because she was so responsible and honest, Amy Sue made the perfect house sitter. When her parents' friends Jim and Diane Wada left the state for a short time, they asked Amy Sue to stay at their house. The Wadas lived outside of Wasilla in a secluded subdivision near mile 46.5 of the Parks Highway, the highway that connects Anchorage to Fairbanks.

On Saturday, September 21, 1991, the Wadas' son, William, arrived at his parents' home to leave some of his belongings. William's friend, Kyung Yoon, a Korean American chemistry student at the University of Alaska Anchorage, accompanied William to the house. The pair spoke briefly to Amy Sue.

The following night, Amy Sue was at the Wadas' house, talking on the phone to her boyfriend, Bob, when she heard someone at the door. She told Bob that William had arrived, and her boyfriend assumed she meant that William Wada had returned to his parents' house to drop off more of his things. Amy Sue asked Bob to stay on the phone while she answered the door. A few minutes later, Amy Sue returned to the phone and asked Bob to hold on a bit longer. Then, a few minutes later, someone hung up the phone and disconnected the call. Bob attempted to call Amy Sue back. He let the phone ring thirteen times, but no one answered.

When Amy Sue did not show up for her shift at the Country Kitchen on Monday, September 23, Kevin Harrington, her boss, knew something was wrong, He contacted Amy's parents, who called her boyfriend. When Bob told her parents about the strange phone call the previous evening, they called the Alaska State Troopers.

Sergeant Bill Tandeske assigned Amy Sue's case to Investigative Troopers Dallas Massie and Tom Clemons. Trooper David Churchill also assisted in the investigation. When the troopers arrived, Amy Sue was not at the Wadas' house, and the investigators did not believe she'd left the premises voluntarily. Although they saw no signs of a struggle in the house, too many things at the residence did not make sense. Amy Sue's car was parked in front of the house. Did this mean she'd left with someone else?

The investigators found Amy's purse, car keys, and wallet in the home. A half-eaten meal sat on the kitchen table. Upstairs, Amy Sue's clothes littered the floor. A towel lay on the floor in the bathroom, and a packet of birth control pills sat on the counter. The troopers were concerned when they saw that Amy Sue had last taken a pill on Sunday. If Amy was okay, then why hadn't she taken a pill on Monday? When Massie and Clemons questioned Amy Sue's parents, they said their daughter was a neat freak and would never leave her clothes or a towel on the floor.

The investigators immediately believed Amy Sue was a victim of foul play. She did not fit the profile of a young woman who would walk away from her life. Someone had taken Amy Sue against her will. The troopers questioned Bob Marhenka, but her boyfriend had a strong alibi, and they dismissed him as a suspect.

The troopers learned that the Wadas' son, William, had been at his parents' house on Saturday. They couldn't find William but did locate his girlfriend in Anchorage. She said William was currently working at his job on the North Slope, but she didn't know what day and time he had flown north to return there. Massie asked the girlfriend for the names of any of Wada's friends, and she suggested they call Kyung Yoon. The girlfriend said he was with William when they went to his parents' house on Saturday.

The troopers located Yoon at his home in midtown Anchorage. Yoon told them that William Wada had several girlfriends and a kinky sex life; he said he didn't know if William had a sexual relationship with Amy Sue, but he thought it was possible. Yoon said he'd accompanied William to his parents' home and saw Amy Sue for just a moment. The investigators noted how nervous Yoon seemed while talking to them, but they assumed he was uncomfortable telling them about his friend's sexual exploits.

The investigators began to suspect that William Wada had something to do with the disappearance of Amy Sue Patrick. Amy

Sue had told her boyfriend over the phone that William was at the door, and a short while later, someone disconnected the call. Did William Wada abduct and possibly kill Amy Sue?

The troopers soon dismissed Wada as a suspect, however, when they learned he'd left for his job on the North Slope on Sunday, September 22, hours before Amy Sue's last phone conversation with her boyfriend. The investigators flew to the North Slope and tracked down Wada for an interview. He could tell the investigators nothing about the disappearance of Amy Sue Patrick. The situation baffled him.

When they returned to Anchorage, Massie and Clemons recalled their interview with Kyung Yoon. They remembered how he had pointed the finger at his friend, subtly suggesting to the troopers that Wada could have done something to Amy Sue. They decided to wait to approach Yoon again until they could study the phone records for the Wadas' house.

According to the phone log, someone placed a call from Yoon's apartment to the Wadas' residence on Sunday, September 22. Yoon made the call one hour and ten minutes before Bob Marhenka said Amy Sue put him on hold so she could answer the door. The troopers knew the travel time between midtown Anchorage and the west side of Wasilla ranged from fifty to sixty minutes.

The investigators began delving into Kyung Yoon's life, but they found little in the student's background to suggest he was the type of person who would kidnap and possibly kill a young woman. Yoon had attended Dimond High School in Anchorage, and his high school teachers described him as intelligent and an excellent student. Friends said he was shy until you got to know him. They said Yoon was funny and easygoing and never showed any signs of aggression. Yoon lived with his mother, who said her son had returned home on the evening of Sunday, September 22, at the usual time, and he acted normal.

The only chink the investigators could find in Yoon's armor was a 1989 arrest for shoplifting, when he'd stolen a cassette tape and a Nintendo game from a Sears store. The judge had ordered him to stay out of trouble for six months and pay a $200 fine. At the end of the six months, the charges were dropped.

Yoon worked part-time at the Chemical and Geological Laboratories of Alaska in Anchorage, where he analyzed soil samples. He had a bright future but was painfully shy around women. Kyung Yoon was a lonely young man.

Troopers Massie and Clemons knew they had little evidence tying Yoon to Amy Sue Patrick, so they decided to visit him at his chemistry lab at the university. They assured Yoon he was not under arrest and then began a friendly conversation with him. Yoon told the officers that he loved to play the game Dungeons & Dragons, and he enjoyed painting fantasy figurines.

The officers steered the conversation to the night of September 22 and asked Yoon about his alibi for the time when Amy Sue Patrick vanished. Yoon said he went to an arcade at 6:00 p.m., and then he went home to watch television. Massie asked Yoon what TV program he'd watched. When Yoon answered, Massie knew he'd caught Yoon in a lie. Massie said he knew the show Yoon mentioned, and it wasn't on TV on Sunday night.

Massie quietly said, "You know you weren't at the arcade on Sunday night."

Yoon's gaze dropped to the floor, and he could no longer look Massie in the eye. Massie and Clemons turned up the heat. They said they knew he'd abducted Amy Sue Patrick. Massie told Yoon to close his eyes and tell him about his dreams and what he saw. Massie had successfully used this technique before on suspects, and it worked well with Kyung Yoon.

Yoon closed his eyes, took a deep breath, and in a calm voice, he said, "I pull up to the house and knock on the door. She answers and lets me in. I cover her mouth with an ether rag, and she passes out. I walk through and check the house. I find the phone is off the receiver, and I hang it up. Then I load her into the car, and I drive toward Anchorage."

Yoon said he drove down the Glenn Highway (the road connecting Anchorage to Palmer and Glenallen) and turned off at Pilot Road. He drove half a mile down the road and stopped. When Massie asked him what he did next, Yoon replied, "I snapped her neck, then I dumped her on the side of the road and covered her over with brush."

The confession shocked the troopers, but they had no physical evidence to back up Yoon's words. Massie asked Yoon if he would take them to Amy Sue's body, and Yoon said he would, but he asked if he could first go to his locker and put his stuff away. The officers waited while Yoon went to his locker, and then he accompanied them to their cruiser.

The trio drove to Pilot Road north of Eagle River off the Glenn Highway. Clemons stopped the vehicle at the spot Yoon indicated, but they saw no sign of a brush pile or a concealed body. Massie began to get angry and asked Yoon, "What's going on?"

The three men sat in the cruiser, and Clemons turned on a tape recorder and told Yoon to tell them his story from the beginning. This time Yoon said he'd originally placed Amy Sue's body at the spot he had indicated. Then, he drove to his home, grabbed some garbage bags, and returned. He put Amy Sue's body in the bags, covered her with brush, and drove to his apartment. The following morning, Yoon went to his scheduled class at the university and then drove to Pilot Road to retrieve Amy Sue's body. He then headed to the Anchorage City Refuse Station and dumped her body, wrapped in garbage bags, in a dumpster.

Troopers Massie and Clemons arrested Kyung Yoon while he sat in their cruiser at 11:44 p.m. on Saturday, October 5. They booked Yoon into the Mat-Su pretrial facility at 4:05 a.m. on Sunday, October 6.

When they handed off Yoon to the officer at the jail, Massie said, "Put this guy on suicide watch. Really, I'm not kidding. Watch him carefully." The receiving officer said he understood. The jailer then strip-searched and processed Yoon.

Later that morning, at 10:15, the guards moved Yoon from his cell to get him ready for his arraignment on the murder and kidnapping charges, and they noted that he seemed ill. A nurse examined

Yoon and sent him to the nearby Valley Hospital. Three hours later, an ambulance with lights flashing and sirens blaring sped Yoon to Providence Hospital in Anchorage. Kyung Yoon died at 6:35 p.m.

An autopsy revealed that Yoon had ingested enough arsenic to kill several people. The doctors could do nothing to save him. Arsenic affects most of the major organs in the body. It first attacks the stomach and intestines, then the kidneys, and finally the nerves. Arsenic does not attack the brain, so the victim is in horrible pain but alert. Yoon told a doctor at Valley Hospital that he wanted to kill himself. When in the ambulance on his way to the hospital, Yoon's heart rate soared, and his breathing increased. At 2:25 p.m., his blood pressure dropped to zero. At the hospital, the doctors hooked him to a ventilator and kidney machine, but by then, the arsenic had fatally damaged his organs.

Yoon often used arsenic at the chemical lab where he worked. He possibly also had access to arsenic at the university, but how did he manage to smuggle a bottle of the poisonous compound into the jail? The guards had strip-searched him when he entered the facility. Investigators believed Yoon had removed a small vial of arsenic oxide from his locker at the university when he asked the troopers if he could put his books in his locker before showing them where he'd killed Amy Sue Patrick. He then hid the vial inside his sock in his shoe, so the officers would not find it during a weapons search. They thought he'd ingested some of the arsenic while riding with the troopers. He then poured the rest into his sock and took it while waiting in the corrections room.

When the troopers learned of Yoon's condition, one of them quickly checked the vehicle Clemons and Massey had used to transport Yoon to the jail. On the floor of the cruiser, the officer found a small empty vial and white powder on the floor mat.

Despite Massie's warning to the jail guard to put Yoon on suicide watch and observe him at all times, the guards on shift ignored the orders, and they did not inform the next shift that Yoon was a suicide risk.

Yoon's death was a heavy blow to the troopers because he could not help them locate Amy Sue's body in the landfill. Trooper Tom

Clemons, accompanied by trooper volunteers and National Guardsmen, searched for Amy's body for three long weeks, spending nearly sixteen hours a day sifting through garbage. The refuse manager informed the troopers that a dead horse and elephant dung from the zoo had been dumped at nearly the same time Yoon said he'd dumped Amy Sue's body. If they could find the horse or the manure, then Amy Sue's remains should be in the same area of the refuse pile.

After a week of searching the dump, the troopers requested the assistance of dogs and dog handlers from Germany. The German handlers had trained the dogs to find human remains deposited in trash. The dogs reportedly could detect the scent of a human buried under fifteen feet of garbage, but the dogs did not find Amy Sue. Troopers wondered if Yoon had lied to them about leaving her body at the dump.

Investigators were about to call off the search at the refuse center when they found the horse's body that had been dumped around the same time Yoon said he'd brought Amy Sue to the dump. They decided to search one more day, and on Saturday, October 26, a backhoe unearthed a plastic bag with a woman's leg protruding from it. Amy Sue's family could finally lay her to rest.

Why did Kyung Yoon, a brilliant young man, confess his crime so readily to Massie and Clemons? He knew the troopers did not have a body nor any physical evidence against him for the kidnapping and murder of Amy Sue Patrick. Yet it took little prodding from Massie before the story of his crime spilled from his mouth. Massie said he believed Yoon wanted to relieve himself of the burden of guilt he felt. Massie said, "I believe that once you face your responsibilities, no matter what you've done, that's the first step to recovery and making yourself feel better."

Yoon's suicide left many questions unanswered. In his confession, Yoon said he'd used ether to subdue Amy Sue, but in a letter he left for a friend, he said he'd lied to the troopers about the ether. Troopers believed Yoon had used ether or a similar chemical to gain control over Amy Sue. If conscious, the young woman would have fought, but there was no sign of a struggle at the house, and Yoon had no scratches or other defensive wounds.

Yoon also said he'd murdered Amy on the spur of the moment. He claimed he'd planned to burglarize the Wadas' house, and he killed Amy Sue because she'd witnessed his crime. This explanation made little sense, though. Nothing was missing from the house, and Yoon knew Amy Sue was at the home because he'd placed a phone call from his home in Anchorage to the Wadas' residence. He'd stayed on the phone just long enough to hear Amy Sue answer, and then he jumped in his car and drove to Wasilla. His actions suggest a premeditated event aimed at attacking Amy Sue.

The big question left unanswered by Yoon's death was why Kyung Yoon would go to his friend's house and kidnap and murder a woman he'd only met briefly on one previous occasion. Yoon said he did not abduct Amy Sue to have sex with her, but the investigators who questioned him did not believe him. They said Yoon was very shy around women and incapable of forming intimate relationships. His pal, William Wada, bragged about his sexual conquests to Yoon, who must have found it challenging to listen to his friend's exploits. The troopers believed Yoon fixated on Amy Sue when he'd met her the previous day, and he decided he would have her at any cost. The medical examiner could not determine if Yoon had sexually assaulted Amy Sue because her body had decomposed by the time of the autopsy.

After an internal investigation into Yoon's suicide while in custody, investigators cleared Massie and Clemons of any wrongdoing. Still, they issued them a reprimand for not completing a more efficient search of Yoon.

The Chulitna Charmer

People move to the Alaska wilderness either because they enjoy solitude and crave a subsistence lifestyle or they wish to escape society. Many people who fall into this second category are either misfits who don't know how or don't want to blend in with others, or they are criminals seeking to escape arrest and hoping to disappear into the vast wilderness. Some people run to Alaska from a life of crime elsewhere. They might wish to turn their lives around in Alaska, but instead, many bring their problems and sociopathic tendencies with them.

Until Memorial Day weekend in 1997, Paul Stavenjord seemed to have succeeded at escaping his criminal past, but then something in him snapped, leaving two people dead and forever altering the course of Stavenjord's life.

Paul Stavenjord endured a rough childhood, first at the hands of an alcoholic father and then with his mother's two subsequent husbands. In 1965, Paul and his family moved from Everett, Washington, to Seward, Alaska. Not long after arriving there, Paul was expelled from school for hurling racially charged insults at other students. He never returned to school and became an insolent, moody teenager. He was arrested five times in two years for breaking into cabins, stealing a skiff and a car, and for breaking into his girlfriend's house and stealing a gun. While serving time in an Anchorage juvenile facility in 1966, Stavenjord escaped, stole a car, and led police on a high-speed chase through the streets of Anchorage. He was captured and incarcerated at the McLaughlin Youth Center until 1968.

Six months after being released from the youth center, Stavenjord brandished a gun and robbed a downtown Anchorage liquor store. The robbery netted him $190, but he was soon arrested and sent back to jail. By this time, Stavenjord was addicted to heroin and used LSD.

Soon after he was released from prison, twenty-year-old Paul Stavenjord and two friends decided to rob the Seward branch of the First National Bank of Anchorage. The robbery was such a ridiculous crime that it's laughable now to think about it. Only one road leads out of Seward, and that's a forty-mile spur road that runs south from an intersection on the Seward Highway and winds through the rugged Chugach Mountains. The robbers knew they would never make their getaway by vehicle because the police could easily set up a roadblock and intercept them before they reached the Seward Highway. Instead, Stavenjord and his buddies hatched what to them must have seemed like a brilliant escape scheme. They planned to rob the bank and then blow up a stolen car to create a diversion for the police. While the police investigated the exploding car, the thieves then planned to escape on foot into the wilderness and hike over the mountains to the Kenai Peninsula. Stavenjord wanted to take his share of the loot and settle near the Yukon River, where he could hunt, trap, and live in peace.

As soon as the trio robbed the bank, they headed up Mount Marathon, but they were unprepared for the steep, rugged terrain, and they had no idea that $150,000, their haul in the robbery, would weigh more than forty pounds. The three men ended up stashing their loot in an alder thicket and planned to return for it later. Unfortunately for them, their escape did not go unnoticed, and the police pursuing them recovered the money and returned it to the bank.

Even without the money weighing them down, the robbers found the mountain trail too difficult and decided to return to Seward and attempt to blend in with the other residents. The three men split up, thinking this would make them more difficult to track. By this time, though, a posse of twenty-five FBI agents, Alaska State Troopers, Seward police, and local citizens were scouring the wilderness for the trio.

Three days after the bank robbery, Paul Stavenjord staggered out of the brush fifty feet from the Seward police chief, parked beside a roadblock. Stavenjord failed to see the chief's police cruiser when he stepped out onto the highway, and he was arrested without incident. Stavenjord's two cohorts were captured at a Seward diner while they ate chili. All three men were convicted of the federal crime of armed bank robbery and sentenced to six years in prison. Stavenjord was released on probation from the federal penitentiary in Lompoc, California, in 1975.

After serving time for the bank heist, Stavenjord vowed to turn his life around and go straight. He took a job with the Alaska Railroad, repairing and inspecting tracks, and he worked for the railroad and stayed out of trouble for the next twenty years. Stavenjord loved the area near Chulitna, a wilderness area and railroad stop forty miles north of Talkeetna. He met and married a waitress for the railroad, and they had a daughter and built a cabin near Chulitna, where they lived for eleven years. Stavenjord supplemented his railroad salary by casting small pewter animals and buttons, carving flutes, and doing scrimshaw work on ivory, bone, and antlers. He sold his craftwork to souvenir shops and at the Alaska Fur Rendezvous. Stavenjord not only carved flutes but also became skilled at playing and writing music for the flute.

Paul and his wife, Peggy, had a son in 1984, but by 1991, Peggy had grown tired of the frontier lifestyle with no electricity, no running water, no plumbing, and no communication with the outside world. Peggy filed for divorce in 1991, but she and Paul remained friends, and Paul played a significant role in his children's lives.

* * *

A neighbor of Paul's in Chulitna named Rick Beery grew up in Alaska, leaving only when he served in the US Navy for two tours of duty in Vietnam. In 1997, Rick was working as an electrician and lived in Big Lake in the Matanuska Valley, north of Anchorage. Rick was forty-eight years old.

Debbie Rehor grew up near Denver. She married young, had a son, divorced, and moved to Wasilla, near her brother, Don Tidwell. Debbie was forty years old and worked in customer service for the Matanuska Electric Association.

Rick swore he would never get married, but he fell hard for Debbie Rehor, and they soon became a couple. After living together for eight years, they married in 1995. Debbie and Rick shared a home in Big Lake, but their dream when they retired was to move to their second home, a large cabin in Chulitna built on land homesteaded by Rick's father. Both Rick and Debbie loved the outdoors and looked forward to spending their retirement years in quiet, secluded Chulitna. For now, though, they escaped to their dream cabin every chance they got.

No roads lead to Chulitna, but it is a whistle stop for the Alaska Railroad. Once a day, a train travels this remote stretch of rural Alaska, halting when the engineer sees people standing beside the tracks. The only other way to access a remote cabin in Chulitna is to park a vehicle near the Parks Highway and travel the remaining distance on an all-terrain vehicle. Rick and Debbie's cabin sat eight miles from the Parks Highway. Their nearest neighbor, approximately one mile from their cabin, was Paul Stavenjord.

Rick and Debbie had an uneasy relationship with Stavenjord, whom they suspected of stealing fuel from their cabin. When Rick had sold Stavenjord a cellular antenna, Stavenjord helped himself to a cable that was not part of the deal. Rick told Stavenjord he wanted fifty dollars for the cable, and Stavenjord returned the cable, cut into pieces. Rick also suspected Stavenjord of taking a snowmachine and a .22 rifle from their cabin. Rick, a big man with a hot temper, confronted Stavenjord, but they did not resolve their issues.

Rick and Debbie decided to spend Memorial Day weekend of 1997 at their cabin. Rick headed to the cabin a day early, and Debbie followed on Friday after she got off work. Debbie parked off the road near the Parks Highway, where Rick met her on his four-wheeler, and they headed toward their cabin for a quiet weekend.

Both Rick and Debbie planned to return to their jobs on Tuesday, and when neither of them showed up for work, their bosses and coworkers found their absences curious. Debbie's boss contacted her brother, and alarm bells immediately sounded in Don's head. He rushed to Rick and Debbie's remote Chulitna cabin to check on them. When he arrived, he found their two dogs in the cabin. The dogs had gone to the bathroom in the cabin and had not eaten in some time. Don knew something terrible must have happened to his sister and brother-in-law. They loved their dogs and would never leave them closed in the cabin. Tidwell worried that perhaps Rick and Debbie had run into a bear or gotten stuck on the other side of the river by rising water.

Tidwell walked to Stavenjord's cabin and asked him if he had seen Rick and Debbie. Stavenjord told Tidwell that he and Rick had argued, and they hadn't spoken in over a year. Tidwell later said he picked up a strange vibe from Stavenjord and quickly thanked him and left the cabin. As Tidwell continued down the trail to search for his sister and brother-in-law, he heard a noise in the brush behind him and quickly turned to see Stavenjord following him down the path. Tidwell asked the other man what he was doing, and Stavenjord said he'd decided to join in the search for Rick and Debbie. Tidwell felt certain Stavenjord knew more about their disappearance than he had let on.

When Tidwell returned to Rick and Debbie's cabin that night, he huddled in the back of the cabin with his gun in his lap. He suspected Paul Stavenjord had done something to them, and he did not plan to be his next victim.

On Wednesday morning, Don Tidwell contacted the Alaska State Troopers and reported Rick and Debbie missing. The troopers responded immediately and discovered Rick's body in a creek two miles from his cabin and two hundred feet from his four-wheeler. Someone had shot Rick in the head execution-style at point-blank range. The authorities found no sign of Debbie and her four-wheeler, so she became a preliminary suspect in Rick's murder. Debbie's brother and friends assured the troopers that Debbie would never harm Rick, and Don feared his sister had met the same fate as her husband.

Electrical workers installing fiber-optic cable along the railroad tracks told troopers that they'd noticed Rick's four-wheeler partially in the creek on Saturday, and it was still there on Sunday. When they passed by the area again on Tuesday, the four-wheeler had been pulled out onto dry land. The electricians also mentioned seeing a recent campsite near the spot where the troopers had found Rick's body.

Twenty-one-year-old Gavin Saha called troopers and said he'd camped over the weekend in the Chulitna area. He said he'd seen the four-wheeler in the creek and pulled it out, helping himself to a soft drink and some gum stashed in a bag on the four-wheeler while he was at it, but he claimed he never saw Rick's body. Troopers determined that Saha had pitched his tent and slept only yards from Rick's corpse. The investigators immediately suspected Saha of murdering Rick, but where was Debbie?

A week after Rick's body was discovered, troopers found Debbie Rehor's body. Her body was downstream from Rick's, partially covered with grass and tree limbs. She was naked from the waist down. Debbie also had a bullet hole in her head, and an autopsy revealed she had been subjected to rough sex around the time of her death. DNA from semen found on her body did not match Gavin Saha's DNA, ruling him out as the perpetrator.

Paul Stavenjord told the authorities that he'd gone to Fairbanks for the Memorial Day weekend, even providing troopers with details of the restaurants where he'd eaten and establishments where he'd stopped to get gas on his travels. When troopers followed up, though, nothing checked out. Not only did no one remember seeing him at the places where he claimed he'd stopped on his trip to Fairbanks, but Gavin Saha also recalled seeing smoke curling out of the stack on Stavenjord's Chulitna cabin. Troopers asked Stavenjord to give them a DNA sample, and when he refused, they obtained a court order for his DNA. Stavenjord allowed a trooper to swab his mouth for DNA, but soon after they'd left his cabin, he disappeared.

After Stavenjord provided his DNA sample and left his cabin, railroad workers reported seeing him walking along the tracks. He had shaved his beard and mustache. A railroad security guard saw Stavenjord crash a red four-wheeler into a bridge and run into the woods. When troopers followed up on the story, they discovered that the crashed four-wheeler was Debbie's missing vehicle.

When the DNA test results came back, the sample from the saliva in Paul Stavenjord's mouth was a match for the semen collected from Debbie's body. Troopers obtained warrants charging Stavenjord with the first-degree murders of Rick Beery and Debbie Rehor and the sexual assault of Debbie. Stavenjord was nowhere to be found, though, so troopers began an intense manhunt, scouring the wilderness near Chulitna for Paul Stavenjord. Troopers searched Stavenjord's cabin and found what they believed was a script he had planned to memorize to tell police if they arrested him. He wrote that he'd run into Debbie while on a walk on the Friday afternoon before Memorial Day. He charmed her by playing his flute and said they had a romantic sexual encounter. He said she then called her husband at 7:30 p.m. to tell him she would be late. Unfortunately for Stavenjord, Debbie's phone records showed she'd placed no calls on Friday evening.

Paul's friends and family did not believe Paul would murder two people. They felt certain the troopers had made a terrible mistake, and since Paul was now a hunted man, they feared for his life. His family hired Carmen Gutierrez, a top criminal defense attorney in Alaska, to defend Paul. Gutierrez immediately issued a plea, asking Stavenjord to surrender.

The manhunt continued for over a month. Finally, on July 12, nearly seven weeks after the shootings, Stavenjord called Gutierrez and met with her in Anchorage before surrendering to the troopers.

Stavenjord told troopers he returned to his cabin the day after the search began and then again after it ended. He went back the first time for Debbie's four-wheeler. When a security guard waved to him, he thought the guard was a trooper, and he attempted to flee, wrecking the four-wheeler. He then fled on foot before hopping a freight train. He made his way to Fairbanks, where he stayed for a week, and then took a van to Anchorage and on to Homer, where he camped for two weeks. Finally, he took a shuttle back to the Chulitna area and hiked to his cabin, where he stayed for two days before surrendering.

Stavenjord went on trial in April 1998. In addition to Gutierrez, Stavenjord's defense team included Jim McComas, another leading Alaska criminal defense lawyer. According to the narrative told by Stavenjord's lawyers and Stavenjord's testimony, Rick Beery had surprised his wife and Stavenjord while the pair were engaged in a sexual encounter in the middle of the wilderness. Stavenjord claimed Debbie scrambled for her clothes while her husband pulled his gun and started shooting. Stavenjord then grabbed his .22 pistol from his vest pocket and returned fire, hitting Beery in the forehead. Stavenjord said when he looked back at Debbie, he saw her lying on the ground, dead, killed by one of her husband's bullets. Stavenjord's attorneys argued that Beery killed his wife and that Stavenjord shot Beery in self-defense.

Stavenjord said he panicked. Due to his criminal past, he didn't think the troopers would believe his story, so he carried Debbie's body to a grassy spot near the creek and covered her with branches. Rick's body floated to a deep pool in the creek, so he left him there. At the end of Stavenjord's testimony, his lawyers asked him to play the song on the flute he had played for Debbie just before she was killed. The judge dismissed the jury while Stavenjord played his melody.

Prosecutor Bill Estelle told the jury not to believe a word Stavenjord had said. Estelle characterized Stavenjord's testimony as "lies, lies, and more lies." Stavenjord's trial lasted two months, and in the end, the jury found him guilty on the two counts of first-degree murder.

Before the trial's sentencing phase several months later, Stavenjord's two attorneys, Gutierrez and McComas, asked to withdraw from the case, citing a breakdown in the attorney/client relationship.

They were replaced by a public defender who requested a new trial, claiming that Stavenjord lied while testifying, and his attorneys knew he was lying. Gutierrez and McComas admitted Stavenjord had lied to them, but they said at the time, they had believed him. Stavenjord was denied a new trial and was sentenced to 198 years in prison.

In an interview, Rick Beery's sister said that Paul Stavenjord expected people to believe he had played his flute for Debbie, and she was so mesmerized that she agreed to have relations with the man. She said Debbie hated Stavenjord and would have been more likely to copulate with an alligator than with him.

Investigators believed Rick Beery had arrived at his cabin the day before the Memorial Day weekend and found items missing, so he confronted Stavenjord. Paul Stavenjord knew Beery planned to meet Debbie on Friday evening at the highway and bring her back to their cabin, so he hid in the brush and waited on them, ambushing the pair when they drove down the trail to their cabin. The troopers believed Stavenjord had molested Debbie after she was dead.

ANCHORAGE AND
SOUTH-CENTRAL ALASKA

A nchorage lies at the head of Cook Inlet, in south-central Alaska. The state's largest city sits on a peninsula formed by the Knik Arm to the north and the Turnagain Arm to the south. Due to the population boom related to the building of the Trans-Alaska Pipeline, the area around Anchorage grew rapidly in the 1970s. In 1975, the City of Anchorage merged with the Greater Anchorage Area Borough, creating the Municipality of Anchorage. As of 2020, Anchorage had a population of approximately 291,000.

Oil, transportation, the military, government, tourism, and regional and multinational corporations all help support the economy of Anchorage. The city is equidistant from New York, Tokyo, and Frankfurt, and it lies within a ten-hour flight of 90 percent of the industrialized world. Because of this, Ted Stevens Anchorage International Airport is a major refueling hub for global air travel, and it is one of the major hubs for FedEx.

For many, Anchorage is a great place to live because they can enjoy the benefits of an urban center while being only hours or minutes away from the Alaska wilderness. Unfortunately, though, Anchorage suffers from many of the same problems facing cities across the United States. It has a high rate of alcoholism and drug abuse, leading to an increased incidence of crime. Anchorage has a total crime rate 99 percent higher than the national average and a violent crime rate 213 percent above the national average. Residents of Anchorage have a one in twenty-two chance of becoming a victim of violent crime.

THE HUNTER

Robert Hansen is arguably Alaska's most notorious serial killer. Several television shows have portrayed Hansen's life, numerous books have detailed his horrific deeds, and a 2013 movie, *The Frozen Ground*, starring John Cusack as Hansen and Nicolas Cage as an Alaska State Trooper, chronicles Hansen's crimes and dramatizes the police investigation and apprehension of Hansen.

This is not a tale of Alaska's criminal justice system at its finest. Hansen should have been caught and prosecuted years before he was, but a perfect storm of circumstances allowed him to remain free and continue killing. Robert Hansen was a skilled liar, able to talk his way out of nearly any situation. He owned a bakery and maintained a reputation as a respected businessman with powerful friends he could convince to lie for him and provide him with critical alibis. He was married with a family and had strong ties to his church. Hansen was intelligent and adept at navigating the wilderness. He was a pilot with his own plane, allowing him to kill and dump bodies in remote locations. He was also an avid big-game hunter with a small arsenal of guns he could use well. Several of his animal trophies scored high in the record books, and his hunting buddies admired him. Hansen did not fit a typical criminal profile, and on those occasions when he was caught doing something wrong, the justice system repeatedly gave him the benefit of the doubt, despite his criminal record.

Anchorage, in the early 1970s, was a frontier town with growing pains. Construction began on the Trans-Alaska Pipeline in 1973, and it was completed in 1977. During this time, 28,000 people worked on the pipeline. Oil field workers made good money, and while many pipeline employees hailed from Alaska, others came from the lower forty-eight. The high wages created boomtown conditions in Fairbanks and Anchorage, and unemployment dropped to nearly zero in those cities. Off-duty workers spent lavishly, and crime rates spiked. Mobsters, drug dealers, prostitutes, and topless dancers followed the money to Alaska. Fourth Avenue in Anchorage became a string of endless taverns, and "the Avenue" was known as the longest bar in the world. Several topless bars opened in Anchorage. The dancers and prostitutes who worked on Fourth Avenue lived a high-risk, nomadic lifestyle, often working a while in Alaska, moving back to Seattle for a spell, and sometimes even traveling to Hawaii to work before perhaps again returning to Alaska. Few people noticed when a prostitute disappeared, and their absences rarely were reported to the police. This pool of transient young women willing to climb into a stranger's car for the promise of money created the perfect atmosphere for a monster like Robert Hansen.

Law enforcement in Anchorage and throughout the state was not prepared for the rapid influx of people and the increase in crime in the early 1970s. As the population of Anchorage exploded, the city quickly expanded past the city limits in every direction. The Anchorage Police Department patrolled the city itself, but the Alaska State Troopers, with a smaller force, were not only responsible for policing the portions of Anchorage outside the city limits but were also charged with patrolling most of the rest of the state of Alaska. Criminals quickly learned they were less likely to get caught if they committed crimes outside the Anchorage city limits. By 1970, the Alaska State Troopers had developed no protocols for dealing with sexual assault cases, and Alaska lacked a decent crime lab for processing evidence. The Hansen case would change all this, but the changes came at a horrible price.

Robert Hansen grew up in Pocahontas, Iowa, 125 miles northwest of Des Moines. By most accounts, he had an average childhood, but a pronounced stutter made him self-conscious. After graduating from high school, he joined the Army Reserves and received advanced military training at Fort Knox, Kentucky. Hansen returned to Iowa and worked at his father's bakery in 1959. In 1960, he was arrested for setting fire to the bus barn at a local school, convicted of arson, and sentenced to three years in prison. A psychiatrist diagnosed Hansen with infantile-personality disorder and said Hansen imagined committing violence against girls who rejected him. Two years later, another psychiatrist reported that Hansen's antisocial behavior had improved, and he was paroled a year early.

Hansen soon met Darla Henrichson, who was studying to be a teacher, and they married in 1961. Hansen then took a series of jobs in bakeries in Minnesota and North Dakota. In 1965, he was arrested for shoplifting from a sporting goods store, but Darla persuaded the pastor at her Lutheran church to vouch for her husband, and the charges were soon dropped. The Hansens then moved to Anchorage, where Darla took a job as a teacher, and Robert worked as a baker. Darla was active in her church, and the couple enjoyed the outdoors. Robert was a serious hunter, and he shot record-book mountain goats, caribou, and Dall sheep. He soon met and became hunting buddies with John Sumrall, a well-respected Anchorage insurance man.

In 1971, Hansen approached eighteen-year-old Susie Heppeard as she got out of her car at her apartment. He pointed his gun at her face and said, "Shut up, sweetheart, or I'll blow your head off." Susie screamed, and one of her roommates looked out the window, saw what was happening, and called the police, while another roommate yelled at Hansen and told him the police were on the way. Hansen pushed his gun into Susie's back and forced her toward the street, but when the police arrived, Hansen ran away into the night. The authorities quickly apprehended him, but he was released on his own recognizance. A month later, the grand jury charged him with assault with a deadly weapon.

Three days later, Hansen kidnapped a topless dancer and took her to a cabin on the Kenai Peninsula, where he raped her. On the way back to Anchorage, he stopped the car, pointed his pistol at her, and told her to start running. She pleaded with him not to kill her, and Hansen finally relented and took her back to Anchorage. To keep her quiet, Hansen wrote down her parents' names and address and said he would kill them if she reported this incident to the police. If Hansen had known her father was an Alaska State Trooper, she might not have been so lucky. On Christmas Day, when the half-naked body of a college freshman was found in a ravine near where Hansen had taken the young dancer, she decided she couldn't remain silent. She went to trooper headquarters, reported her abduction and rape, and identified Hansen from a photo.

Hansen was arrested again, and the latest charges were added to those that had already been filed against him. On December 29, he was arraigned and held on $50,000 bail. Hansen's family minister, as well as John Sumrall and another influential friend, appeared as character witnesses for him and stated that Bob Hansen would not harm anyone. They argued that the dancer must have been mistaken. Hansen's attorney attacked the topless dancer's reputation and pointed out that she used drugs. The charges in the case of the dancer were finally dropped, and Hansen received a five-year sentence for assaulting Susie Heppeard. He would be eligible for parole once his doctors determined he was psychologically fit.

A psychiatrist diagnosed Hansen with schizophrenia and said he would commit violent acts and then not remember them later. He learned how to manipulate the prison system and was a model inmate, effortlessly convincing psychiatrists and jailers that his condition had improved. He was released to a halfway house after serving only three months and soon was allowed to move home with his family.

Hansen owned a boat he moored in a small harbor at Seward, 125 miles south of Anchorage. Megan Emerick was last seen on July 7, 1973, folding her laundry at a dormitory in town. The police believed Hansen murdered her and buried her on the shore of Resurrection Bay, near Seward.

In the summer of 1975, friends drove Mary K. Thill to Seward. She got out of the car, and they never saw her again. Troopers believed Hansen also buried her near Seward.

A few weeks after Mary Thill disappeared, Hansen lured a dancer away from the Kit Kat Club on the Old Seward Highway near Anchorage. He drove her to Chugach State Park, raped her, and then let her go. The woman reported the rape but refused to press charges. The trooper who took her statement notified Hansen's parole officer, but Hansen claimed he thought he and the dancer were on a date, and the parole officer let the matter drop.

In November 1976, security guards caught Hansen trying to shop-lift a chainsaw from a store in Anchorage. The court sentenced him to five years in prison and sent him to the Juneau Correctional Institute. After he'd served only sixteen months, the Alaska Supreme Court re-viewed his case and decided that since his other offenses had occurred several years in the past, and since Hansen provided well for his family and was a respectable member of the community, he should be released. The judge who had initially sentenced Hansen expressed outrage at the court's decision. Soon after Hansen was released from prison, investiga-tors believed he committed a series of rapes and murders.

In 1982, Hansen opened his own bakery. Business thrived, and he soon made enough money to purchase a small airplane. The plane offered Hansen increased mobility. He no longer had to drive his vic-tims into the wilderness to kill them. He could now fly them there.

The body of Joanna Messina was found in a gravel pit near Seward in May 1980. Two months later, a second body was discov-ered over a hundred miles away in a shallow grave on a remote road outside Anchorage. Troopers could not identify the second victim. The two bodies were found so far apart that the authorities assumed two different people had murdered the women.

On September 13, 1982, two off-duty Anchorage police offi-cers were moose hunting on the Knik River when they found the re-mains of Sherry Morrow on a sand bar. When Alaska State Trooper Sergeant Lyle Haugsven arrived to examine the remains, he thought about the growing list of missing dancers in Anchorage. Was a seri-al killer stalking the streets of Anchorage? Haugsven compiled a list of women who had been reported missing, and then he created a suspect list. More than thirty names made his list, including Robert Hansen. Still, as the months passed and no more bodies surfaced, the police rejected the idea of a serial killer and decided the murder of Sherry Morrow had been an isolated event.

On June 13, 1983, a trucker encountered a seventeen-year-old girl named Cindy running down a street near an airfield in Anchor-age. A man with a gun was chasing her. Cindy was barefoot and handcuffed, and when the trucker stopped, she climbed into his truck. The trucker tried to convince her to go to the police, but she was confused and terrified and demanded he drop her off at a motel. He complied with her demands but then continued to the police station, where he reported the incident. When Anchorage police officer Gregg Baker arrived at the motel, he found Cindy still in handcuffs and hysterical. Cindy led Officer Baker to the airfield, pointed out a plane, and told Baker that her assailant had tried to force her to climb into it. The aircraft was registered to Robert Hansen.

The police went to Hansen's home, but he denied the incident, saying he and another friend had been at John Sumrall's home. Both friends backed up Hansen's story, providing Hansen with an alibi for the time when Cindy said she was abducted. The prosecutor had to weigh the testimony of a teenage prostitute against the testimony of two highly regarded Anchorage businessmen, and he dropped the case before charges were brought.

On September 2, 1983, another woman's body was found on the Knik River near the spot where Sherry Morrow's body had been found, and Alaska State Trooper Sergeant Glen Flothe was assigned the case of the Knik River murders. Flothe remained convinced that a serial killer was stalking the streets of Anchorage, and Robert Hansen topped his list of suspects. He ordered twenty-four-hour surveillance on him, and Flothe made up a list of twenty-two missing women he felt were possible victims of the murderer.

Flothe contacted the FBI's Behavioral Sciences Division and asked for their assistance in identifying the murderer. Agents John Douglas and James Horn came up with a profile in which they noted that the murderer stuttered and was an excellent hunter. They said the unknown subject was a hardworking, successful businessman, and his wife was probably religious and not aware of her husband's activities. Their profile perfectly described Robert Hansen and his wife, Darla. The FBI agents also told Flothe that their killer likely had a stash of items, such as jewelry or clothes, taken from his victims and saved for trophies.

Flothe convinced a judge to issue a search warrant for Hansen's bakery and house. Behind the headboard of Hansen's bed, officers found an aviation map with twenty-four X's marked on it, but at the time, the map meant nothing to them. An officer searching the attic in Hansen's home found a cache of weapons, including a rifle the authorities matched to the shell casings found near the bodies on the Knik River. The officer also found a bag of jewelry—the souvenirs the FBI agents believed the murderer would have.

When confronted with the mounting evidence, John Sumrall and Hansen's other buddy recanted their testimony, saying Hansen was not with them when Cindy was abducted after all. After several days of interrogation, Hansen finally confessed to killing fourteen women over the course of twelve years, but when Flothe reviewed the evidence in the case, he came across the aviation map covered with the twenty-four X's, and he realized each X might represent the burial spot of one of Hansen's victims.

State troopers recovered the remains of twelve of Hansen's victims, and they positively identified ten of the women. They referred to the two remaining victims by nicknames. The authorities believed the woman they called "Eklutna Annie" was Hansen's first victim. Her body was found near Eklutna Lake, just north of Anchorage.

In 1984, investigators were unable to identify the skeletal remains of a young woman found near Horseshoe Lake and the Little Susitna River, northwest of Anchorage. They found no ID near her body, so they nicknamed her "Horseshoe Harriet." When detectives asked Hansen about this victim, he remembered abducting her from downtown Anchorage sometime in the winter of 1983. He flew her to the lake in his airplane, murdered her, and discarded her body. He didn't know her name or anything else about her. To him, she was just an object he could use and then throw away.

An autopsy confirmed that Horseshoe Harriet was a white woman between the ages of seventeen and twenty-three. Detectives found no missing person report to match her description, so they buried her as an unknown in the Anchorage municipal cemetery.

Cold case detectives took another look at Harriet's case in 2014, the same year Robert Hansen died in prison. The investigators exhumed Harriet's body and took samples, which they sent off to a lab to create a DNA profile. They then entered the profile into the FBI's national missing person database, but they didn't get a hit. They were no closer to identifying Harriet.

In September 2020, cold case detectives decided to take another stab at identifying her. This time, forensic genealogy experts compared Harriet's DNA to a familial genetic database, and they hit paydirt. They discovered several close genetic matches and constructed a family tree for the victim. The familial links suggested that Horseshoe Harriet's real name was Robin Pelkey.

Troopers traced Robin to Anchorage, where she lived in the early 1980s, but they found no evidence indicating she was alive after 1984. Investigators talked to Robin's close relatives, who lived in Arkansas and Alaska. Family members told troopers that Robin had lived in Anchorage in the late 1970s but moved to Arkansas as a teenager and then returned to Alaska in 1981 to live with her father and stepmother. Sadly, Robin ended up living on the streets of Anchorage, but by late 1982 or early 1983, she had vanished. Robin's parents are now deceased, and her living relatives have no idea why her parents never reported her missing.

The authorities suspect that Robert Hansen murdered more than thirty women, and some speculate he also murdered men. Although Hansen never admitted it, investigators believe from studying the evidence of where Hansen's victims started and where he finally killed them that Hansen would abduct a woman, take her into the wilderness, rape her, and order her to run while he hunted her down as if she were one of his big-game trophies.

Hansen was sentenced to 461 years, plus life without parole. With the aid of the marked aviation map of south-central Alaska, troopers found human remains near seventeen of the X marks on Hansen's map.

Hansen was incarcerated at the Spring Creek Correctional Center in Seward, where he died from natural causes on August 21, 2014. After his conviction, his wife and children moved back to Arkansas to be near her family.

As an interesting side note, a few investigators believe Hansen could have been responsible for some of the murders attributed to the Green River Killer in Seattle. Hansen denied any connection.

During the Hansen case, Alaska State Troopers began developing protocols for dealing with sexual assault cases and started building and supporting safe houses around the state for victims of abuse. Also, Alaska's Department of Safety built a state-of-the-art, $56 million crime lab for evidence processing.

Serial Murderer Gary Zieger

G ary Zieger, another brutal serial killer, stalked the streets of Anchorage in the early 1970s. We'll never know how many people Zieger killed, but he eventually made a fatal mistake.

During the period when serial killer Robert Hansen was terrorizing Anchorage and south-central Alaska, another vicious murderer roamed the same area. While Hansen selected and hunted his prey, Gary Zieger used women and men for his satisfaction and then simply discarded them. Zieger seemed unwilling or unable to control himself, and the authorities knew it was only a matter of time before he self-destructed.

When two hikers discovered the body of Celia Beth van Zanten at McHugh Creek State Park south of Anchorage, they knew she had suffered a horrible death. Someone had gagged her and tied her hands behind her back with speaker wire. She was naked below the waist. The pathologist later determined that Beth had been raped and her chest slashed with a knife. She was still alive when she was either thrown or fell into a ravine. She tried to climb out of the steep-walled crevice, but with her hands tied behind her back, she had no way to pull herself up the cliff, and she repeatedly fell until she froze to death in the frigid December weather.

Investigators discovered tire tracks turning lazy circles in the campground parking lot, and they deduced that Beth had escaped her attacker, run down the steep slope, and probably fallen into the ravine. Her abductor circled the parking lot, waiting for her to reappear, but when she never did, he finally left.

Beth disappeared on December 23, 1971, while walking from her house to a local convenience store. What happened during her short walk down the street?

Soon after the hikers discovered van Zanten's body on Christmas Day, eighteen-year-old Sandra Patterson, the daughter of an Alaska State Trooper, came forward to report her own abduction on December 19. Sandra worked as a prostitute to support her heroin addiction. She was working in the parking lot of the Nevada Club in Anchorage when a man pointed a gun at her and told her he would kill her if she didn't do what he wanted. She described her attacker as a slender man in his midtwenties wearing horn-rimmed glasses. The man drove Sandra to a motel on the Kenai Peninsula, nearly a hundred miles south of Anchorage, and raped her. On the drive back to Anchorage, he threatened to kill her if she reported him to the police. Sandra complied with his demands to remain silent until she heard about Beth van Zanten's murder, and then she knew she had to come forward and tell the authorities about her abduction.

The police asked Sandra to study a book of photos of known sex offenders to see if she could pick out the man who had kidnapped and raped her. She immediately identified her attacker as Robert Hansen. Hansen's photo was in the book because he was awaiting trial for the attempted kidnapping of a young Anchorage woman.

Hansen was initially charged with kidnapping and raping Sandra Patterson, but prosecutors considered Patterson an unreliable witness, and the charges were eventually dropped. Meanwhile, nothing tied Hansen to the murder and abduction of Beth van Zanten. To this day, the authorities remain unsure whether Beth was murdered by Hansen, by someone she knew, or by another brutal killer named Gary Zieger.

The police knew about Gary Zieger. In 1970, the girlfriend of a young man urged him to tell Anchorage police detectives what he had witnessed. The boyfriend confessed he had been riding in Zieger's truck six months earlier when Zieger picked up a male hitchhiker. Zieger asked to borrow the young man's gun and then drove to a secluded area, placed the barrel of the weapon against the hitchhiker's head, and forced him to perform oral sex on him. Zieger then shot the hitchhiker and threw his body into a pit at the Anchorage landfill. Investigators used a metal detector at the dump to find the empty rounds from a 9mm pistol. Their next step was to see if they could match the markings on the cartridges to the barrel of the young man's gun and substantiate his story. An officer drove to the man's apartment to collect the weapon, but while waiting for the warrant to arrive, he watched Zieger show up at the home, go inside, and leave a short while later. Officers were never able to locate the pistol in question, and with little evidence and only the eyewitness testimony of one person, prosecutors declined to press charges against Zieger.

Two months after the discovery of Beth van Zanten's body, eighteen-year-old Shirley Ann Jones was seen leaving an Anchorage nightclub with a man. The next morning, her body was found in a truck yard on the east side of Anchorage. Someone had severely beaten and raped her. She was alive and unconscious when found, but she died a short time later.

In August 1971, Zingre "ZeZe" Mason decided to hitchhike from her home to an auto body repair shop to pick up her car. When she didn't show up to work the next day, her boss contacted her family, and when her parents called the repair shop, they learned that ZeZe had never retrieved her car. Six days later, children playing in a gravel pit near the intersection of Sand Lake Road and Dimond Boulevard found the body of ZeZe Mason hidden under a tree. She was naked below the waist. According to the medical examiner, her killer had brutally beaten her face and then stabbed her numerous times.

At the gravel pit, detectives found blood and drag marks leading from a set of tire tracks to ZeZe's body. They believed the perpetrator had killed her elsewhere and then dumped her body in the pit. The unusual tire tracks gave investigators their first lead in the case. The tracks had been made by the heavy tread of tires used to gain traction in mud, snow, or soft sand, but what made the tracks unusual was that three of the four tires appeared to have been mounted backward.

A gravel-truck driver called the police and reported seeing a young woman hitchhiker, matching the description of ZeZe Mason, climb into a pickup truck with two men. The driver said he saw the same truck later parked at the back of the gravel pit where ZeZe's body was found. The second time the driver saw the vehicle, only a man and woman were in the truck, and they appeared to be kissing.

A man named Ralph Keiner called the police to tell them he was riding with Gary Zieger the afternoon ZeZe disappeared. Keiner said Zieger had picked up a young woman hitchhiker and then dropped off Keiner near an Anchorage fire station. Keiner reported that Zieger had a large knife on the dashboard of his truck.

Gary Zieger's boss at Arctic Pipelines said another employee reported seeing Zieger washing his pickup at Campbell Creek on the day of ZeZe's murder. The police found the unusual tire tracks near the creek and felt they were making progress in the investigation.

Since the gravel pit where the children had found ZeZe's body was outside the Anchorage city limits, both the Alaska State Troopers and the Anchorage Police Department investigated the murder. The troopers obtained a search warrant for Zieger's truck and noted that three of the wheels were indeed mounted backward on the pickup. The vehicle's interior had been cleaned, but investigators found small spots of blood in the truck, including a smear on the inside of the driver's door. Detectives arrested Zieger and held him at the state jail on $75,000 bail. In the era before DNA analysis, lab technicians tentatively matched the blood smear in Zieger's truck to ZeZe Mason's blood type.

Due to the excessive press coverage and public outcry over the murders of Beth van Zanten, Shirley Ann Jones, and ZeZe Mason, the judge ruled that an impartial jury could not be found in Anchorage for the Zieger trial, and he moved the proceedings to Kodiak, a town on a large island 250 miles southwest of Anchorage. Concerned about the influence of news coverage surrounding the trial, the judge ordered the jurors sequestered in a hotel in Kodiak where they could be isolated from news reports.

Zieger's lawyer, Jon Larson, admitted that on the day ZeZe disappeared, Zieger had picked up a young woman and drove her around in his truck, but he claimed Zieger had dropped off the woman a while later. Larson said Zieger was unsure whether the woman was ZeZe Mason.

Analysts determined that the blood on the door of Zieger's truck was human, but they could not definitively match it to ZeZe. An expert testified that the other bloodstains found in the vehicle belonged either to a human or a higher primate, but he could not determine the blood type nor the sex of the source of the blood. He also did not know how long the blood had been in the truck.

An FBI lab technician testified that Zieger's tires were similar to the casts made from the treads left in the gravel pit, but he wasn't certain whether the tires on Zieger's truck had made the tracks there.

Zieger's boss, Michael Beaver, retracted his statement about Zieger washing his truck in Campbell Creek on the day of the murder. Despite the substantial circumstantial evidence, nothing directly tied Zieger to ZeZe's murder. The defense put three witnesses on the stand who claimed they'd seen ZeZe alive and well several hours after she'd supposedly climbed into Zieger's truck.

Finally, Zieger himself took the stand and calmly denied harming ZeZe Mason. The jury deliberated six hours and returned a not guilty verdict on all counts. One juror said Zieger might be guilty, but she and the other jurors didn't feel the prosecution had proved its case.

After the jury acquitted Zieger, he returned to his job at Arctic Pipelines, but he failed to stay out of trouble, and the Alaska State Troopers and Anchorage police kept a close eye on him, knowing he would kill again.

Zieger aspired to join the Brothers motorcycle gang. In Anchorage, the Brothers had recently merged with the Hell's Angels. Zieger hoped to gain admittance to the inner circle of the group, but with his explosive temper and violent tendencies, there was little chance he would ever be anything other than a probationary member.

The Brothers wished to get involved in the lucrative business of strip clubs and massage parlors in the Anchorage area. These types of clubs had blossomed after work began on the Trans-Alaska Pipeline, when young, well-paid men flooded the state. The motorcycle gang thought they could siphon off some of the profits and perhaps even control the flow of dancers into the state. Gang members contacted club owners and demanded the owners pay them "protection" money.

Jimmy Sumpter was one of the club owners the motorcycle gang approached. Sumpter owned two clubs. One was the Sportsman Too in Muldoon, and the other was a larger club called the Kit Kat Club a few miles out on the Old Seward Highway from Anchorage. Sumpter turned down the gang's offer of protection and told them he had no desire to deal with them. A short while later, someone broke into Sumpter's house, murdered his wife, Marguerite, and his stepson, Richard Merck, and then set the house on fire.

A grieving and enraged Jimmy Sumpter vowed to find the man or men who had killed his wife and stepson, and according to a rumor, Sumpter put the word out on the street that he wanted the killer or killers dispatched as soon as possible. Sumpter might have suspected members of the Brothers motorcycle gang, but some members thought they knew who had murdered Marguerite Sumpter and Richard Merck. The police had no doubt who had committed the murders and arson.

Although Zieger had been acquitted for the murder of ZeZe Mason, the Alaska State Troopers believed he was a vicious killer who would soon murder again. Major Walter Gilmour ordered his troopers to keep an eye on Zieger. On the evening of November 25, 1973, a trooper named Mcycrs called Major Gilmour and told him he'd been on the way to see a movie with his wife when he spotted Zieger driving an unfamiliar truck. Meyers quickly wrote down the license plate number of the vehicle.

A few hours later, not far from where Meyers had seen Zieger, someone murdered Marguerite Sumpter and her son and set the Sumpters' house on fire. While interviewing neighbors, the police questioned a woman who lived across the street from the Sumpters. She told the detectives that she'd been up late on the night of the murders and had seen a strange truck parked along the road in front of the Sumpters' house. The truck made her nervous, so she wrote down the license plate number. The number she'd recorded matched the plate on the pickup Meyers had seen Zieger driving a few hours earlier.

The police knew Gary Zieger had shot Marguerite Sumpter and her son, but they were not sure why. The killer stole $20,000 in cash and jewelry from the Sumpters' house, so robbery appeared to be the most apparent motive. Zieger was also trying to gain admittance to the inner circle of the Brothers motorcycle gang, so perhaps the murders were an effort to impress others in the gang. Zieger had recently been convicted of stealing dynamite in Cordova. The high-priced attorney he hoped to hire for his appeal demanded a $10,000 retainer before he would handle his case. Zieger did not have $10,000, so investigators believed he broke into the Sumpters' house to steal the cash. It was no secret Sumpter kept large sums of money in his home.

No matter Zieger's reason for breaking into the Sumpters' house and killing Jimmy's wife and stepson, he made a big mistake by crossing the players in the hardened Anchorage underworld. Within hours, motorists discovered Zieger's body near Potter's Marsh along the Seward Highway. A shotgun blast to the chest had ended his life.

After Zieger's death, the police solved another Anchorage mystery involving the killer. On August 22, 1973, Anchorage resident Johnny Rich disappeared. Rich had recently purchased Cindy's Massage Studio in Anchorage, and Wesley Ladd, another Anchorage club owner, felt he had been double-crossed in the deal. Ladd believed he owned a portion of Cindy's, but Rich disagreed with this assertion. When Rich's pregnant sixteen-year-old wife and his fifteen-year-old daughter contacted the authorities to report him missing, the police immediately suspected Ladd in his disappearance. With no evidence, though, they had no cause to arrest him.

A few months after Zieger's murder, the police arrested a heroin addict named Benny Ramey for receiving and selling stolen property. Ramey claimed he knew where Johnny Rich was buried. He confessed that Wesley Ladd had hired him and Gary Zieger to kidnap Rich. They then drove him to a remote cabin, where Ladd attempted to force Rich to sign over Cindy's Massage Studio and his other properties to Ladd's attorney. When Rich refused to sign, his captors put a clamp on his testicles and squeezed until he autographed the documents. Ladd was prepared to release Rich, but Zieger shot Rich in the chest. The shot did not kill him, so Ladd shot him in the heart, and the men then buried him near an abandoned coal mine.

Today, the authorities don't know how many people Gary Zieger killed, but some believe he murdered at least a dozen people. Did he murder Beth van Zanten? The police found wire similar to that used to bind Beth's wrists in Zieger's house, but a definitive match could not be made. A composite sketch made by witnesses who claimed they saw Beth with a man on the night she disappeared resembles Zieger, but the observations were tenuous.

One of the most shocking details about Gary Zieger and his reign of terror in Anchorage was that when he was found dead near the Seward Highway with a shotgun blast to his chest, he was only twenty years old.

What Happened to Congressmen Hale Boggs and Nick Begich?

Plane crashes occur far too frequently in Alaska, with poor weather contributing to many of these accidents. To make a living, though, commercial pilots in Alaska often must fly in marginal weather. Mysteries abound in the Last Frontier about airplanes vanishing into thin air without leaving a clue as to their fate. The following is a story of one of the most famous airplane disappearances in the state's history.

On October 16, 1972, a Cessna 310 with the tail number N1812H, operated by Pan Alaska Airways, disappeared somewhere between Anchorage and Juneau. Thirty-eight-year-old Don Jonz, the owner of Pan Alaska, piloted the plane. Jonz was a military veteran with more than seventeen thousand hours of flight time, and he had logged fifteen years as a pilot in Alaska. The passengers on the doomed plane were Alaska's sole congressman, Nick Begich, forty; his aide Russell Brown, thirty-seven; and Louisiana congressman Hale Boggs, fifty-eight, the majority leader of the US House of Representatives. The three men planned to attend an election rally for Begich in Juneau.

The plane left Anchorage at 9:00 a.m., and Jonz filed a visual flight rules (VFR) flight plan, stating that he planned to fly southeast over the Turnagain Arm of Cook Inlet, through Portage Pass, over Prince William Sound to Johnstone Point, and then on to Yakutat. From there, he would fly directly to Juneau. The flight should have taken approximately three and a half hours, and the airplane carried six hours' worth of fuel. The weather was marginal throughout the entire area on October 16. Yakutat had a seven-hundred-foot ceiling and visibility of only 1.5 miles with fog. Juneau also had fog. In addition to poor visibility, the forecast called for icy rain and fierce headwinds en route.

Portage Pass is a flight route through the mountains on the eastern end of Turnagain Arm. At 8:40 a.m. on October 16, 1972, a helicopter pilot flying through the pass reported severe turbulence on its west side with headwinds of fifty-five knots, a low overcast, and reduced visibility. Visual flight was not recommended through the pass due to the low ceiling and poor visibility. Don Jonz was flying under VFR, but still, he chose to fly through Portage Pass. Shortly before entering the pass, Jonz contacted the Anchorage Flight Service Station. It was the last official radio broadcast anyone heard from Cessna N1812H.

When the plane failed to arrive in Juneau and was declared missing, the United States launched the largest search-and-rescue mission on record up until that time. The search lasted thirty-nine days and included forty military aircraft and fifty civilian planes, covering over 325,000 square miles. Pilots flew a thousand sorties, totaling thirty-six hundred flight hours. The search area encompassed massive glaciers and the jagged Wrangell–St. Elias Mountains, as well as a large portion of the coastlines of Prince William Sound and the Gulf of Alaska. In addition to the air operation, ground patrols searched Portage Pass twice. No piece of the aircraft was located during the initial search or since, and officials at the time decided the plane likely crashed and either sank into Prince William Sound or was buried in ice and snow.

Did the plane hit a mountain obscured by fog, or did turbulence play a role in the disaster? Icing on the wings could have affected lift and maneuverability, or any combination of these factors might have caused the plane to crash.

An Alaska law passed just months before the plane disappeared required all small commercial aircraft to carry an emergency locator transmitter (ELT). Such a device would have sent out a signal if the plane had crashed on land. Officials claimed no signal was ever received, and they determined there was no locator device on the downed aircraft. Jonz owned a personal ELT, but it was found in another Pan Alaska Airways airplane. Pan Alaska employees who were on N1812H shortly before takeoff saw no sign of an ELT, and they also reported seeing no survival equipment in the aircraft.

Officials terminated the search for the airplane on November 24 and declared the four men dead on December 29. Even though Boggs and Begich were presumed dead, both men were reelected to the House of Representatives. Boggs's widow, Lindy, went on to replace her husband in Congress and served eight more terms. Alaska held a special election, and the voters chose Republican Don Young, who had initially lost to Begich. Young remained Alaska's congressman until his death in March 2022. Oddly, Congressman Young died of natural causes while riding on an airplane on his way home to Alaska.

Once the search for the plane ended and the authorities declared the men dead, most people assumed the Cessna had crashed because the pilot had pushed the boundaries too far. Under pressure perhaps from the congressmen to get them to the political rally in Juneau on time, Jonz chose to fly in marginal weather conditions. Demanding passengers sometimes ask pilots to fly in poor weather. When those passengers are high-ranking politicians, a pilot might find it difficult to refuse them. Don Jonz was an experienced aviator, but some pilots considered him a risk-taker who pushed the boundaries when it came to flying in poor weather.

Several reports of strange radio calls and other electronic communications baffled investigators in the days following the disappearance of the Cessna 310 carrying Boggs, Begich, Brown, and Jonz. Immediately after the plane went missing, the US Coast Guard station in Long Beach, California, received a call from an anonymous tipster claiming he knew where the plane had crashed. The man said he had access to experimental electronic equipment, and he provided detailed directions to the coordinates of the downed airplane. According to documents released nearly fifty years after the crash, the FBI found the source believable, and one agent wrote, "The source of the aforementioned information is reliable." Agents who interviewed the man reported that he "appeared rational, extremely intelligent, but somewhat strange." It is not clear whether searchers checked the coordinates the tipster provided.

Also, in the hours and days following the plane's disappearance, several independent ham radio operators in Northern California reported hearing a transmission from someone on the downed aircraft broadcasting that there were survivors on the plane. Searchers were never able to pinpoint the location of the origin of these transmissions.

According to the FBI file, the day after the plane vanished, a search plane picked up a signal for forty minutes some distance from Juneau emitting from what searchers believed was a crash locator beacon. The searchers heard another, weaker signal 150 miles northeast of Anchorage, but search planes could not pinpoint the source of either signal.

Today, most investigators believe the plane crashed somewhere between Portage Pass and Johnstone Point, about an hour into the flight. One question remains, though. What caused the plane to crash?

Nick Begich was only a freshman congressman from a sparsely populated state. Hale Boggs, however, was a colorful, outspoken representative from Louisiana who likely would have become the next speaker of the House of Representatives. Many people refused to believe that he disappeared accidentally, and conspiracy theories swirled around his untimely death. To this day, many think he was the victim of foul play instead of an unfortunate passenger on an ill-fated flight.

Hale Boggs, a Democrat, was first elected as a US representative from Louisiana in 1946, and the voters reelected him thirteen times. Boggs was the youngest member of the Warren Commission, which investigated the assassination of John F. Kennedy. In a 1966 interview on *Face the Nation*, Boggs defended the commission's findings and said he believed Lee Harvey Oswald had acted alone when he killed President Kennedy. Despite this assertation, though, a persistent rumor suggested Boggs was not happy with the Warren Commission's findings and was seeking to reopen the Kennedy investigation.

Around 11:30 p.m. on July 23, 1970, two years before Boggs disappeared in Alaska, a Lincoln Continental ran his car off the road in Washington, DC. Boggs chased the car, wrote down the license plate number, and called the police. No record exists to indicate if the police ever investigated the incident, however. Washington's Metropolitan Police Department would have been the agency in charge of the investigation, but they now say they can find no relevant records relating to the case.

In April 1971, Boggs claimed the FBI had tapped his telephone; he also said several other US representatives also believed their phones had been tapped. Boggs said he knew why the FBI had tapped his phone and how they intended to use the conversations they heard. He refused to say what the conversations entailed but said once his lawyers finished their investigation, he would release the details to the public. Boggs then called for the immediate resignation of FBI Director J. Edgar Hoover. Attorney General John Mitchell denied Boggs's allegations about the FBI, but Boggs said he was "absolutely certain" the FBI had placed a tap on his phone.

Freelance writer Jonathan Walczak has spent a great deal of time and money investigating the disappearance of Pan Alaska Airways N1812H. He believes that if someone sabotaged the plane, the likely target was Nick Begich, not Hale Boggs.

Walczak learned that on March 4, 1974, less than seventeen months after the disappearance of her husband, Pegge Begich, the widow of Congressman Nick Begich, married Jerry Max Pasley, a Mafia-connected killer and bomber. The marriage lasted only two years. In 1994, when Pasley was in prison in Arizona for murder, he spoke with investigators from the Anchorage Police Department, the Alaska State Troopers, and the Arizona Department of Public Safety. Pasley provided details about several unsolved murders and made various shocking claims, but the most surprising thing he said was that he'd transported a bomb to Alaska in 1972.

Pasley worked for various mobsters, including Peter Licavoli Sr. and Joe Bonanno Sr., and he admitted to several bombings and murders. He was in prison in 1994 for gunning down a man in a Tucson hotel. At his trial, Pasley told the jury that he was ashamed he had killed people. Pasley knew he would spend the rest of his life in prison and said he wanted to come clean about several other killings, including the murder of his ex-wife's first husband, Nick Begich.

Pasley told investigators that in 1972, a Bonanno lieutenant in Arizona handed him a locked briefcase. The man ordered Pasley to take the briefcase to Anchorage and give it to two other men. Pasley followed the instructions and then flew back to Arizona the following day. He said the men told him "something big" was about to happen, and soon afterward, the plane carrying Begich and Boggs disappeared.

Pasley said he then moved to Anchorage and began dating Pegge Begich, a woman he had met through mutual friends in Arizona. Pasley claimed Pegge gave him lavish gifts, including coownership in a bar. His partners in the bar were Pegge and one of the men he had handed the briefcase to in 1972. Pasley said he and this man were fishing one day when the man got drunk and told Pasley that the case he'd carried from Arizona contained a high-tech bomb. According to Pasley, the man said he'd placed the bomb on Pan Alaska N1812H before it left on its final flight with Begich, Boggs, Brown, and Jonz on board.

Pasley's claims shocked the investigators, who immediately notified the FBI, who in turn sent agents to interview Pasley in 1995. Retired Anchorage police sergeant Mike Grimes told Walczak that he was stunned by Pasley's claims. When he returned to Anchorage from his interview with Pasley in the Arizona prison, Grimes said he immediately contacted an FBI agent he knew in Anchorage. When Grimes did not hear back from the agent for several weeks, he again contacted her, and she insisted they meet somewhere other than her office. The agent told Grimes that when her boss called FBI headquarters in Washington with the information

Grimes had provided her, his superiors told her boss, "You will do nothing there. You will send everything you have to us."

Other investigators also told Walczak that they were surprised the FBI had not vigorously investigated Pasley's claims of a bomb. Pasley agreed to take a polygraph, but no evidence indicates the FBI ever administered one to him. The FBI immediately shut down the investigation.

Max Pasley died in prison in 2010 at the age of sixty-nine. Was he telling the truth about the bomb? It is a fact that Pasley married Pegge Begich less than seventeen months after her husband disappeared, and Pasley had no upside in claiming he'd carried the bomb to Alaska. By confessing that someone in the Bonanno crime family handed him a bomb to take to Alaska, Pasley likely put himself in danger in prison. Why would he fabricate this story? If Pasley was telling the truth, though, then why did someone put a bomb on the plane, and who would want to murder Nick Begich? If Pasley knew the answers to these questions, he never told anyone.

The disappearance of N1812H remains as much of a mystery today as it was in 1972. The tragic deaths of the four men make us wonder what they would have accomplished with their lives and what the congressmen might have done to shape the future of the United States.

As a story, this tale has everything you could want, including power, intrigue, spies, danger, pushing the limits of nature, incredible scenery, and a tragic ending. No wonder people still want to hear about the extraordinary lives and horrible deaths of Congressmen Hale Boggs and Nick Begich.

Since 1962, more than forty cases of missing aircraft have remained open in Alaska. No missing airplane case is closed until substantial evidence provides information about the plane's location. Maybe one day, we will know what happened to Pan Alaska N1812H.

A Car Bomb in Downtown Anchorage

Neil Mackay was ruthless in his personal and business dealings, and associates learned not to cross him. When a car bomb instantly killed his ex-wife, Muriel Pfeil, the police knew Mackay had planned her murder, but they could not find enough evidence to charge him with the crime.

Neil Mackay grew up in California, and shortly after the Japanese bombed Pearl Harbor, he enlisted in the military and became a Marine pilot and flight instructor. According to Marine records, Mackay suffered severe injuries from a plane crash during the war, receiving back, shoulder, and head wounds. Doctors were forced to place a steel plate in his skull to repair it.

Mackay married his high school sweetheart, Barbara, and after the war, he enrolled in law school in California. Once he'd received his law degree, he and Barbara moved to Anchorage, where he took a job as vice president of the First National Bank of Anchorage.

When Mackay attended high school in California, he'd worked as a driver for a mortuary, and from what he saw, he believed he could make a fortune in the mortuary business. After passing the Alaska bar exam, allowing him to practice law in the state, he opened a mortuary on Fourth Avenue in Anchorage and had his law office in the back of the business. Before long and in accordance with his plan, Neil Mackay became a millionaire.

After twenty-five years of marriage, Barbara Mackay filed for divorce from Neil in 1965. Neil opposed the divorce and refused to sign a settlement agreement for three years, until ordered to do so by a judge. Forty-five-year-old Neil Mackay did not remain alone for long. He soon married thirty-three-year-old Muriel Pfeil.

Muriel was the daughter of a wealthy Anchorage couple who had made their fortune in the local real estate market. Muriel owned a successful travel agency in downtown Anchorage. Like Neil, Muriel had a temper, and the two often clashed. To make things worse, Neil suffered seizures and had severe headaches from the injuries he'd sustained in the plane accident in the war. To ease his pain, he took powerful painkillers, and the narcotics fueled his temper.

In 1973, Neil and Muriel had a son named Scotty, but two months after Scotty's birth, the couple separated and decided to divorce. Their temper tantrums and wild accusations during their divorce proceedings provided a daily court drama where little was accomplished. The judge finally barred Muriel and Neil from the property-settlement hearings, saying the two had tied up the court system for months, and he felt it was time to bang their heads together and settle the divorce. In the final agreement, the judge awarded Muriel $757,000 plus $500 a month for Scotty's support.

Neil fumed over the divorce settlement, and Muriel's attempts to keep him away from Scotty infuriated him. Muriel tried to convince the judge to suspend Neil's visitation rights with their son, claiming he abused drugs and had an explosive temper. The judge limited Neil's time with Scotty to a partial weekend per month. The ruling enraged and depressed Neil, who genuinely seemed to love his son. He tried to have his visitation rights expanded, but Muriel fought him at every turn.

On the afternoon of September 30, 1976, when Scotty was only three years old, Muriel Pfeil left her travel agency, unlocked her Volvo, and then died instantly when her car exploded. Explosive experts determined that someone had placed a powerful charge underneath the hood of her car. Witnesses to the explosion said the hood was blasted a hundred feet in the air, and shock waves shook the ground and shattered windows in the buildings near the parking lot. Police detectives quickly concluded a remote device had been used to detonate the bomb. Someone watched Muriel's car until she got inside before pushing the button to ignite the bomb.

Muriel had driven Scotty to a babysitter's house only ninety minutes before the explosion, and the device must have already been in the car at the time.

Because of the animosity between Neil Mackay and Muriel Pfeil, Mackay became the immediate focus of the police investigation. Still, they could find nothing to tie him to the murder. The Anchorage police, the Alaska State Troopers, and the US Bureau of Alcohol, Tobacco, and Firearms worked the case. Investigators sent pieces of Muriel's car to the FBI crime lab in Washington, DC, but analysts found no useful evidence.

The police could not solve the murder of Muriel Pfeil, but Muriel's brother, Bob Pfeil, a senior pilot for Alaska Airlines, believed he knew who had killed his sister, and he was determined to honor her wishes and not allow Neil Mackay to gain custody of Scotty.

Mackay petitioned the court for full custody of Scotty, but Bob Pfeil hired attorneys to fight the petition. Pfeil offered a $20,000 reward to anyone with information on the murder of his sister, but no one came forward to claim the money.

In December 1977, Mackay took Scotty to Micronesia and left him there with friends. The police arrested Mackay when he returned to Honolulu, but he refused to divulge Scotty's whereabouts. Despite this bizarre behavior, Mackay won full custody of Scotty in 1978, and he immediately moved from Anchorage to Honolulu, where Scotty joined him.

Bob Pfeil was the administrator of Muriel's estate, and Scotty was her only beneficiary. Mackay felt Bob had inappropriately used money from Muriel's estate, and he even believed he had used his sister's money to hire a private detective to locate Scotty in Micronesia. Mackay thought Pfeil was stealing from Scotty, and the idea angered him. Mackay became a recluse in his penthouse on Waikiki Beach and reportedly spent his hours obsessed with his battle with Bob Pfeil.

On October 12, 1985, only thirty-eight days after Bob Pfeil had won the court battle with Mackay over nearly $142,000 in expenditures from Muriel's estate, Bob Pfeil was driving home from his job as a pilot with Alaska Airlines when another car pulled alongside him. The man in the passenger seat of the second car pushed a .45-caliber automatic handgun out the window and shot at Bob Pfeil five times. Three of the bullets hit him, but he lived to tell detectives he was sure his former brother-in-law, Neil Mackay, had ordered the shooting. Pfeil gave investigators a good description of the car and the man who'd leaned out the window to fire the gun. Pfeil suffered critical wounds, and to receive better care, he was transferred to the Mayo Clinic in Minnesota. Nearly a month later, while undergoing surgery to remove bullets from his spine and lungs, Bob Pfeil died when a blood clot became lodged in his lungs.

Soon after the shooting, Pfeil's neighbors described an old, mustard-colored Lincoln parked near his home on the night of the shooting. This description of the car matched the one Pfeil had given the detectives. A few days after the attack, eighteen-year-old Tyoga Closson bragged to his friends that he knew something about the shooting of the Alaska Airlines pilot. The police brought Closson in for questioning, and he admitted he'd provided the gun used to shoot Pfeil. He said he'd taken it from a house where his girlfriend was babysitting. Closson claimed he had nothing to do with shooting Pfeil, but he knew the men involved in the crime.

Closson told the detectives that his friend, Bob Betts, nineteen, had driven the car while another young man, John Bright, twenty-one, had fired the fatal shots. In exchange for the verbal promise of a reduced sentence, Bob Betts soon agreed to tell the detectives all he knew about the crime. Betts admitted that he, John Bright, and thirty-four-year-old Larry Gentry had been hired to murder Bob Pfeil. He said that they had been hired by Gilbert "Junior" Pauole, the thirty-eight-year-old manager and part-owner of the Wild Cherry, a strip club in Anchorage. Betts, Gentry, and Bright had once worked for Pauole at the club. Betts said Gentry had helped them plan the hit on Pfeil, and he'd provided the car and a backup gun.

Betts agreed to wear a wire to try to get Gentry to incriminate himself. When Gentry realized Betts had recorded their conversation, Gentry admitted his involvement in the crime to the police. Detectives next promised Gentry a deal for a lighter sentence if he wore a wire to record Bright and Pauole.

When Gentry approached Bright and Pauole, both men seemed suspicious of him and remained cautious about what they said, but the detectives felt they had said enough to incriminate themselves. They arrested five men for the shooting of Robert Pfeil, but they still did not have Neil Mackay, the man they wanted.

Once the detectives had arrested Junior Pauole, he seemed eager to talk in exchange for a promise of leniency in his sentence. He told the police that Neil Mackay owned the building where he operated the Wild Cherry. He said Mackay often visited his club, and the two men had gotten to know each other well.

According to Pauole, Mackay told him his ex-wife caused him trouble, so he took care of her. He said a war buddy planted a bomb in her car and detonated it from half a block away. Mackay then told Pauole he was now having problems with his former brother-in-law and wanted him to disappear. Pauole said he and Mackay talked for two years about arranging Pfeil's murder. Mackay thought Pauole had mob connections and could hire pros for the hit, but in the end, Pauole hired young, inexperienced hoods to murder Bob Pfeil.

After Bright shot Pfeil, Pauole said he called Mackay in Hawaii to let him know Pfeil had "been taken care of." He said Mackay was happy to hear the news. Mackay was less pleased a few days later to learn the shots had not immediately killed Pfeil, who in fact was still alive.

Detectives instructed Pauole to place a call to Mackay while they listened to and recorded the conversation. Pauole told Mackay that he felt scared and was hiding from the Anchorage police. Mackay hesitated to say anything and told Pauole to be careful of what he said, or he would implicate himself.

Pauole placed two more calls to Mackay, who finally asked him if he had ground up the metal thing.

"What?" Pauole asked. "You mean the car?"

Mackay answered, "Yeah."

Then, Mackay stunned the detectives when he asked Pauole, "What about the G-U-N?"

Junior replied that he didn't know anything about the "G-U-N."

Since the detectives listening to the call knew G-U-N spelled gun, they felt they had enough evidence against Mackay to take him into custody. Later the same day, the Honolulu police arrested Neil Mackay in his Waikiki penthouse, and the authorities held him on a bail of $25 million.

Prosecutors charged Neil Mackay, John Bright, Larry Gentry, and Bob Betts with first-degree murder. Because of his plea agreement, they charged Junior Pauole with attempted murder. Betts and Gentry believed they also had made deals with the prosecution for reduced charges in exchange for wearing wires to incriminate the others. Only Pauole and Closson had signed formal agreements with the prosecutors, though, so Gentry and Betts received no leniency.

The judge decided each defendant should be tried separately, and Larry Gentry was tried first. His trial was held in March 1986, and the jury found him guilty of first-degree murder. The judge sentenced Gentry to forty years in prison. He would be eligible for parole in fifteen years.

Two weeks after Larry Gentry's trial, Tyoga Closson received a sentence of eighteen months in jail for stealing the .45-caliber handgun used to murder Bob Pfeil.

Bob Betts's trial began in August 1986. The jury convicted him of first-degree murder, and he was sentenced to fifty years in prison. He would be eligible for parole in twenty years.

On October 17, 1986, a jury convicted John Bright, the man who had pulled the trigger, of first-degree murder, and the judge sentenced him to ninety-nine years in prison. He would not be eligible for parole for forty years.

Because of the enormous amount of publicity surrounding Neil Mackay's trial, the judge ordered the court proceedings moved from Anchorage to Fairbanks, and the trial began in January 1987. Mackay chose the best defense lawyer money could buy, and since they had no direct evidence against Mackay, the prosecution knew his case would be hard to prove. Their evidence consisted of only Junior Pauole's word and Mackay's suspicious comments on the taped phone conversation.

Junior Pauole was not an upstanding citizen, and Mackay's attorney easily discredited him. The judge weakened the case against Mackay by not allowing Pauole to testify that Mackay had once told him he'd had his wife murdered. The judge also ruled out some of the recorded conversations between Pauole and Mackay and did not allow documentation of the court battle between Mackay and Pfeil into evidence. The judge did allow the tape on which Mackay asked Pauole what he'd done with the "G-U-N." To explain away this comment, though, Mackay's attorney argued that Mackay was only playing along with Pauole because he believed Pauole was trying to extort money from him by threatening to frame him for Pfeil's murder.

Making this bizarre case even stranger, the judge abruptly declared a mistrial three months into the trial and three days after jurors had started their deliberations. Somehow, a thick file of material on Mackay relating to his ex-wife's murder had ended up in the jury room. The file was intended for the judge to use as background information on the case, but instead, it landed in the hands of the jurors. The information confused the jurors because they didn't remember the prosecution discussing or admitting any of it into evidence. When it became clear that several of the jurors had read at least part of the file, the judge had no choice but to declare a mistrial.

The court retried Mackay in November, and on February 7, 1988, the jury found him not guilty.

Junior Pauole received only an eighteen-year prison sentence as a reward for his assistance in secretly recording and testifying against Mackay and the other defendants.

On September 24, 1994, Neil Mackay was found dead in his condominium at the Ilikai Hotel on Waikiki Beach. He died of natural causes and had been dead for several days when his body was discovered.

As an interesting side note to this story, ghost hunters believe Muriel Pfeil's spirit haunts the Snow City Café in downtown Anchorage, where her travel agency was once located and near where she died.

THE NEWMAN FAMILY MURDERS

The brutal murders in 1987 of a mother and her two daughters terrified the residents of Anchorage. Who could commit such a barbaric act, and would he strike again?

People move to Alaska for various reasons, including adventure, the opportunity to make good money, a desire to live in the wilderness, and a chance to escape the problems in their lives. As referenced in earlier stories, Alaska is not a good refuge for people with serious issues. Harsh weather and endless winter nights lead to depression. If people have psychological problems to begin with, they are likely to get worse in Alaska. Kirby Anthoney was so flawed before he moved to Alaska that it is difficult to say whether his condition worsened once he lived here for a while, but from his actions, we can guess it did.

Nancy Newman and her sister, Cheryl Chapman, were waitresses at Gwennie's, a popular Anchorage restaurant still in business today. Nancy's husband, John, worked as a heavy equipment operator for MarkAir until he was seriously injured in a forklift accident. Workers' compensation paid to have him retrained in California as a locksmith, and he was in California for his training in March 1987. Meanwhile, Nancy and her two daughters, eight-year-old Melissa and three-year-old Angie, stayed in Anchorage, where Nancy worked as a tax accountant in addition to her job at Gwennie's.

At 6:00 p.m. on Friday, March 13, 1987, Nancy joined Cheryl and her husband, Paul Chapman, for dinner at Gwennie's. Meanwhile, Cheryl's daughter took Nancy's children swimming. Nancy rode with the Chapmans to their house, where they sat and talked. Later, they drove to Nancy's apartment and sat around her kitchen table, smoking and drinking coffee. Melissa and Angie returned home at 9:00 p.m. and went to bed, and the Chapmans departed a while later. Nancy had left her car at Gwennie's that night and told the Chapmans she would get a ride to the restaurant the following day to retrieve it. Her next shift at Gwennie's was not until 6:00 a.m. Sunday.

At 8:00 a.m. on Sunday, a ringing telephone startled the Chapmans awake. Nancy's boss at Gwennie's apologized for calling so early but said Nancy was two hours late for her shift. Nancy's car was still parked at the restaurant, and no one had moved it since Friday night. Her boss was concerned because Nancy was never late for work. Cheryl immediately knew something was wrong, and she and Paul hurried over to the Newmans' apartment. Cheryl had keys to her sister's apartment, so they let themselves in, and Cheryl, a nervous wreck, sat at the kitchen table while Paul searched the apartment.

Paul opened the door to Melissa's room, where he found the little girl's body on the floor. She lay on her back with her right arm under her back and her left arm out to her left side. Both legs were bent at the knees and spread wide. Her attacker had pulled her nightgown up above her waist. In the second room, Paul found Nancy dead on the bed with a pillowcase around her neck and her nightshirt pulled above her breasts. The horror got worse when he opened the third door and found three-year-old Angie Newman covered in blood. The killer had severed both her left carotid artery and her jugular vein.

Paul fought to remain calm as he returned to the kitchen and told his wife, "Don't go down the hall; they're all dead." Cheryl can be heard screaming in the background on the 911 tape when Paul called to report the crime.

Detective Sergeant Mike Grimes, head of the Homicide Response Team of the Anchorage Police Department, led the investigation into the Newman murders. He assigned two groups of detectives to the case. One group was responsible for gathering evidence from the crime scene, while the other would concentrate on leads and suspects. It was one of the most intensive murder investigations in the state's history.

The forensic team spent two weeks combing the apartment for blood, hair, fluid samples, fingerprints, and footprints. According to Paul Chapman, Nancy had borrowed their vacuum cleaner on Friday, March 13, and cleaned her apartment. The freshly cleaned apartment allowed the detectives to vacuum again and gather any recently shed hair and fiber. The detectives meticulously collected, labeled, and shipped all the evidence to the state crime lab or the FBI lab.

The detectives noticed two cereal bowls in the kitchen sink, a coffee cup on the kitchen table, and a few cigarette butts in the ashtray. According to Cheryl Chapman, the girls liked to get up early on Saturday morning, watch cartoons, and eat cereal while Nancy drank coffee and smoked. This information led the authorities to believe the murders had occurred sometime Saturday morning.

A large, empty cookie jar also sat on the kitchen table, and according to John Newman, Nancy kept her tip money in the jar, the coins packaged in rolls. Also missing from the apartment were Nancy's purse and jewelry, John's keys, a checkbook, a wallet, and an expensive 35mm camera. Despite the missing items, the apartment looked tidy; it had not been ransacked. The perpetrator seemed to have known exactly where to find the things he took, and he disturbed nothing else.

The murderer had struck Nancy in the face several times with a blunt object and then strangled her to death. The police found blood and a small amount of fecal matter on her sheets and green wool gloves near her body. They discovered blood on the underside of the bathroom light switch and a damp washcloth wadded up in the sink. Investigators recovered three pubic hairs on Melissa's bed and thirteen more on or near her body. They found one pubic hair on Angie and collected two more from floor sweepings. They found an additional hair on the washrag in the bathroom sink.

The killer had sexually assaulted all three victims, and Sergeant Grimes felt certain the perpetrator not only knew the victims but had enjoyed himself while committing these atrocities. After he'd murdered Nancy and her daughters, he splayed their bodies as if displaying his handiwork. Grimes believed the killer was a sexual psychopath, and he consulted the FBI's Behavioral Science Unit.

FBI analysts told him the murders probably were committed by someone close to the family and someone who had spent enough time at their apartment that his presence in the neighborhood early in the morning would not arouse the neighbors' suspicions. According to the profile, the killer could likely keep himself under control when things were going well, but he fantasized about rape and murder and probably had assaulted other young girls. They noted that this type of person could commit a brutal murder and then act normal an hour later.

The police immediately suspected John Newman's nephew, twenty-three-year-old Kirby Anthoney. Anthoney and his girlfriend had moved to Anchorage from Twin Falls, Idaho, in 1985, when the authorities in Idaho accused him of raping and brutally beating a twelve-year-old girl at a campground near town. Prosecutors never filed charges against Anthoney because the young girl was the only witness to the crime, and the beating she'd received had left her so brain-damaged that she could not identify her attacker. Anthoney had denied raping and beating the girl, but a few years earlier, in 1982, he'd confessed to robbing an elderly, wheelchair-bound woman in her house. Before leaving the woman's house, he'd tied her up and sprayed Mace in her face. When he later withdrew his confession to robbing and assaulting the woman, prosecutors dismissed the case against him. Anthoney had also been arrested numerous times for burglary.

When his problems escalated in Idaho, Anthoney fled to Anchorage, where his uncle John and aunt Nancy lived. He and his girlfriend stayed with the Newmans for a month in 1986 before taking jobs on a fishing boat in Dutch Harbor. Once aboard the *Arctic Enterprise*, Anthoney's girlfriend broke up with him when she grew tired of his abusive behavior, and a short while later, Anthoney was fired.

Two months after leaving Anchorage to work on the *Arctic Enterprise*, Kirby Anthoney returned to Anchorage and took a taxi to Nancy Newman's apartment. By this time, John was in California training as a locksmith. Kirby asked Nancy if he could stay at her apartment for a while, and she reluctantly agreed. His volatile temper and drug use concerned her, and she didn't like having him around the girls. John was unhappy when he heard Kirby was living in their apartment, and he told Nancy to kick him out. Nancy asked Anthoney to leave, and while he complied, he reportedly was furious with his aunt.

According to Anthoney, he'd spent the night of March 13 drinking alcohol and using cocaine at a dice-playing party across the street from where he lived. He'd stayed up all night and returned to his apartment the following morning when his roommate was getting ready for work. The roommate said Anthoney left again around 8:45 a.m. Anthoney said he then went to the home of his friend Kirk Mullins and arrived there around 9:00 a.m. Mullins said Anthoney didn't come to his place until between 10:00 and 11:00 a.m. He did say, however, that when Anthoney arrived, he acted normal, as if nothing were wrong. If Kirby Anthoney was the murderer, the police wondered, then how could he savagely rape and murder three family members and then carry on a casual conversation an hour later?

The detectives asked Anthoney for the clothes he had been wearing Friday night and Saturday morning, and they then searched his apartment, where they found John Newman's camera. Anthoney claimed Nancy had let him borrow the camera. The clothes they collected were reasonably clean, but analysts found a drop of blood on his shoe and discovered a spot of feces on his shirt. In the era before DNA analysis, the investigators determined the blood was human, but the sample yielded no other information.

While the crime lab continued to test the evidence, the Anchorage police task force played mind games with Anthoney. They sporadically tailed him, making sure he saw the tail, and two of the detectives talked to him frequently, playing good cop–bad cop with him. By April 15, Anthoney felt the pressure, and he climbed in his truck and fled for the Canadian border, asking his roommate not to tell the police where he'd gone. His roommate immediately called the Anchorage police, and the authorities stopped Anthoney at the border. The police brought Anthoney back to Anchorage and arrested him for the murders of Nancy, Melissa, and Angie Newman.

The detectives knew they had the killer in custody, but they had no witnesses and no direct pieces of evidence to tie Anthoney to the crimes. They had uncovered no murder weapon, nor were they lucky enough to find Anthoney's bloody fingerprints in the apartment. Anthoney's conviction weighed heavily on the forensic evidence and its analysis. He had lived with the Newmans, though, so it was likely the police would find his fingerprints in the apartment. But there was not a good reason why his prints were on the empty cookie jar, where Nancy stashed her tip money. After the murders, witnesses saw Anthoney use rolls of coins to pay for things.

Pubic hairs removed from the victims' bodies and found on the damp washcloth in the bathroom sink looked identical to those collected from Kirby Anthoney. Still, the hairs could not be matched definitively to one person. More damning were the lice-egg casings clinging to some of the pubic hairs collected from the bodies and to the one collected from the rag in the sink. At the time of the murders, Anthoney had pubic lice. The washcloth also had green wool fibers on it, and the fibers matched the gloves found near Nancy Newman's body. The gloves were covered with hair pulled from Nancy's head. It appeared as though the perpetrator had attacked Nancy while wearing the green gloves. He then removed the gloves and went into the bathroom to clean himself with the washcloth, leaving behind the wool fibers and a pubic hair covered with lice-egg casings. The detectives also believed Anthoney had gotten feces on his shirt from the spot on Nancy Newman's bed.

The prosecution struggled with the task of explaining to the jury how anyone could brutally murder three people and then act perfectly normal an hour later. FBI agent John Douglas, with the Behavioral Science Unit, explained that the FBI categorizes acts such as those perpetrated against the Newman family as "sex-power killings." These premeditated acts are committed by a sane person with a character disorder. While the perpetrator knows the difference between right and wrong, he doesn't care; he lacks a conscience. If he feels no remorse, then he has no reason to act guilty after committing a brutal act.

Once the attorneys had presented all the evidence, the jury deliberated for two days before returning a verdict of guilty on all counts. Kirby Anthoney's sentence was so long that he would not even be eligible for parole for 120 years. When handing down the sentence, the judge stated that Kirby Anthoney was the most dangerous offender ever to enter his courtroom.

The Newman murders understandably outraged the city of Anchorage, and Kirby Anthoney received numerous death threats. The crime even sparked a movement to reinstate the death penalty in Alaska, but the movement never gained traction.

This case is an excellent example of the use of forensic evidence to capture and convict a murderer. Thanks to the many hours the crime scene investigators spent combing through the Newman apartment collecting evidence, the prosecution was able to build a solid circumstantial case and put Kirby Anthoney behind bars, where he belonged.

A Monster Named Israel Keyes

A monster moved to Anchorage in 2007. Israel Keyes didn't look evil. He appeared normal. He seemed like a dedicated businessman, a doting father, and a loving boyfriend to those who crossed his path. No one could see the darkness lurking inside him, but by the time he moved to Alaska, Israel Keyes was already a thief, an arsonist, a rapist, and a serial killer. He did not give up these hobbies when he arrived in Anchorage.

With 2.8 specialty coffee shops per ten thousand people, Anchorage has more coffee shops per capita than anywhere else in the US, including Seattle. Some of these shops are walk-in establishments, but many are small drive-through shops. The Common Grounds Espresso stand at 630 East Tudor Road in Anchorage was a small drive-through shop, measuring eight feet in length and a little more than that in width. Usually, only one employee at a time worked at the coffee stand, and customers either drove or walked up to the window to place their orders.

Eighteen-year-old Samantha Koenig was thrilled when she landed a job as a barista at the coffee stand. It was the perfect job for a friendly young woman who loved being around people. Her father, however, did not share her enthusiasm. He wasn't pleased to learn his daughter would be working alone at night, but Samantha pleaded and assured him the stand was equipped with surveillance cameras as well as a panic button should a barista need to summon the police.

Samantha was a beautiful, brown-eyed brunette with a bubbly personality and a dazzling smile. After working at the coffee stand for only a month, she already had several loyal customers. On February 1, 2012, Samantha worked the late shift and was scheduled to be there until closing time at 8:00 p.m. She didn't have a car, but her boyfriend had promised to stop by the stand and give her a ride home.

Israel Keyes had been planning to burglarize the coffee stand for several days, and on the snowy night of February 1, he pulled a ski mask over his face, parked his car down the road, and walked to the stand. He hadn't decided what he would do when he reached the stand. He planned to rob the shop, and if conditions were right, he would kidnap the barista. Keyes arrived at the stand at 7:55 and calmly ordered a large Americano. Samantha prepared the drink, but when she turned around to hand it to him, she gasped at the .22 Taurus handgun Keyes pointed at her. He told her to turn out the lights and then hoisted himself through the window and inside the coffee stand. Samantha apparently was so terrified by the intruder and his gun that she forgot to push the panic button.

Keyes told Samantha this was a robbery, and when she said her boyfriend or father would be there any moment to pick her up, Keyes thought twice about abducting her. He had two ground rules: never hunt close to home and never use his own vehicle for an abduction. He had already broken the first rule, and he hesitated to break the second. After all, he had parked down the road, so he would need to walk Samantha down the street to his vehicle. Keyes later told investigators that he lost control, and with a rush of adrenaline, he decided to take the chance.

Keyes walked Samantha out of the coffee stand, and with his arm around her and his gun pointed at her side, he forced her to continue down the road. Samantha nearly broke away from him once, but he caught her and told her he would kill her if she tried to escape again. Once he'd secured her in his truck, he asked Samantha if she had a debit card, and she told him her card was in her boyfriend's truck, which would be parked on the street in front of her father's house later that evening.

Keyes drove Samantha to the house he shared with his girlfriend and young daughter and tied her up in a shed next to the house. He told Samantha he would kill her if she screamed, and then he turned on a radio in the shed to cover up any noise she made. Next, Keyes drove to Samantha's father's house, located her boyfriend's truck, broke into the vehicle, and took Samantha's debit card. Her boyfriend was already on edge and worried about Samantha because she wasn't at the coffee stand when he'd arrived to pick her up from work. When he heard a noise outside the house, he opened the door and saw Keyes near his truck. He called to him and asked him what he was doing, but Keyes managed to get away with the debit card.

Once Keyes had Samantha's debit card, he returned to his home, and being careful not to wake his girlfriend, he poured himself a glass of wine and took it back to the shed with him. He sipped wine and then raped Samantha while she sobbed. After he was finished with her, he slowly strangled her to death, wrapped her body in a tarp, and stuffed her in a cabinet in the freezing shed. By then, it was morning, and he woke his daughter, got her dressed, and called a cab to take them to the airport, where the two departed for New Orleans and a cruise he had booked months earlier. Keyes's girlfriend flew separately and met Keyes and his daughter for the cruise.

After the cruise, Israel Keyes left his daughter with relatives and drove to Aledo, Texas, where he burglarized and burned down a house. He then went to Azle, Texas, and robbed the National Bank of Texas. Next, he drove to Houston, where he and his daughter flew back to Anchorage.

On February 19, Keyes dropped his daughter at school, returned to his home, removed Samantha's body from the cabinet, and had sex with her frozen corpse. A few days later, he applied makeup to Samantha's face to make her appear alive, sewed her eyes open with fishing line, and photographed her with a recent newspaper. He then included the photo with a ransom note to Samantha's family, telling them to deposit $30,000 into Samantha's bank account if they wished to see her alive again. He planned to use her debit card to withdraw the $30,000 from her account. A few days later, Keyes cut up Samantha's body and dumped her remains in Matanuska Lake, near Anchorage.

In early March, Keyes flew to Las Vegas, rented a car, and drove to Wilcox, Arizona, where he used Samantha's debit card to withdraw $400. Ninety minutes later, he withdrew money in Lordsburg, New Mexico. Keyes wore a disguise when he made the transactions, but an ATM security camera recorded an image of the white Ford Focus rental car he was driving. The image did not capture the license plate, but it was clear enough to determine the make and model of the vehicle. Ironically, Keyes had mechanical problems with the car and returned it to the rental agency in exchange for another vehicle, but to his bad fortune, the rental agent issued him another white Ford Focus.

Two days later, on March 9, Keyes withdrew money from an ATM in Humble City, Texas, and the FBI alerted Texas law enforcement officials to be on the lookout for a white Ford Focus. On March 13, Texas Highway Patrol corporal Bryan Henry spotted a white Ford Focus parked at a motel in Lufkin, Texas. When Keyes left the motel, Henry followed him and noticed the car was traveling three miles over the speed limit. Henry leaped at the excuse to stop the car, and when Keyes handed him an Alaska driver's license, Henry called for backup. He knew the perpetrator they were looking for was wanted in connection with a crime in Alaska, and the driver of the Ford Focus was not only from Alaska but also looked like the photos of the disguised person who had used Samantha's card at the ATMs. Henry felt he had probable cause to hold Keyes and search the vehicle. In the Ford Focus, police found a dye-stained roll of bills from a bank robbery, the mask Keyes had worn while withdrawing the money from the ATMs, a gun, and Samantha's debit card. They arrested Keyes, and a few days later, Alaska State Troopers escorted him back to Anchorage.

At first, Keyes refused to talk to investigators, but on March 31, he admitted he had abducted Samantha Koenig from the coffee stand. He said he would give the authorities more details eventually, but he would talk only if they could promise to keep the details from the press. He did not want his daughter to read about everything he had done to Samantha. Keyes had friends and neighbors in Anchorage and a list of happy clients from his construction business, and he said he needed to get used to the idea that now these people would know who he really was.

When the federal prosecutor pressed Keyes on the issue of whether Samantha was dead or alive, Keyes told him she was dead but said he wasn't yet ready to give them the details of her murder. He said, "I'll tell you everything you want to know. I'll give it blow by blow if you want. I have lots more stories to tell." His words stunned the investigators in the interrogation room as it slowly dawned on them that they were sitting across the table from a serial killer.

Keyes demanded two things. First, he wanted a speedy trial and the death penalty, and he wanted the death penalty carried out within a year. Second, he wanted to keep the details of his crimes secret from the news media. He told investigators that unless they met those two demands, he would not divulge any information about other crimes he might have committed. He did agree to tell the investigators the details of his abduction and murder of Samantha Koenig and where to find her body. A few days later, the police recovered her remains from Matanuska Lake. Samantha's family had her cremated and held a memorial service for her on Easter Sunday.

When investigators discovered information on Keyes's computer about a missing Vermont couple, they confronted him with the evidence and asked him what he knew. He smiled and told the investigators they were lucky because he had planned to throw the computer into a landfill when he returned to Anchorage from Texas. At first, he told them he would only talk about the Vermont case if they scheduled his execution date and promised he would be executed within a year. Finally, though, he told them that he'd left the bodies of Bill and Lorraine Currier in an abandoned farmhouse near Burlington, Vermont. When the prosecutor asked Keyes how he knew the Curriers and why he'd decided to murder them, Keyes became annoyed with what he considered a stupid question. He said he didn't know the Curriers. "It was just random."

Keyes explained that his usual routine was to fly to an area of the country, rent a vehicle, and then drive, sometimes hundreds of miles, to find a victim. He buried murder kits around the country in areas he found interesting, and he often buried these kits years before he carried out a crime in that area. He placed each kit in a plastic, five-gallon bucket with a tight-fitting lid and included such items as a shovel, plastic bags, money, weapons, ammunition, and bottles of Drano to help dispose of the bodies.

Two years before killing the Curriers, Keyes had stashed a murder kit near Essex, Vermont. Then, on June 2, 2011, Keyes flew to Chicago, rented a car, and drove nearly one thousand miles to Vermont. After spending a few days fishing and relaxing, Keyes began scouting the area for a victim. He ultimately chose the Curriers' house because it had an attached garage, providing covert access into the home. He also chose the house because no children lived in the residence. Keyes said the only rule he had for himself as far as victims were concerned was to never kill children.

Keyes entered the Curriers' garage and broke into the house through the door leading from the garage to the house. He attacked the couple in bed while they slept and took them to an abandoned farmhouse. He restrained Bill in the basement, but when he tried to escape, Keyes lost his temper and shot and killed him. Keyes then sexually assaulted Lorraine and strangled her. He stuffed the Curriers' bodies into black garbage bags and left them in the basement of the abandoned house. A few months later, when the farmhouse was demolished, the bags containing the bodies were unwittingly transported to a landfill. After Keyes admitted to the crime and specified where he'd left the bodies, Vermont law enforcement officials searched the landfill, but the Curriers' bodies were never found.

Keyes hinted about some of his other crimes to investigators, including a bank robbery in New York, the burglaries of twenty to thirty homes across the US, a rape, and several homicides, but he loved playing games with his interrogators and only offered minor details of these crimes. He claimed he'd abducted a girl in the summer of 1997 or 1998 while she and her friends were tubing on the Deschutes River in Oregon. Keyes said he sexually assaulted her and then sent her on her tube down the river. He estimated she was between fourteen and eighteen years old. According to police records, no one ever reported such a crime.

Keyes said he'd committed his first homicide between July and October 2001, not long after being discharged from the Army. He did not tell investigators the victim's identity nor where he'd left the body. Between 2001 and 2005, he said he'd murdered a couple in Washington State, but again he provided no information about the couple, except to say they were buried near a valley. Between 2005 and 2006, Keyes said he'd committed two separate murders and disposed of at least one of the bodies in Crescent Lake in Washington. He admitted that on April 9, 2009, he'd abducted a woman from a state on the East Coast and transported her over multiple state lines into New York, where he buried her somewhere upstate. On the same trip to New York, Keyes had robbed the Community Bank in Tupper Lake. In April and May of 2011, Keyes admitted to staking out two spots near Anchorage where he'd considered killing people but then changed his mind. In June 2011, he'd murdered the Curriers in Vermont, and on February 1, 2012, he'd abducted and murdered Samantha Koenig.

FBI agents believed Keyes murdered at least eleven people and possibly more. He traveled extensively around the US between 2005 and 2012 and made several trips outside the country. According to Keyes, only two of his victims' bodies had been recovered. One was Samantha Koenig's, and the other was the body of a victim he'd staged to make it appear as if she'd died from an accident. He claimed that when the authorities recovered her body, they had indeed ruled her death accidental.

On May 23, Keyes appeared before US district judge Timothy Burgess in federal court for a hearing to set a new trial date. Samantha Koenig's family and friends were in attendance. Partway through the hearing, Keyes somehow broke free from his steel leg shackles and jumped over the railing into the first row of seats in the gallery area. Spectators screamed, "Get him!" and "kill him!" while deputies tackled Keyes and used a Taser to subdue him. The deputies later learned that Keyes had removed the chain from one of his ankle cuffs, but they couldn't figure out how he had managed to do it.

When the FBI relayed the information that Keyes had told them about the Curriers' murders to law enforcement personnel in Vermont, FBI agents asked the Vermont officials not to release Israel Keyes's name to the public, explaining that he had agreed to talk about his other victims only as long as his name was kept out of the press. In July, Vermont investigators announced that the murderer of Bill and Lorraine Currier had been arrested and was in prison in another state after being charged with a crime in that state. They said they could not release more details at the present time. As soon as the press conference ended, though, WCAX-TV in Burlington released a story reporting that anonymous sources had identified Israel Keyes as the Curriers' killer.

Keyes was furious when he learned the press had connected him to the Curriers' murders. He felt betrayed and stopped talking to the FBI and Anchorage police detectives. He became increasingly concerned that if he admitted to crimes in other states, each jurisdiction would want to try him separately, and the judicial process would drag on for years. He wanted only to stand before a federal judge, admit he was guilty of abducting and murdering Samantha Koenig, and receive a death sentence, scheduled to be carried out within a few months. He now felt the entire process spiraling out of his control and saw no reason why he should talk about his other crimes.

Keyes said he felt no moral obligation to the families of his victims to explain what he'd done to their loved ones. He expressed no remorse for his crimes. Investigators who questioned Keyes said he was arrogant and sometimes seemed bored while relating the details of his crimes, but when talking about an abduction or murder, he'd get excited and sit on the edge of his seat, adrenaline coursing through him while he described every minute, grisly detail of what he had done.

In late November, Keyes again met with investigators, but he seemed distracted by the end of the interview and told them he might be willing to talk to them the following week. Two days later, at 5:57 a.m. on December 2, 2012, a corrections officer performing a security check in the Anchorage Correctional Complex noticed a strange, red-colored streak on the floor of cell three. He instantly realized the streak was blood, and when the inmate did not respond to his calls, the guard summoned medical assistance. When medics pulled back the blanket from the inmate's bed, they found Israel Keyes lying face-down, covered in blood. Keyes was pronounced dead at 6:13 a.m.

Keyes had slit open his left wrist along the vein, and a razor blade attached to a pencil rested under his body. Wanting to make sure he succeeded in killing himself, Keyes lay on his stomach and tied a bedsheet noose around his neck. Then, with his left leg bent back toward his buttocks, he tied the other end of the sheet around his left ankle. This configuration ensured that when he lost consciousness due to blood loss, the force of his leg lowering back down to the bed would tighten the noose around his neck and strangle him. To keep the guards from noticing the blood as it flowed from his wrist, Keyes had collected his blood in two milk containers and two cups until he passed out, and he did all this while remaining nearly motionless under his blanket. Investigators noted that Keyes had carried out his own death with the same methodical planning he had used to abduct and murder his victims. His suicide method was so successful that the medical examiner could not determine whether he had died from blood loss or strangulation. Prison officials still have not determined how Keyes obtained a razor blade while locked in a segregation cell.

Investigators were crestfallen when they heard about Keyes's suicide. Now they would never know the details of his other crimes and the locations of the bodies of his other victims. Keyes left a four-page suicide note on a yellow legal pad that was so saturated with his blood it was unreadable until the FBI lab in Virginia restored most of it. Even after the restoration, though, parts of the note remained indecipherable. After studying the suicide note, the FBI concluded that there was no hidden code in the message, nor did the note offer any investigative clues to the identity of other possible victims. The note seemed to describe a victim's final moments, and it provided a glimpse into the arrogant, evil mind of Israel Keyes.

Israel Keyes did not like being called a serial killer, even though he knew the term applied to him. He admitted he admired Ted Bundy, but he stated he did not copy Bundy, and his ideas were his own. He resembled Bundy in several ways, though. Both killers felt they possessed their victims, and both were methodical planners. Both chose and killed victims in different areas of the country instead of in one particular city or region, but Bundy's murders were spread throughout the US because he often moved from one location to another. Keyes purposefully chose to murder in places far away from where he lived in order to avoid detection. He often traveled partway to his chosen location by airplane and the rest of the way by car. Also, while Bundy targeted only attractive young women, Keyes had no victim profile. He admitted his victims ranged from young to old and were both male and female. He had no connection to and did not know his victims before abducting and murdering them. Keyes was also careful to turn off his mobile phone and pay for items in cash when on a murder trip. A national expert on serial killers stated that Israel Keyes was one of the most organized and intelligent serial killers he had ever studied.

Like Ted Bundy, Israel Keyes was a heavy drinker, and also like Bundy, as his appetite for murder and the adrenaline rush he got from taking risks increased, he became more careless. He took chances he had never taken before when he abducted Samantha Koenig. First of all, he chose a victim near where he lived instead of traveling across the country to find his prey. Secondly, he told himself that if the barista working at the Common Grounds coffee stand did not have a car he could use to abduct her, he would simply rob the stand and leave. He couldn't stop himself, though, and he abducted her anyway, despite the risk. Finally, using Samantha's debit card to extort ransom from her family proved his downfall. He disguised himself when withdrawing money from the ATMs, but he carelessly allowed the ATM camera to photograph his rental car. Keyes admitted to investigators that when he saw Samantha Koenig, he could not walk away from her. Killing had become an addiction for him, and in the end, he couldn't control his addiction.

What Happened to the Fandel Children?

Sterling, Alaska, is located on the western side of the Kenai Peninsula, 136 miles southwest of Anchorage. In 2020, it had a population of approximately six thousand. The famous Kenai River runs past Sterling, making it a popular destination for salmon sport anglers. In 1978, when the following story about the disappearance of the Fandel children took place, Sterling had a population of only nine hundred.

Most parents can imagine no nightmare worse than the disappearance of a child, but how can parents possibly cope when both of their children vanish, swallowed by the Alaska wilderness?

Sometime during the late-night hours of September 5 or the early-morning hours of September 6, thirteen-year-old Scott Fandel and eight-year-old Amy Fandel disappeared from their Sterling home. The mystery of what happened to the Fandel children has baffled the Alaska State Troopers for over four decades. How can two kids vanish from their home without a trace?

At 10:30 p.m. on September 5, 1978, as darkness settled on Sterling, Scott and Amy Fandel seemed safe and happy. Less than four hours later, they were gone, never to be seen again. Where did they go? What could have happened to them? Investigators spent thousands of hours running down hundreds of leads, but they led nowhere. One former Alaska State Trooper said they chased "quirks and spider web leads," but they never got any closer to finding the children.

The children's parents had recently battled through a bitter divorce. Their father, Roger Fandel, loved his kids but was unfaithful to his wife, Margaret. Margaret began drinking more alcohol as Roger strayed before finally leaving her. She worked long hours waiting tables to pay the bills, and when Roger moved to Arizona, the kids often stayed unsupervised at the family's small cabin in the woods near Sterling.

Scott Fandel was little more than a child, but according to those who knew him, he was mature for his age, and he was a good babysitter for his little sister. September 5, 1978, promised to be a big day for the Fandel children because their mother's sister, their aunt Cathy Schonfelder, was moving from Illinois to live with them. Aunt Cathy arrived on schedule, and after dinner at their cabin, the family drove to a bar called Good Time Charlie's. The bar had video games to entertain the kids, and Scott and Amy drank Cokes while their mother and aunt drank beers and talked.

Around 10:00 p.m., Margaret and Cathy took the kids home and then drove to another bar. Before the night was over, the sisters had visited at least one more bar. Margaret told the kids not to stay up late, and Cathy told them to lock the door. This last comment caused Scott to laugh because the lock on the cabin door was broken. The Fandels' cabin sat in a grove of birch trees. It was nearly invisible from the road, but a bright light mounted on a pole illuminated the front of the cabin.

The Fandels' closest neighbors were Nancy and Bill Lupton and their five children, who lived in a Quonset hut approximately two hundred yards from the Fandels' cabin. The Fandel and Lupton children were good friends and spent most of their time together. As soon as Margaret and Cathy dropped off Scott and Amy at home, the kids walked over to the Luptons' hut to play with the neighbor kids. According to Nancy Lupton, Scott and Amy seemed in great spirits that evening and were very excited about their aunt coming to live with them. The kids played and were making too much noise, so Nancy sent the Fandel children home after a while. Nancy said it was a typical evening, and she heard nothing unusual.

Residents driving home noted lights blazing in the Fandel cabin around 11:45 p.m. This was not unusual because both Scott and Amy were afraid of the dark and usually turned on every light in the house. When Margaret and Cathy arrived home at 2:00 a.m., though, the cabin appeared dark and empty. A package of macaroni and an open can of tomatoes lay on the kitchen counter, and a pot of hot water sat on the stove. Scott liked to eat a macaroni snack before going to bed and had started to make his snack when something interrupted him.

Margaret thought the kids probably were spending the night with the Lupton children, so she and Cathy went to bed. Margaret went to work at 8:30 the following morning, and once she arrived at her job, she called the school to leave a message for Amy, telling her she was in trouble for not stopping by home before going to school. The school informed Margaret that Amy was not at school. Margaret began to worry about Amy, but her boss wouldn't let her leave work until the afternoon. Margaret later said she was concerned but not alarmed by Amy's absence at school.

Meanwhile, Cathy became worried when the kids didn't arrive home on the school bus. The Lupton children told her that Scott and Amy hadn't been in school all day. Cathy called Margaret, and Margaret raced home. Now she felt frightened and knew something was wrong. She frantically called the kids' friends, and when she learned that no one had seen Scott and Amy all day, Margaret called the Alaska State Troopers at 5:14 p.m. on September 6, at least fifteen hours after the children had disappeared.

At first, Margaret suspected her ex-husband. She couldn't reach him in Arizona, but when she talked to his family, they said he didn't have the children. Roger Fandel had a reputation as a tough guy, but he loved his kids, and he soon flew to Alaska to help search for them. Over the next decade, the authorities would consider Roger a person of interest in this case. If he hadn't snatched the kids himself, perhaps someone else had kidnapped the kids for him. As the years passed, though, the troopers eventually dismissed Roger as a suspect.

Teachers and friends remembered Amy Fandel as sweet and beautiful, and they characterized Scott as smart and as his sister's devoted protector. Scott would have intervened if someone had tried to take Amy against her will.

Troopers found bullet casings outside the Fandel cabin, but no one could tell them if the casings were new or had been there for a long time. No one reported hearing shots the night the kids disappeared. Volunteers scoured the woods for any sign of the Fandel children, and the troopers brought in search dogs from Anchorage.

Investigators searched ferries leaving Homer and informed the Canadian Mounties to be on the lookout for someone crossing the border with the children. The kids disappeared at the height of the oil boom during the construction and early operation of the Trans-Alaska Pipeline, and sketchy characters frequented the bars on the Kenai Peninsula. Did someone at Good Time Charlie's hear Margaret and Cathy talk about taking the children back to the cabin and leaving them alone for a few hours? Troopers tried to run down every lead, but there seemed to be no end of suspects, and tips flowed in from every direction.

Early in the investigation, Trooper Sergeant Tom Sumey found a witness who said that on the night the children vanished, he saw a black sedan speed away from the road in front of the Fandels' cabin. The witness thought the driver of the sedan might have been a vandal or a thief, so he followed the sedan and watched the driver pull into a driveway and shut off the car's headlights. The witness drove down the road and then turned around in time to see the black sedan pull out of the driveway and speed away. Sumey learned that the car belonged to two carnival workers from the East Coast who had visited the Kenai in late August. Margaret had allowed the men to crash at her house for a night.

Sumey felt he had a solid lead and eventually ran down the men in Maryland. They admitted they had been in the area of the Fandel cabin and had considered stopping, but they said they were in Sterling on September 6, not September 5. The men worked at the Alaska State Fair on September 4, picked up their paychecks in Anchorage on September 6, and then drove to Sterling. When Sumey reinterviewed the witness who'd followed the black sedan, the man admitted he could have seen the car the night after the children had vanished. Troopers did not dismiss the carnival workers as possible suspects, but they never found any evidence to incriminate them.

Investigators discovered another promising lead during the first days of the investigation. On the night the children disappeared, a friend had introduced Margaret to a man involved in the Anchorage sex trade. "Mr. W," as he was called in a newspaper article, was in the process of moving one of his "motels" from Anchorage to Soldotna, a town near Sterling. A few days later, when the public first heard about the disappearance of the Fandel children, Mr. W showed up at Margaret's house with one of her sisters. The two had taken the same plane from Anchorage, and he offered to give her a ride to Margaret's home. Troopers immediately focused their interest on Mr. W, and when he offered a $5,000 reward for information leading to the children's whereabouts, their suspicions only grew. Soon, rumors circulated about a pornography ring in Sterling, and people wondered if someone had sold the Fandel children into sexual slavery.

When Mr. W buried his car on the property where he was building his motel, troopers obtained a search warrant, dug up the vehicle, and popped the trunk, expecting to find the bodies of two children. The trunk was empty, and Mr. W explained that he'd grown tired of the car and had to put it somewhere. With no other evidence leading to Mr. W, the troopers dismissed him as a suspect.

Numerous other leads plagued investigators. Roger Fandel's family wasted no time pointing their fingers at each other. Roger suspected that his uncle Herman had killed the kids, while Herman suggested that Roger had done something to them. When investigators dug up Herman's yard to look for the bodies of Scott and Amy, Herman wept about the public humiliation.

People hounded Margaret and blamed her for the disappearance of her children, and psychics continuously called her with false leads. Margaret spiraled into depression and alcohol abuse after her children disappeared. In 1980, she moved back to the Midwest, met a nice man, quit drinking, and remarried. When interviewed in 1988, Margaret said she still hoped Scott and Amy would return to her someday. She wanted to believe her kids were still alive. In an interview near the same time, Roger did not sound as hopeful. He thought Scott would have found a way to contact him if they were alive.

You don't have to spend much time online to find active discussions about this case. Margaret's relatives maintain a Facebook group devoted to the kids and their disappearance. They hope to learn anything that might lead to finding Scott and Amy. Margaret's brother believes Scott was killed soon after the children were abducted, but he thinks Amy is still alive. Others in the family do not agree.

In these online discussion groups, internet sleuths are quick to blame Margaret for leaving the children alone in an unlocked cabin and then not checking on them when she got home. Others point out that Scott was mature for thirteen, and he was undoubtedly capable of babysitting his little sister. Margaret worked hard to keep a roof over her family's head.

The pan of water on the stove remains one of the strangest elements in this mystery. When Margaret and Cathy arrived home around 2:00 a.m., they found a package of macaroni and an open can of tomatoes on the counter, and a pan of water on the stove. Some accounts say the water was boiling, but others indicate the pan felt hot or warm. How hot was the water, or if it was boiling, was there much water left in the pan? Wouldn't the water temperature offer a significant clue to the time the children disappeared? Did Scott leave the house so quickly he didn't have time to turn off the stove? If he did turn off the burner, how long would it take the water to cool? Perhaps the troopers used this information to narrow down the time frame for when the children disappeared, but nothing they've said to the public suggests they considered it.

Scott and Amy Fandel would be in their fifties if they are still alive in 2022. If you know anything about the disappearance of Scott and Amy Fandel, please contact the Alaska State Troopers.

KODIAK

The Kodiak Archipelago consists of twenty-five islands. The island of Kodiak is the second-largest island in the United States, after the "Big Island" of Hawaii, and it lies 250 miles southwest of Anchorage. Much of Kodiak is part of the Kodiak National Wildlife Refuge. There are seven towns on the island, but most of the 13,500 residents live in the city of Kodiak, located on the northeast corner.

Kodiak has a wet, mild maritime climate. The primary industry is commercial fishing, and Kodiak yearly ranks as one of the top fishing ports in the United States.

MURDER AT A FISH SITE

Forty-four commercial fishermen died at sea near Kodiak in 1988, which is the deadliest fishing year on record. That was also the year fishermen earned $2.40 per pound for sockeye salmon, the highest price ever paid to fishermen for sockeyes before or since. Commercial fishing proved lucrative but dangerous that year.

Alaska fishermen know their jobs involve risk. (While many women fish commercially, the industry is dominated by men.) They work on the North Pacific, often in big seas and brutal weather, but no fisherman expects to be murdered by his crewman.

During the summer of 1988, whispers spread across the island, first about two missing brothers who were fishermen in Uganik Bay and later about the mother of those two men discovering their bodies buried in a shallow grave near their fish site. It was the first double homicide in recorded history on Kodiak Island.

As noted earlier, the two main methods of commercial salmon fishing practiced along coastal Alaska are purse seining and gill netting. Purse seining is done from a fishing boat. A typical purse-seine boat measures approximately forty-two feet in length with a cabin, a wheelhouse, a galley, and sleeping quarters. A crew of three or four live on and fish from the boat all summer. Purse seiners follow the fish. When the captain spots a school of salmon, he orders the crew to make a set. With the aid of a smaller boat, the crew deploys the purse seine, circles the school of fish, and pulls the salmon into the large boat. When the net is stored back onboard, and the crew secures the smaller boat behind the seiner, the captain heads off in search of another school of salmon. Once or twice a day, the captain delivers the catch to a much larger boat (a tender), and the tender delivers its cargo of salmon to the fish-processing plant, usually once a day.

Gill net (or setnet) fishermen live on shore. They anchor their nets to the shore on one end and then extend the nets out from shore for a maximum of nine hundred feet. The nets measure thirty feet deep. Salmon swim into the gill net and get caught in the mesh, and the fishermen pull along the net in an open skiff to pluck the salmon from the mesh. The fishermen hold the salmon on ice, and the tender visits their fish site twice a day for a delivery. Since setnet fishermen live on shore and remain there all summer, a setnet site often is not only a business but also a summer home for the entire family.

In the summer of 1988, forty-two-year-old Daniel Nickerson and his thirty-six-year-old brother Robbin, both from Bothell, Washington, operated a setnet site in Uganik Bay, a large bay on the west side of Kodiak Island. The Nickersons had fished this site since the 1970s. Daniel's wife and two young sons often joined him at the site, but in 1988, Daniel and Robbin hired a crewman from Kodiak named Robert Shepard. Like the Nickerson brothers, Shepard was a Vietnam veteran.

The Nickerson brothers had reputations as heavy drinkers, and Daniel reportedly possessed a volatile temper, especially when he was drunk. Other set netters in Uganik Bay admitted that you did not want to cross Danny Nickerson, especially if he had been drinking.

Before the salmon season began, tempers flared between the Nickersons and their new crewman. The brothers sent Shepard out to their setnet site in Uganik Bay from Kodiak with a boatload of supplies, but when Shepard encountered bad weather and heavy seas, he beached the skiff and waited for help. Several witnesses spotted the Nickersons berating Shepard after the incident, and the crewman's relationship with the brothers went downhill from there.

On June 22, 1988, friends of Daniel and Robbin stopped by their fish site for a visit. They didn't see the brothers, but Shepard told them that the Nickerson brothers had been drinking all night and were now asleep in their bunks. A few days later, Shepard told these same friends that he had not seen the Nickersons since the morning of June 23, when he said the brothers headed out in their boat to go to a party.

The friends worried something had happened to the brothers, and when they found the Nickersons' skiff badly damaged and aground on a beach, they believed their worst fears had been confirmed. Other fishermen in Uganik Bay assumed the Nickersons got drunk, fell out of their skiff, and drowned. On June 29, the Coast Guard and the Alaska State Troopers launched an intensive search for the brothers, but they suspended the search in mid-July when no further trace of the brothers materialized.

Soon after the Nickerson brothers were reported missing, their mother traveled from her home in Washington State to stay at their site and take charge of the fishing operation. Robert Shepard also remained at the site and continued to fish the Nickersons' gear. Mrs. Nickerson believed her sons had too much boating experience to fall overboard and drown, and she told other fishermen in the bay she did not think her sons had accidentally disappeared but felt sure they had met with foul play.

Mrs. Nickerson dismissed Shepard and hired a young couple to help her run the fish site. In early August, she told a visitor to the site that she had noticed someone had moved some of the banya rocks (small, round rocks used in their steam bath) to a grassy ravine behind the cabin. The visitor investigated and found the bodies of Daniel and Robbin Nickerson bundled in a sleeping bag and buried beneath the rocks.

Mrs. Nickerson contacted the Alaska State Troopers, and on August 9, 1988, they removed the bodies of the Nickerson brothers from the fish site. The troopers noted that someone had shot the men, and when they sprayed the inside of the setnet cabin with luminol (a chemical that reacts with the iron in hemoglobin and glows blue, revealing even trace amounts of blood), the walls and the floor glowed, evidence of a recent bloody battle inside the cabin. The troopers confronted Ron Shepard, the only other person known to have been at the cabin before the brothers disappeared. Shepard admitted he had killed Daniel and Robbin Nickerson, but he claimed he had acted in self-defense.

At trial, the prosecution argued that if Ron Shepard shot Daniel and Robbin Nickerson in self-defense, then why did he concoct such an elaborate cover-up? Why did he deliberately damage the Nickersons' boat and beach it; tell the Nickersons' friends that Daniel and Robbin set out by skiff for a party and hadn't been heard from since; bury their bodies; clean up the scene; and tell everyone, including the Coast Guard, the troopers, and Mrs. Nickerson, that he had no idea what had happened to the brothers? If the murders were self-defense, why didn't Ron Shepard contact the troopers and report what had happened?

Ron Shepard took the stand in his defense. He claimed Daniel and Robbin Nickerson were extremely violent and unstable. Daniel always carried a gun and enjoyed using it to frighten and shoot at people. According to Shepard, on the morning of June 23, while the brothers were passed out drunk, he took their skiff out to work the nets. Shepard said that when he returned to the cabin, Daniel confronted him and yelled at him for taking the skiff without permission. Shepard said Daniel then pulled a pistol and told Robbin to move out of the way so he could get a clear shot at Shepard. Shepard said he grabbed Robbin and used him as a shield between himself and Daniel. Shepard backed into his bedroom, released Robbin, grabbed his rifle, and shot Daniel once, killing him. According to Shepard, Robbin then lunged at him with a knife, and Shepard shot him in the shoulder. Shepard said he then went for a towel and water to treat Robbin's wounds, but Robbin grabbed a shotgun. When the two men struggled over the gun, it discharged, the shot killing Robbin instantly.

Shepard's attorney presented physical evidence and expert testimony to back up the details of Shepard's story, but this evidence failed to explain why Shepard had covered up the murders and buried the bodies. According to Shepard, he hid his crime not out of guilt but because he suffered from post-traumatic stress disorder (PTSD). When he was a Marine in Vietnam, Shepard said he was confined for several weeks to the Marine brig at Da Nang, where he claimed he was brutally mistreated, including one incident in which he was sexually assaulted with a nightstick by a guard. This mistreatment by the authorities, he said, left him distrustful of the police. He said that his violent encounter with the Nickersons and the shooting had brought back the trauma from Vietnam, and once he'd killed the Nickerson brothers, all he wanted to do was return to normal life as quickly as possible. He believed the police would not listen to his side of the story and would arrest and attack him if he tried to report the incident.

Shepard's attorney hoped to call Dr. Raymond Scurfield to testify. Dr. Scurfield was one of the leading experts in the country on the psychiatric symptoms and treatment of PTSD, but since Dr. Scurfield had never treated Shepard, the judge did not allow the doctor to testify. Dr. Robert Alberts, a psychiatrist from Anchorage who had treated Shepard for PTSD, was allowed to testify instead. Dr. Alberts said he had diagnosed Robert Shepard with PTSD and explained that PTSD is a recognized form of anxiety disorder experienced by some people who are exposed to extremely traumatic events such as military combat. The effects of PTSD can last for years, and even after remaining dormant for a long period, PTSD may be retriggered by another traumatic incident. According to Alberts, people who have PTSD often avoid and distrust authority figures. He said Shepard's behavior after he shot the Nickerson brothers was consistent with what a person living with PTSD who had acted in self-defense might do.

The prosecution then called Dr. Francis Criswell, a forensic psychiatrist with the Alaska Psychiatric Institute, to the stand. Dr. Criswell testified that he had treated several veterans who had PTSD, and he said the condition was difficult to diagnose because the diagnostic category of PTSD is so broad. He said it was nearly impossible to prove whether or not someone suffered from the disorder. Dr. Criswell added that he believed PTSD had become a "fad in legal defenses," and he thought psychiatric professionals, such as Dr. Alberts, who did not often work with criminal defendants, proved gullible and easily swayed by defendants who claimed they had committed crimes because of a PTSD flashback. Dr. Criswell said he had evaluated Shepard before the trial and was not convinced he had PTSD.

After Dr. Criswell finished testifying, Shepard's attorney again requested that Dr. Scurfield be allowed to testify, but the judge denied his request.

The judge handed the case to the jury, and, to the surprise of many Kodiak residents, the jury acquitted Shepard of all charges related to the death of Daniel Nickerson. In the death of Robbin Nickerson, the jury found Shepard guilty of the lesser offense of manslaughter. Sheppard was sentenced to fifteen years in prison.

Many Kodiak residents felt Shepard should have been happy he was only convicted of one count of manslaughter, but he appealed his conviction, claiming the judge should have allowed Dr. Scurfield to testify. The Court of Appeals of the State of Alaska found in Shepard's favor and reversed his conviction for manslaughter. According to the court, Scurfield should have been allowed to testify as an expert witness because the jury could have found his description of PTSD more helpful than the description provided by Dr. Alberts. Dr. Scurfield also had more expertise than Alberts in dealing with Vietnam veterans who had PTSD, so the jury "may have deemed his views more credible than Alberts'."

Rather than retry Shepard, the state allowed him to plead guilty to criminally negligent homicide and covering up the crime. He was credited with the four and a half years he had already served and was released from prison on ten years' probation in August 1993. Shepard quit drinking while in prison and earned a college degree. He later said the years he spent in jail were the best of his life. He now lives in eastern Washington.

Some Kodiak residents believe Shepard got away with murder. This case highlights how difficult it is to convict someone of a serious crime in an isolated setting with no witnesses. People have plenty of time to clean up the crime scene, and there's no one to dispute the defendant's version of the events preceding the crime. The troopers probably would have never arrested Shepard had he weighted the bodies and dumped them at sea.

In most ways, 1988 was an excellent time to be a commercial fisherman on Kodiak Island. Salmon prices exploded, and most salmon fishermen made a great deal of money, more than they have ever made in a single season before or since. No one could foresee the disaster lurking on the horizon. In March 1989, the fuel tanker *Exxon Valdez* hit Bligh Reef in Prince William Sound, and wind and ocean currents carried some of the oil all the way to the waters around Kodiak Island. The Alaska Department of Fish and Game closed commercial salmon fishing around the island for the summer of 1989 because they feared the oil would contaminate the salmon. Salmon prices still have not rebounded to what they were in 1988.

As mentioned earlier, this was the first double homicide ever recorded on Kodiak Island. Read the following story about the second double homicide on the island. It occurred in 2012, when two men were murdered on the US Coast Guard base near the town of Kodiak.

Double Murder at a US Coast Guard Base

"Cold and miserable" describe the winter of 2011/12. It was one of the harshest winters on record in Alaska. In the town of Kodiak, the ground froze nearly six feet deep, down to where the water lines are buried. The frigid temperatures made life difficult, and in addition to being cold, Kodiak's snowfall during the winter of 2011/12 measured 212 percent above normal. Instead of the average 68.9 inches, Kodiak received 145.9 inches of snow. By the end of the winter, people were cranky and on edge.

The US Coast Guard base on Kodiak Island, established in 1972, is the largest Coast Guard base in the United States. The base supports approximately a thousand active-duty members, seventeen hundred family members, and several hundred civilian employees, many of whom have retired from active duty with the Coast Guard. Not only is the Coast Guard a vital employer in the community, but it is often the lifeline for one of the largest fishing fleets in the country. The Coast Guard base on Kodiak is responsible for covering nearly four million square miles of the roughest oceans and most inhospitable terrain in the world. When a fishing boat takes on water in heavy seas, or a fisherman receives a head injury from a swinging crab pot, the Coast Guard speeds to the scene to offer assistance.

The residents of Kodiak respect and welcome the Coast Guard as an essential asset to their island community. On those rare occasions when members of the Coast Guard die during a daring rescue, residents mourn those who gave their lives to protect them. The 2012 double murder at the Coast Guard Communications Station shocked and saddened the residents of Kodiak. It is tragic but understandable when a guardsman dies during a high-risk rescue attempt, but a double murder at a repair station made no sense.

The US Coast Guard base is located six miles south of the town of Kodiak via the Chiniak Highway. The USCG Communications Station is not part of the main USCG base but is a small installation down a side road on the other side of the highway. The turnoff to this side road is one mile north of the main base. The Kodiak airport and the Comfort Inn are also crucial to this story, and they sit on the same side of the highway as the main base and are between the main base and the road leading to the communications station.

Among other duties, guardsmen and women working at the communications station track aircraft, receive and relay messages from and to ships in distress, and transmit weather reports. The 2012 murders occurred in the rigger shop next to the communications station. Those working in the rigger shop are responsible for servicing and repairing the approximately forty antennas for Coast Guard communications stations across Alaska. It is essential to note that in 2012, the main Coast Guard base was closely guarded and the communications station was located behind a secure fence, but the rigger shop was protected only by a grainy security camera.

On April 12, 2012, meteorologists predicted the temperature on Kodiak would soar to 50°F (10°C), and if it did, the island residents would enjoy the warmest day since October. Spirits lifted in Kodiak with this promise of spring, but the upbeat mood didn't last long. Around 8:30 that morning, rumors spread through the town. There had been a murder at the Coast Guard base. When the rumors became more specific, and the whispers suggested the shooting had happened at the rigger shop, the families of the small crew of men who worked there waited with dread. Soon, those rumors were confirmed. Not only had one man been killed, but two men were dead. Someone had shot Petty Officer First Class James Hopkins, forty-one, and civilian employee Richard Belisle, fifty-one, multiple times. They died in the rigger shop, their bodies discovered around 8:00 a.m. by a fellow employee. Richard Belisle had served in the Coast Guard for twenty-three years and had retired as a chief boatswain's mate before returning to the Coast Guard to work as a civilian.

Belisle, Hopkins, and a fellow civilian employee, James Wells, were scheduled to begin their shifts at 7:00 a.m. Wells had left two phone messages saying he would be late for work because he had a flat tire. He did not report for duty until after the bodies had been discovered.

Residents of Kodiak responded to the shootings with rage and fear. Rich Belisle, a well-liked member of the community, was married with three daughters. James Hopkins was married and had a son and daughter.

At the time of this incident, the only other murder of a guardsman on a base in the US had occurred in 2001 on St. Paul Island, Alaska, a tiny island in the Bering Sea. The guardsman shot in that incident was reportedly having an affair with the shooter's wife.

The US Coast Guard is attached to the Department of Homeland Security. Since the murders occurred on a US Coast Guard base, the FBI assumed control of the investigation. The Alaska State Troopers aided the FBI in their inquiries. The FBI chose not to relay any information to the public about the progress of the investigation. When they did not immediately arrest a suspect for the murders, their silence angered many Kodiak residents and created an atmosphere of fear and distrust in a community whose nerves already were stretched to the breaking point by the harsh, unrelenting winter.

FBI spokesman Eric Gonzales issued a statement saying, "Nothing in this investigation has led the FBI to believe that anyone is in danger." While he said the residents of Kodiak were not in danger from the unknown killer, he didn't bother to explain how the FBI knew this or what the FBI was doing to apprehend the killer. The FBI simply expected the residents of Kodiak to trust them, but nothing the FBI did earned the residents' respect or trust. Instead, people carried weapons, looked over their shoulders, and listened to rumors.

The day after the murders, US Secretary of Homeland Security Janet Napolitano issued a statement saying her department placed a high priority on solving this crime and bringing the perpetrator to justice. She said she had directed the full resources of her department to support the investigation of these murders.

On April 23, the FBI issued a news release describing two vehicles and asking citizens to come forward if they had information concerning the whereabouts of these vehicles on April 12 and 13. Residents were quick to note that the descriptions of the cars matched those owned by James Michael Wells, the other civilian employee who should have been at his post in the rigger shop at the time of the murders. Wells claimed he was late for work that morning because he'd had a flat tire. James and his wife, Nancy, lived in Bells Flats, a small community about ten miles from the town of Kodiak and a few miles down the Chiniak Highway south of the Coast Guard base.

While the FBI volunteered no information, residents inferred much from their actions. They knew the FBI had searched the house of James and Nancy Wells after the shootings, and the Wellses' vehicles had been towed away but then returned to them. Residents—especially those in Bells Flats, where murder victim Richard Belisle had lived and his coworker, James Wells, still lived—knew that both men were retired from the Coast Guard. Until the murders, they'd worked together as civilian employees in the rigger shop. Rumors circulated about the animosity between Wells, Belisle, and Hopkins. Wells, who had worked at the rigger shop for twenty years, had been disciplined several times in recent months, and he seemed to blame Belisle and Hopkins for his problems. Residents believed Wells was the obvious suspect in the murders, but the authorities refused to name him or arrest him. According to the local newspaper, the *Kodiak Mirror*, two FBI agents sat in a car across the road from the Wellses' house and watched it around the clock.

On May first, nearly three weeks after the murders, the Coast Guard made a request on Facebook for community volunteers, especially those with metal detectors, to help search the area around the rigger shop. The FBI said the search was related to the murders, but they did not tell the searchers what they were hoping to find. Residents recalled Secretary Napolitano's promise to deploy the total resources of the Department of Homeland Security to investigate this crime. But it seemed that instead of the town receiving help from a huge government agency, the Coast Guard and FBI were asking citizens to bring their personal metal detectors to search for something near the crime scene. Residents began to wonder if the Homeland Security and FBI agents knew what they were doing. If they didn't, were Kodiak's citizens truly safe, or were they in danger from an unknown killer who had already murdered two men?

The public believed the purpose of the search was to look for the gun used in the murders, and when a hundred residents showed up to search, everyone hoped they would find the weapon and the authorities would finally arrest the killer. Unfortunately, no gun was found that day, and if anyone discovered anything of interest, the FBI did not report the find to the community. Agents reviewed the books of the gun shops on the island, but again, they did not reveal what (if anything) they found.

The investigation dragged on for several months, and still, no arrest was made. The residents of Bells Flats became more and more convinced that James Wells had murdered his coworkers, and Wells still lived in and moved about their community, making everyone nervous, angry, and frustrated with the slow progress of the investigation.

Finally, on February 15, 2013, ten months after the murders, the authorities arrested James Michael Wells. They charged him with two counts of first-degree murder, two counts of murdering an officer or employee of the United States, and two counts of possession and use of a firearm in relation to a crime of violence. Wells pleaded not guilty.

At Wells's February 19 arraignment, FBI Special Agent Elizabeth Oberlander portrayed James Wells as a substandard Coast Guard civilian employee who had feuded with his coworkers and supervisors. Hopkins, the enlisted guardsman, was in charge of the rigger shop, but Wells refused to take orders from him. Wells failed to follow regulations and guidelines, and at one point, he'd sabotaged several trees at the station so he could cut them down and use them for firewood for his home. In December 2011, a supervisor told Wells he needed to shape up or retire. A month later, the same supervisor told Wells he would not be sending him to the national conference for tower erectors, a conference Wells usually attended. Instead, the supervisor planned to send Belisle and Hopkins to the conference. Belisle and Hopkins were murdered less than three months later. Oberlander admitted that there were no eyewitnesses to the murders, and no murder weapon had been found. Still, she said enough circumstantial evidence existed to provide probable cause that James Michael Wells had "willfully, deliberately, maliciously, and with premeditation" killed Hopkins and Belisle.

The trial of James Michael Wells took place in April 2014 at the US District Court in Anchorage. The jurors were selected from around the region, and the trial lasted twenty days.

First responders testified that when they arrived at the murder scene, they saw no evidence of a break-in or robbery at the rigger station, and they said both men appeared to be victims of a targeted killing. US Attorney Karen Loeffler, the lead prosecutor in the case, played tapes of two interviews with Wells conducted by FBI agent Kirk Overlander (not to be confused with Special Agent Oberlander) shortly after the murders. In the first interview, Wells said he'd started to drive to work for his 7:00 a.m. shift at the rigger shop but detected a soft tire and pulled into the parking lot of the Comfort Inn near the Kodiak airport. He checked the tire, saw a nail in it, and returned home to change the tire.

Wells did not know that a security camera on the main gate of the Coast Guard station recorded his truck heading toward the rigger shop at 6:48 a.m. and then returning in the opposite direction toward his home at 7:22 a.m., a time frame of thirty-four minutes.

During the second interview, Agent Overlander told Wells that he'd driven the same route Wells claimed he'd followed, and the trip took him only ten minutes. He then asked Wells why it took him thirty-four minutes to stop, check his tire, and turn around to drive home. Wells stated, "I don't have a reasonable explanation for it; I don't have a theory at the moment."

At trial, Wells's defense attorney said his client suffered from chronic diarrhea as the result of recent gallbladder surgery. After checking his tire on the morning of the murders, he drove to the airport to use the bathroom at a commuter airline. The prosecution provided evidence showing that no one at the airline remembered seeing Wells, and if this was Wells's explanation for the thirty-four-minute time frame, then why hadn't he told this to the FBI when they first interviewed him?

The FBI learned that James Wells's wife, Nancy, was in Anchorage during the murders, and she left her blue SUV parked in the Kodiak airport parking lot during her absence. James Wells drove a white truck to work on the morning of the murders. A blurry video taken by a camera near the rear of the rigger shop showed a blue SUV arriving at the shop just before the murders occurred. No one reported seeing the blue SUV, either on the road or parked at the communications station, but this one blurry video proved it was there.

The FBI agents believed James Wells left home in his white pickup truck, drove to the airport, parked, switched to his wife's SUV, and drove to the rigger shop. He then shot Belisle and Hopkins, returned to the airport, left his wife's SUV there, and drove home in his white truck. During this period, he made two calls to work to report he had a flat tire and would be a few minutes late arriving for his shift.

To support its argument, the prosecution played the two videos, one from the gate at the main base and the other from the camera outside the rigger shop. Attorneys said when Wells's wife returned from Anchorage, she told the detectives her car had been moved while she was gone. An expert who examined the flat tire with the nail in it stated that someone had shot the nail into the tire with a nail gun. The nail had not been picked up by driving over it on the road, as Wells claimed. According to the expert witness, the tire had not been driven on after the nail was embedded in it. Finally, while investigators never found the murder weapon, they determined that a .44-caliber gun was used in the shootings, and they found .44-caliber ammunition in James Wells's house. A witness testified that Wells had borrowed a .44-caliber handgun from him several years earlier and never returned it.

After a ten-month investigation and a twenty-day trial with over a hundred witnesses called to testify, a jury of six women and six men deliberated only six hours before finding James Michael Wells guilty on all six counts of the indictment. The judge sentenced Wells to four consecutive ninety-nine year terms: two for killing James Hopkins and Richard Belisle and two more for using a firearm in a violent crime. After Wells received his sentence, he made a brief statement. He maintained his innocence, claiming a tragedy had occurred and that "we have all suffered for it." Nancy Wells stood by her husband throughout the trial, and even after he was convicted and sentenced, she continued to say she believed he was innocent of the crime. The judge in the case condemned Wells for allowing his family to think he was innocent when he knew better. Nancy Wells simply shook her head after this comment.

After the trial ended, US Attorney Karen Loeffler, the lead prosecutor, praised the investigators and her legal team. She said:

> This was a long road to justice for the families of Richard Belisle and James Hopkins, the United States Coast Guard community, and the citizens of Kodiak. The guilty verdicts were the result of the superb investigative effort of the FBI and Coast Guard Investigative Service, and I am very proud of the work of the members of the United States Attorney's Office for the District of Alaska and our Special Assistant US Attorney from the US Coast Guard Judge Advocate General. We are very pleased that the lengthy and meticulous investigation of this brutal crime has resulted in the conviction of the person responsible.

Loeffler had a right to be proud about convicting James Wells with only circumstantial evidence. There were no witnesses, and no weapon was ever found, but she and her associates presented such a compelling case that the jury returned a guilty verdict in only six hours. It is unfortunate, though, that the FBI and the other investigators in this case could not have either arrested Wells sooner or released enough information to the Kodiak community to calm people's fears and assure the residents that the investigation was moving forward.

Their silence took a toll on the community and the victims' families. At the sentencing hearing, Rich Belisle's wife, Nicola, said she'd lived in fear for more than ten months while her husband's killer remained free, and she said that more than once, she'd huddled in her house with a loaded firearm because her dogs had barked at something outside the home. Maybe if the authorities had released more information or arrested Wells sooner, Nicola Belisle would not have suffered the double insult of losing her husband and her security.

In August 2016, Nicola Belisle and James Hopkins's widow, Deborah, filed a suit against the United States of America for the wrongful deaths of their husbands. They asked for one million dollars each. They alleged that the US Coast Guard knew or should have known James Wells was a dangerous, disgruntled employee with several reprimands and disciplinary sanctions, and he posed a serious threat to other employees.

The saga of James Wells continued in 2017, when the Ninth US Circuit Court of Appeals overturned Wells's conviction and ordered a new trial. The court cited several problems with the original trial, but their biggest concern was the testimony of a forensic psychologist. They believed the testimony should not have been allowed at trial.

The subsequent trial for James Wells took place in Anchorage, and on October 8, 2019, the jury again found Wells guilty on all counts.

It seemed as if the winter of 2012 would never end. On May 13, snow again fell on the island, and then, finally, the temperatures began to rise. Most of the winters since 2012 have been unseasonably warm, and now, those few brutal months remain a distant memory.

CONCLUSION

Alaska has a reputation for independence and lawlessness. This reputation draws fine, strong newcomers who want to enjoy nature and pursue a wilderness lifestyle. Unfortunately, it also attracts misfits and criminals. In the early twentieth century, Ed Krause boldly took what he wanted from his neighbors and then murdered them. With very little law enforcement present in Alaska in 1912, Krause and his gang felt they could do whatever they wanted. Sixty years later, Robert Hansen kidnapped and murdered women in Anchorage over a period of twelve years before he was finally caught. The police and troopers were so overwhelmed by the influx of criminals to the area that Hansen flew under their radar for several years.

Alaska has always had a high rate of violent crime. From the gold rush to the building of the Trans-Alaska Pipeline, the state's rich resources have attracted eager workers and criminals alike. Alaska also attracts misfits and wanderers. Some hope to turn their lives around by moving to Alaska, but they often bring their problems with them. Others think they will be less likely to get caught perpetrating their crimes in a state with sparse law enforcement. Michael Silka was a drifter with mental issues. We will never know what caused him to start his murder spree. Louis Hastings was obviously unstable when he concocted his convoluted plan to destroy the pipeline, beginning with murdering his neighbors. Kirby Anthoney had severe mental problems as well as substance abuse issues. He came to Alaska for a fresh start, but he couldn't control his violent tendencies.

The Alaska State Troopers are tasked with policing a vast territory. Due to inclement weather conditions in the state, they often can't reach a murder scene for a day or more. The troopers were never able to solve the murders on the *Investor* because, by the time they reached the boat, most of the evidence had burned. Most of the Alaska State Troopers who have served the state over the years have been intelligent, resourceful, and brave. Trooper Jim McCann and his fellow Fairbanks troopers taught themselves how to analyze a crime scene in the days before Alaska even had a crime lab. McCann also seemed capable of climbing into the mind of killers to track them.

The troopers have never shied away from asking for help in a case. They embraced criminal profiling almost at its inception, and they quickly learned that profiling could be a valuable tool, but it is only one of many tools. The FBI's murderer profile did not help in the Richard Bunday case, but it was nearly spot-on for Robert Hansen. In the case of the North Pole serial killer, the FBI told the troopers the murderer was not in the military, but the killer, Richard Bunday, was, in fact, in the Air Force. Only after the troopers had ignored the profile did they look at Air Force transfers and trail Bunday to Texas. On the other hand, the FBI nailed the profile of Robert Hansen down to his stutter.

Even today, the Alaska State Troopers remain on the cutting edge of law enforcement. Cold Case Trooper Investigator Randy McPherron has recently closed several cold cases, including the 1992 murder of Sophie Sergie and the 1996 murder of Jessica Baggen, by using genetic genealogy.

Of course, not all police officers are good, and they do not always do a great job investigating a crime. John Patrick Addis, a trooper based in Fairbanks, handed in his trooper's badge and became a serial killer. Nome PD officer Matthew Owens used his badge to abduct, sexually assault, and murder Sonya Ivanoff. As mentioned earlier, law enforcement did a poor job responding to the murders on the *Investor*, and it took the Anchorage police years to apprehend Robert Hansen.

Policing in Alaska is not an easy job. Troopers must fly to small villages around the state when called to investigate a murder, solve a robbery, or settle a domestic dispute. They never know what to expect when they walk into a village. They are often the lone law enforcement agents within hundreds of miles, and backup remains hours away from them. Troopers Scott Johnson and Gabe Rich probably considered it a routine call to fly to Tanana to handle a domestic dispute. They had no idea they would be gunned down by a misguided young man who'd been taught to hate law enforcement.

When viewed through the lens of history, the Alaska State Troopers and the Alaska city police departments have done an incredible job enforcing the law in a state with too many criminals.

Afterword

I have attempted to portray the crimes in this book as honestly as possible. Sometimes the investigators did an excellent job, and other times they did not. I am an independent author with no loyalties to any investigative agency. I am simply a third-party observer. I have tried but occasionally failed to stay neutral. Any observations or opinions in the book are mine and mine alone.

If you disagree with my depiction of any of the stories in this book or believe I have misrepresented the facts, please email me (robinbarefield76@outlook.com). A few of these crimes and mysteries are controversial. The disappearance of the plane carrying congressmen Hale Boggs and Nick Begich remains the most disputed mystery in Alaska, and from publishing the story elsewhere, I know people have very strong opinions about it. I have attempted to relay some of the more common conspiracy theories, but please don't get mad at me. Before you send me a hate-filled email, I will tell you that I think the plane crashed into a mountain in bad weather, fell into the ocean, and sank.

If you have information on the Fandel case or any other unsolved case in this book, please contact the Alaska State Troopers.

I write a monthly newsletter about true crime in Alaska, and I pulled these stories from those newsletters. Please sign up for my free monthly newsletter if you would like to read more stories of murder and mystery in Alaska. You can sign up at https://mailchi. mp/e34d98f1a569/alaska_mystery_newsletter. You can also sign up on my website at robinbarefield.com.

I also have a podcast called *Murder and Mystery in the Last Frontier*. Please look for it wherever you listen to podcasts, or you can listen to it at https://murder-in-the-last-frontier.blubrry.net.

Thank you to Bill Siever for his brilliant editing. I would be lost without his help. Thank you to Evan and Lois Swensen at Publication Consultants for turning my manuscript into a book. I appreciate all the amazing authors at Author Masterminds (authormasterminds. com) for their support. Last but not least, thank you to my husband, Mike Munsey, for his unending support and encouragement.

SOURCES

ED KRAUSE: ALASKA'S FIRST SERIAL KILLER

"Edward Krause saws bars and makes escape." April 13, 1917. *Alaska Daily Empire.*

Heaton, John W. *Ed Krause: Outlaw Tales of Alaska.* 2010. Guilford, CT: Morris Book Publishing.

Hunt, William R. *Hard to Convict: Distant Justice.* 1987. Norman: University of Oklahoma Press.

"Krause's career of crime was a long and a bad one." November 19, 1915. *Fairbanks Daily News-Miner.*

Story Time with Aunt Phil. "Alaska's first serial killer strikes." 2018. https://auntphilstrunk.com/alaskas-first-serial-killer-strikes/

THE *INVESTOR* MURDERS

Bovsun, Mara. "Murder on a fishing boat—and there was never a conviction." March 31, 2019. *New York Daily News.* https://www.ny-dailynews.com/news/crime/ny-justice-story-investor-boat-kill-ings-20190331-y333ejn4qjd5vnhf33wzxg4jiy-story.html

Dodd, Johnny, and Adam Carlson. "The mystery of who murdered 8, including a family, on a fishing boat in Alaska." December 11, 2017. *People.* https://people.com/crime/people-explains-investor-fishing-boat-murders-alaska/

Hale, Leland E. *What Happened in Craig: Alaska's Worst Unsolved Mass Murder.* 2018. Kenmore, WA: Epicenter Press.

Kahn, Dean. "8 killed in 1982 *Investor* murders remembered in exhibit." April 30, 2016. *Washington Times.* https://www.washingtontimes.com/news/2016/apr/30/8-killed-in-1982-investor-murders-remembered-in-ex/

THE TROUBLED TEEN

Demer, Lisa. "Convicted killer testifies at Waterman trial." January 27, 2011. *Anchorage Daily News.* https://www.adn.com/alaska-news/article/convicted-killer-testifies-waterman-trial/2011/01/27/

Fleeman, Michael. *Love You Madly: The True Story of a Small-town Girl, the Young Men She Seduced, and the Murder of Her Mother.* 2011. New York: St. Martin's True Crime.

Kheiry, Leila. "2015. Alaska Court of Appeals denies Rachelle Waterman appeal." Alaska Public Media. https://www.alaskapublic.org/2015/02/06/supreme-court-denies-rachelle-waterman-appeal/

Larson, John. "Teen blogger murder trial: How could Rachelle Waterman's fantasies spiral into her mom's murder?" *Dateline.* NBC. http://www.nbcnews.com/id/13962555/ns/dateline_nbc/t/teen-blogger-murder-trial/#.XmQ-QEBFweE

Wikinews. "American teenage girl charged with murder of her mother." 2004. https://en.wikinews.org/wiki/American_teenage_girl_charged_with_murder_of_her_mother

THE UNHAPPY WIFE

The Charley Project. "Scott Michael Coville." http://charleyproject.org/case/scott-michael-coville

Grove, Casey. "Mother in cold case describes years wondering about her son." May 31, 2016. *Anchorage Daily News.* https://www.adn.com/alaska-news/article/mother-cold-case-describes-years-wondering-about-her-son/2010/11/28/

Murderpedia. "Jane Reth." n.d. https://murderpedia.org/female.R/r/reth-jane.htm

Pietragallo, James, and Jimmie Whisman. *Small Town Murder.* Podcast #45: "The hottest cold case around in Sitka, Alaska." November 22, 2017. https://www.stitcher.com/podcast/small-town-murder/e/52324451?autoplay=true

FINDING THE MURDERER OF JESSICA BAGGEN

Alaska Department of Public Safety, Public Information Office. "1996 cold case solved: Jessica Baggen killer identified through DNA." August 2020. https://dps.alaska.gov/AST/PIO/PressReleases/1996-Cold-Case-Solved-Jessica-Baggen-Killer-Ident

Boots, Michelle T. "Suspect in 1996 cold-case murder of Sitka girl killed himself last week in Arkansas, troopers say." August 11, 2020. *Anchorage Daily News.*

Boots, Michelle T. "23 years ago, Alaska tried the wrong man for the murder of a Sitka teenager. Now police say they've found the real killer. Why wasn't he a suspect all along?" September 9, 2020. *Anchorage Daily News.*

PBS News Hour. "Genetic genealogy can help solve cold cases. It can also accuse the wrong person." November 7, 2019. https://www.pbs.org/newshour/science/genetic-genealogy-can-help-solve-cold-cases-it-can-also-accuse-the-wrong-person

The McCarthy Massacre of 1983

Bartley, Bruce. "Killings shock a town on mail day." March 4, 1983. *Fairbanks Daily News-Miner*.

Bartley, Bruce. "McCarthy murders trial: Mystery to be unraveled." December 5, 1983. *Sitka Daily Sentinel*.

Court of Appeals of Alaska, no. A-8783. *Hastings v. State*. February 28, 2007. https://casetext.com/case/hastings-v-state-55

Murderpedia. "Louis D. Hastings." n.d. https://murderpedia.org/male.H/h/hastings-louis.htm

The Horrible Misdeeds of Papa Pilgrim

Harden, Blaine. "A bulldozer runs through it." September 28, 2003. *Washington Post*. https://www.washingtonpost.com/archive/politics/2003/09/28/a-bulldozer-runs-through-it/a93f7e3a-eb8f-424e-a6f5-75adc3dcb39d/

Kirby, Mark. "Papa Pilgrim's progress: The dark tale of an Alaskan frontiersman." November 19, 2008. *Outside* magazine. https://www.outsideonline.com/1928141/papa-pilgrims-progress-dark-tale-alaskan-frontiersman#close

Kizzia, Tom. *Pilgrim's Wilderness: A True Story of Faith and Madness on the Alaska Frontier*. 2013. New York: Crown Publisher.

Kizzia, Tom. "Hale clan details abuse at the hand of their father, 'Papa Pilgrim.'" July 1, 2016. *Anchorage Daily News*. https://www.adn.com/projects/article/hale-clan-details-abuse-hand-their-father-papa-pilgrim/2013/07/12/

Murder at the North Pole

Brennan, Tom. *Murder at 40 Below*. Chapter 9: "Having trouble with girls." 2001. Kenmore, WA: Epicenter Press.

Capps, Kris. "Bunday never denied he was killer, trooper recalls." March 17, 1983. *Fairbanks Daily News-Miner*.

Capps, Kris. "Bunday was suspect in 1980." March 17, 1983. *Fairbanks Daily News-Miner*.

Fisher, Susan. "Authorities were awaiting more facts." March 17, 1983. *Fairbanks Daily News-Miner*.

Ice Cold Killers. Season 1, episode 5: "North Pole slay ride."

"Troopers release summary of Thomas Bunday murder case." April 29, 1983. *Fairbanks Pioneer All Alaska Weekly*.

THE HOMICIDAL TROOPER

Cervone, Chellie. "Joann Albenese, Las Vegas woman's death and disappearance." February 15, 2013. *Las Vegas World News*. http://www.lasvegasworldnews.com/joann-albanese-las-vegas-womans-death-and-disapperance/12605/

Puit, Glenn. *Ghost: The True Story of One Man's Descent into Madness and Murder*. 2011. New York: Berkley Books.

Tataboline, Brant. "Ex-trooper linked to second disappearance." August 2, 2003. *Anchorage Daily News*. https://www.tapatalk.com/groups/thecyberseekerssociety/ex-trooper-linked-to-second-disappearance-t1049.html

Zekan, Karen. "Remains identified as those of LV woman." October 19, 1998. *Las Vegas Sun*. https://lasvegassun.com/news/1998/oct/19/remains-identified-as-those-of-lv-woman/

MASSACRE AT MANLEY HOT SPRINGS

Brennan, Tom. *Murder at 40 Below*. Chapter 8: "Manley Hot Springs murders." 2001. Kenmore, WA: Epicenter Press.

Hall, Jeff. "Michael Alan Silka and the firefight at Manley." *Tactical Life* magazine. https://www.tactical-life.com/lifestyle/military-and-police/firefight-at-manley/

Ice Cold Killers. Season 1, episode 5: "Frozen carnage."

Murderpedia. "Michael Alan Silka." n.d. https://murderpedia.org/male.S/s/silka-michael.htm

Murder in a College Dorm

Alaska Department of Public Safety, State Troopers: Alaska Bureau of Investigation. "Cold Case Investigation Unit." n.d. https://dps.alaska.gov/ast/abi/coldcase

Associated Press. "AST cold-case unit faces elimination." April 10, 2015. *Fairbanks Daily News-Miner*.

Bohman, Amanda. "New theory revives old murder case." April 25, 2009. *Fairbanks Daily News-Miner*.

Farneski, Anna. "Sergie was target of opportunity." May 8, 1993. *Fairbanks Daily News-Miner*.

Farneski, Anna. "While troopers hunt Sophie's killer, family tries to cope." July 8, 1993. *Fairbanks Daily News-Miner*.

Nolan, Caitlin. "Genealogy DNA leads to arrest in 1993 murder of Alaska student found dead in dorm bathtub." February 18, 2019. *Inside Edition*. https://www.insideedition.com/genealogy-dna-leads-arrest-1993-murder-alaska-student-found-dead-dorm-bathtub-50844

Williams, Tess. "Jury finds Maine man guilty in Fairbanks cold-case murder." February 10, 2022. *Anchorage Daily News*.

Tragedy in Tanana

Chomicz, Dorothy. "Kangas found guilty of evidence tampering in Alaska State Trooper deaths." April 23, 2015. *Fairbanks Daily News-Miner*.

Chomicz, Dorothy. Arvin Kangas sentenced in case related to Alaska State Trooper killings." September 3, 2015. *Fairbanks Daily News-Miner*.

Chomicz, Dorothy. "Courtroom tenses as Nathanial Kangas murder trial gets underway." May 9, 2016. *Fairbanks Daily News-Miner*.

Chomicz, Dorothy. "Pilot describes scene in Tanana minutes after troopers killed." May 10, 2016. *Fairbanks Daily News-Miner*.

Edge, Josh. "Man convicted in Tanana trooper killings sentenced to 203 years in prison." November 3, 2016. Alaska Public Media. https://www.alaskapublic.org/2016/11/03/man-convicted-in-tanana-trooper-killings-sentenced-to-203-years-in-prison/

Murder on the Yukon River

Associated Press. "More details emerge in killing of postmaster." July 19, 1996. *Daily Sitka Sentinel*. https://www.newspapers.com/clip/10310101/more-details-emerge-in-killing-of/

Murphy, Kim. "Murder in a town full of suspects." August 2, 1996. *Los Angeles Times*. https://www.latimes.com/archives/la-xpm-1996-08-02-mn-30531-story.html

Smithsonian National Postal Museum. "1996 postmaster." n.d. https://postalmuseum.si.edu/exhibition/behind-the-badge-case-histories-assaults-and-murders/1996-postmaster

A Betrayal of Trust in Nome

Associated Press. "Ex-officer jailed 99 years for murder." April 21, 2006. *Whitehorse Daily Star*.

Associated Press. "Ex-officer on trial for the second time." November 30, 2005. *Whitehorse Daily Star*.

Associated Press. "Jury to begin deliberations in Nome murder trial." February 23, 2005. *Fairbanks Daily News-Miner*.

Associated Press. "Murder trial hears final arguments." February 25, 2005. *Whitehorse Daily Star*.

Associated Press. "Murder victim entered police car, women say." January 24, 2005. *Whitehorse Daily Star*.

Associate Press. "Nome cop charged with murder." October 27, 2003. *Fairbanks Daily News-Miner*.

Associated Press. "Nome, family settle suit over woman's murder." December 9, 2005. *Sitka Daily Sentinel.*

Associated Press. "Officer killed woman, staged theft, court told." January 21, 2005. *Whitehorse Daily Star.*

Associated Press. "Suspect demonstrated suspicious behavior." November 10, 2003. *Whitehorse Daily Star.*

Associated Press. "Trial begins for officer charged with murder." January 19, 2005. *Whitehorse Daily Star.*

Associated Press. "Troopers whittle down murder suspects list." October 22, 2003. *Whitehorse Daily Star.*

Brant, Tataboline. "Nome police must work to regain trust after officer charged with murder." October 29, 2003. *Anchorage Daily News.*

Court of Appeals of Alaska, no. A-9640. *Owens v. State.* March 3, 2010. https://casetext.com/case/owens-v-state-590

Mackenzie, Victoria, and Wong, Maye-E. "In Nome, Alaska, review of rape 'cold cases' hits a wall." December 22, 2019. *Spokesman Review.*

Tsong, Nicole. "Jury foreman: Majority voted to convict officer." March 2, 2005. *Sitka Daily Sentinel.*

The Bethel School Shooting

Anderson Cooper 360. "Four wounded in Cleveland school shooting rampage." October 10, 2007. CNN. http://transcripts.cnn.com/TRANSCRIPTS/0710/10/acd.01.html

McBride, Rhonda. "Twenty years after the Bethel school shooting." February 22, 2017. Alaska Public Media. https://www.alaskapublic.org/2017/02/22/20-years-after-the-bethel-school-shooting/

Murderpedia. "Evan E. Ramsey." n.d. https://murderpedia.org/male.R/r/ramsey-evan.htm

MURDER NORTH OF THE ARCTIC CIRCLE

Brennan, Tom. 2001. *Murder at 40 Below*. Chapter 3: "The caribou murders." 2001. Kenmore, WA: Epicenter Press.

Francis, Alfred. "Lone survivor says driver of snowmobile did shooting." January 27, 1970. *Fairbanks Daily News-Miner*.

"Court upholds murder charge, overturns drug conviction." June 16, 1973. *Fairbanks Daily News-Miner*.

"Defense seeks insanity ruling in killing of 3." December 16, 1970. *Fairbanks Daily News-Miner*.

"Johnson charged in triple murder." January 30, 1970. *Fairbanks Daily News-Miner*.

Supreme Court of Alaska. 511 P.2d 118 (1973). *Johnson v. State*. https://law.justia.com/cases/alaska/supreme-court/1973/1477-1.html

"Trooper investigating shootings on way to question lone survivor." January 29, 1970. *Fairbanks Daily News-Miner*.

THE MACHETE KILLER

Associated Press. "Another 189 years for Alaska machete murderer." December 26, 2012. *Fairbanks Daily News-Miner*. http://www.newsminer.com/news/alaska_news/another-years-for-alaska-machete-murderer/article_04ea3828-f472-523f-bed3-d5b2ceae7e02.html

Associated Press. "Man charged with killing father with machete." December 4, 2007. MSNBC. http://www.nbcnews.com/id/22101555/ns/us_news-crime_and_courts/t/man-charged-killing-father-machete/#.XlGWEEBFweE

Court of Appeals of Alaska, no. A-10635. *Rogers v. State*. June 15, 2012. https://caselaw.findlaw.com/ak-court-of-appeals/1607160.html

McKinney, Deborah. "Palmer machete killer's sentences now total 498 years." January 11, 2010. *Anchorage Daily News*. https://www.adn.com/alaska-news/article/palmer-machete-killers-sentences-now-total-498-years/2010/01/11/

Wellner, Andrew. "Hero dog done in by tumor." December 8, 2011. *Mat-Su Valley Frontiersman.* https://www.frontiersman.com/news/hero-dog-done-in-by-tumor/article_7bc08a86-a809-569c-91f3-aa23c18e0fc5.html

Deadly Passion

Associated Press. "Neighbor convicted of Wasilla bomb murder." October 21, 1994. *Daily Sitka Sentinel.* https://www.newspapers.com/newspage/13043179/

Associated Press. "Police followed trail left by blind poodle." March 9, 1994. *Seattle Times.* https://archive.seattletimes.com/archive/?date=19940309&slug=1899341

Enge, Marilee. "Neighbor jailed in bombing of guardsman." November 10, 1993. *Anchorage Daily News.*

Goodman, Peter S. "Affair—fact or fantasy—figures large as bomb victim's widow sues accused man, their relationship takes center stage." May 5, 1994. *Anchorage Daily News.*

Goodman, Peter S. "Bomb suspect pleads not guilty to murder." June 25, 1994. *Anchorage Daily News.*

Goodman, Peter S. "Indicted for murder." November 20, 1993. *Anchorage Daily News.*

Goodman, Peter S. "Murder suspect fights extradition." April 5, 1994. *Anchorage Daily News.*

Komarnitsky, B. J., and P. S. Goodman. "2nd man arrested in truck bombing." March 4, 1994. *Anchorage Daily News.*

Komarnitsky, B. J. "Bomb case bound for federal court—5 charges filed in slaying." December 19, 1996. *Anchorage Daily News.*

Phillips, Natalie, and M. Enge. "Love may be bomb motive." November 11, 1993. *Anchorage Daily News.*

United States Court of Appeals, Ninth Circuit, no. 99-30393. *United States v. Geiger.* August 31, 2001. https://casetext.com/case/us-v-geiger-4

The Kidnapping and Murder of Amy Sue Patrick

"Arsenic found after murder suspect dies." October 9, 1991. *Sitka Sentinel.*

Associated Press. "FBI probes death of suspect in Anchorage." October 14, 1991. *Sitka Sentinel.*

Associated Press. "German dogs to search Alaskan landfill for body." October 20, 1991. *Seattle Times.* https://archive.seattletimes.com/archive?date=19911020&slug=1311977

Associated Press. "Man held in murder falls sick in jail, dies." October 8, 1991. *Sitka Sentinel.*

Associated Press. "Troopers defend way murder case handled." October 16, 1991. *Sitka Sentinel.*

Doto, Pamela. "House sitter, 18, disappears." September 27, 1991. *Anchorage Daily News.*

Doto, Pamela. "Search for body on again." October 26, 1991. *Anchorage Daily News.*

Doto, Pamela. "Teen's body found." October 27, 1991. *Anchorage Daily News.*

Enge, Marilee. "Troopers say Yoon took arsenic." October 9, 1991. *Anchorage Daily News.*

Enge, Marilee. "Yoon's letters ask forgiveness." October 16, 1991. *Anchorage Daily News.*

Mathiesen, Peter B. *Tales of the Alaska State Troopers: Stories of Courage, Survival, and Honor from the Last Frontier.* "The story of Amy Sue Patrick." 2015. New York: Skyhorse Publishing.

"Murder suspect's rights not violated, FBI says." November 15, 1991. *Sitka Sentinel.*

Randall, Gail. "Crime lab can't tell if teen was molested." November 20, 1991. *Anchorage Daily News.*

Randall, Gail. "Troopers call in dogs to search for body." October 19, 1991. *Anchorage Daily News.*

Randall, Gail. "Why did Kyung Yoon confess?" March 22, 1992. *Anchorage Daily News.*

Randall, Gail. "Yoon killed himself, inquest finds." December 4, 1991. *Anchorage Daily News.*

"Suspect apparently took his life after confessing." October 8, 1991. *Anchorage Daily News*.
"Toxicologist tells how arsenic works." October 12, 1991. *Anchorage Daily News*.
Wohlforth, Charles. "Wasilla woman apparent murder victim." October 7, 1991. *Anchorage Daily News*.

The Chulitna Charmer

Brennan, Tom, 2003. *Murder at 40 Below*. Chapter 7: "The bank robber next door." 2001. Kenmore, WA: Epicenter Press.
Court of Appeals of Alaska, no. A-7418. *Stavenjord v. State*. March 28, 2003. https://caselaw.findlaw.com/ak-court-of-appeals/1436854.html#:~:text=Stavenjord%20guilty%20of%20two%20counts,his%20motion%20to%20change%20venue.
Ice Cold Killers. Season 1, episode 3: "Mountain man."
Menerey, Amy. "Convicted murderer's appeal denied." April 8, 2003. *Mat-Su Valley Frontiersman*.

The Hunter

Brennan, Tom. *Murder at 40 Below*. Chapter 1: "The trophy hunter." 2001. Kenmore, WA: Epicenter Press.
Gilmour, Walter, and Leland Hale. *Butcher, Baker: The True Account of an Alaskan Serial Killer*. 2018. New York: Open Road Media.
Murderpedia. "Robert Christian Hansen." n.d. https://murderpedia.org/male.H/h/hansen-robert.htm
"Serial killer's victim identified after 37 years through genetic genealogy and a DNA link. October 23, 2021. CBS News. https://www.cbsnews.com/news/serial-killer-robert-hansen-victim-identified-robin-pelkey/

Serial Murderer Gary Zieger

Brennan, Tom. *Cold Crime*. Chapter 8: "Alaska's Billy the Kid." 2005. Kenmore, WA: Epicenter Press.

Gordon, Mike. "The hired gun." Turnagain Currents. March 26, 2014. https://turnagain.alaskapacific.edu/the-hired-gun/

Hale, Leland. "The lonesome death of Beth van Zanten: The killer is killed." Butcher Baker. October 17, 2018. https://lelandhale.com/butcher-baker/wordpress/2018/10/17/beth-van-zanten-killer-killed/

Hale, Leland. "Lonesome death of Beth van Zanten: Whodunnit." Butcher Baker. October 18, 2018. https://lelandhale.com/butcherbaker/wordpress/2018/10/19/beth-van-zanten-whodunit/

What Happened to Congressmen Hale Boggs and Nick Begich?

Alpert, Bruce. "Author writes about disappearance of plane carrying Hale Boggs 43 years ago over Alaska." June 16, 2015. Nola.com. https://www.nola.com/news/politics/article_45008f3a-4357-5592-962e-3a5b-1f26e5f9.html

Glass, Andrew. "Hale Boggs' plane vanishes in Alaska." October 16, 1972. *Politico*. https://www.politico.com/story/2016/10/hale-boggs-plane-vanishes-in-alaska-oct-16-1972-229692

Liefer, Gregory P. 2011. *Aviation Mysteries of the North*. Chapter 16: "Accident or conspiracy?" Publication Consultants: Anchorage.

"New podcast *Missing in Alaska* takes on 50-year-old mysterious plane disappearance." May 21, 2020. Inside Radio. https://www.insideradio.com/podcastnewsdaily/new-podcast-missing-in-alaska-takes-on-50-year-old-mysterious-plane-disappearance/article_385c65e8-9b81-11ea-b5ae-bb39e1734444.html

A Car Bomb in Downtown Anchorage

Associated Press. "Jury acquits Mackay of murder." February 7, 1988. https://apnews.com/3a33ee9d7d1837d298e5930405c7d10d

Brennan, Tom. *Cold Crime.* Chapter 10: "An angry man." 2005. Kenmore, WA: Epicenter Press.

"Dynamite expected in car bomb killing." October 19, 1976. *Fairbanks Daily News-Miner.*

Jenkins, Paul. "Alleged contract shooting victim dies." November 12, 1985. Associated Press. https://apnews.com/31a0160ee34f2987548f678d-7358cb99

Mroch, Courtney. "The ghost of the Snow City Café." October 27, 2019. Haunt Jaunts. https://www.hauntjaunts.net/the-ghost-of-the-snow-city-cafe/

Turner, Wallace. "Alaskan murder: Enigma within an enigma." June 30, 1987. *New York Times.* https://www.nytimes.com/1987/06/30/us/alaskan-murder-enigma-within-an-enigma.html

The Newman Family Murders

Barer, Burl. *Murder in the Family.* 2016. Denver: WildBlue Press.

Brennan, Tom. *Murder at 40 Below.* Chapter 6: "The Newman family massacre." 2001. Kenmore, WA: Epicenter Press.

"Murder in Alaska: The Newman family slaughter." September 14, 2019. What Lies Beyond. https://whatliesbeyond.boards.net/thread/10150/murder-alaska-newman-family-slaughter

A Monster Named Israel Keyes

Callahan, Maureen. *American Predator: The Hunt for the Most Meticulous Serial Killer of the 21st Century.* 2019. New York: Viking.

FBI. "FBI requests the public's assistance in case of serial killer Israel Keyes." August 13, 2013. https://archives.fbi.gov/archives/portland/

press-releases/2013/fbi-requests-the-publics-assistance-in-case-of-serial-killer-israel-keyes

FBI. "Seeking information regarding serial killer case." n.d. https://www.fbi.gov/video-repository/newss-seeking-info-serial-killer/view

What Happened to the Fandel Children?

The Charley Project. "Amy Lee Fandel." n.d. http://charleyproject.org/case/amy-lee-fandel

The Charley Project. "Scott Curtis Fandel." n.d. http://charleyproject.org/case/scott-curtis-fandel

Dateline Cold Case Spotlight. "The theories of the Fandel children's disappearance." July 1, 2015. NBC News. https://www.nbcnews.com/feature/cold-case-spotlight/theories-fandel-children-s-disappearance-n385361

"The disappearance of Amy and Scott Fandel." July 16, 2015. True Crime Stories. https://truecrimediscussions.blogspot.com/2015/07/the-disappearance-of-amy-and-scott.html?

Scott and Amy Fandel missing. n.d. Facebook page. https://www.facebook.com/scottandamyfandelmissing/photos/

Toomey, Sheila. "Still missing." September 4, 1988. *Anchorage Daily News*.

Murder at a Fish Site

Sullivan, Toby. "Sea stories: Missing brothers turn up dead in Uganik." July 12, 2016. *Kodiak Daily Mirror*. http://www.kodiakdailymirror.com/community/article_37f0be0c-485a-11e6-a26e-6ba696185b1e.html

Court of Appeals of Alaska, no. AP-1283. *Shepard v. State*. February 19, 1993. http://touchngo.com/ap/html/ap-1283.htm

Double Murder at a US Coast Guard Base

Associated Press. "Man arrested in 2012 Alaska Coast Guard base deaths." November 21, 2015. KOMO News. https://komonews.com/news/nation-world/man-arrested-in-2012-alaska-coast-guard-base-deaths-11-21-2015

Grove, Casey. "Wells convicted, again, of Kodiak Coast Guard double murder." Alaska Public Media. https://www.alaskapublic.org/2019/10/08/wells-convicted-again-of-kodiak-coast-guard-double-murder/

Joling, Dan. "Car expert testifies in CG trial." April 10, 2014. *Ketchikan Daily News.* https://www.ketchikandailynews.com/Premium/BC-AK--Coast-Guard-Shooting-2nd-Ld-Writethru2014-04-16T09-20-52/

Saint Louis, Julie. "Ninth Circuit orders new trial for man accused of Coast Guard killings." December 9, 2017. *Courthouse News.* https://www.courthousenews.com/ninth-circuit-orders-new-trial-for-man-accused-of-coast-guard-killings/

Silverman, Adam. "FBI: Coast Guard murder suspect resented co-workers." February 19, 2013. *USA Today.* https://www.usatoday.com/story/news/nation/2013/02/19/coast-guard-murder-suspect-resented-co-workers/1931741/

United States Court of Appeals, Ninth Circuit, no. 14-30146. *United States of America v. James Michael Wells.* January 11, 2018. https://caselaw.findlaw.com/us-9th-circuit/1885650.html

"Wives of murdered tower techs sue the Coast Guard for wrongful death." August 16, 2016. Wireless Estimator.com. http://wirelessestimator.com/articles/2016/wives-of-murdered-tower-techs-sue-the-coast-guard-for-wrongful-death/

www.ingramcontent.com/pod-product-compliance
Lightning Source LLC
Chambersburg PA
CBHW052032090426
42739CB00010B/1880